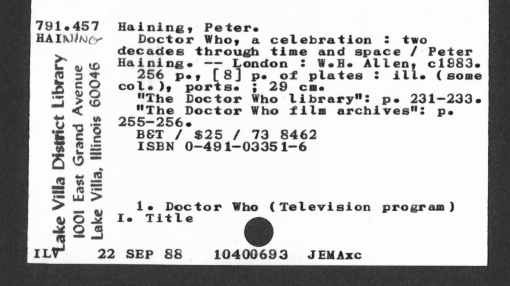

DOCTOR WHO
A CELEBRATION

This book is published by arrangement with
the British Broadcasting Corporation

DOCTOR WHO

A CELEBRATION
Two Decades Through Time and Space

PETER HAINING

W.H. ALLEN · LONDON
1983

Typeset by Phoenix Photosetting, Chatham
Printed and bound in Great Britain
by Mackays of Chatham Ltd, Kent
for the Publishers, W.H. Allen & Co. PLC
44 Hill Street, London W1X 8LB

ISBN 0 491 03351 6

First published September 1983
Reprinted October 1983, February 1984, March 1984, July 1984,
October 1984, November 1984, January 1985, March 1985,
February 1986, July 1987

ACKNOWLEDGEMENTS

Researching and writing this book has been a particular pleasure
because of the help of numerous people so generously given. I should
like to record my special thanks to the following: John Nathan-Turner,
Verity Lambert, Terry Nation, Patrick Troughton, Jon Pertwee, Tom
Baker, Peter Davison, Richard Hurndall, Peter Cushing, Barry Letts,
Terrance Dicks, Jeremy Bentham, Ian Levine, David Saunders, Ron
Katz and Antony Howe. Thanks, too, to the many other people
associated with *Doctor Who* over the past twenty years who helped with
information and photographs relating to what is a remarkable success
story. And, finally, I must just record my gratitude to Bob Tanner,
managing director of W. H. Allen, who sent me off in search of this
incredible time-traveller, and my editor, Christine Donougher, whose
assistance and knowledge of the complex worlds of *Doctor Who* would
make her an ideal companion in anyone's TARDIS!
My sincere thanks to you all.

PETER HAINING
May 1983

Stills from *Doctor Who and the Daleks* and *Dalek – Invasion Earth 2150 AD*
by permission from National Film Archive Stills Library. Diagrams for
construction of a time machine from *Science Digest*. Unless otherwise
credited, all other photographs BBC copyright, used by kind
permission.

CONTENTS

This book is in memory of William Hartnell and for John Nathan-Turner
and Peter Davison – *Who* made it all possible
And not forgetting my children Richard, Sean and Gemma
– who all love *Who*

Doctor Who has a terrific formula. It has a cast of regular, relatable characters, a continually changing environment, and a lasting impression of not knowing what you are going to see next. Perhaps most of all, through its predominantly high standards, it has never lost the ability to fascinate people of all ages in all walks of life.

Verity Lambert
first *Doctor Who* producer
1963–5

INTRODUCTION

THE CHANGING FACE OF DOCTOR WHO

Saturday, 23 November 1963 is a day that remains vividly etched in the memory of all those who were old enough to comprehend world events. It was a time when a large percentage of the population were still numbed with horror at a tragedy – an almost unthinkable tragedy – that had occurred only hours earlier in one of the great cities of one of the supposedly most civilised nations on earth.

The place in question was Dallas in America, and the news which had stunned everyone was the cold-blooded assassination of President Kennedy, the charismatic and youthful leader whose driving ambition for a brighter future had united the young and old of all the free nations in a quite unparalleled way. Now, we were told, he lay dead, victim of a gunman's bullets which had exploded the life from his body as he drove in open cavalcade through the heart of the Texan city.

I remember that day and those hours vividly. Like countless millions of others I can recall *precisely* where I was and what I was doing when news of that terrible event hit Britain on the Friday evening. The next twenty-four hours were overshadowed by horror as the implication of what had happened sank in, and the murder and how it occurred dominated everything that dark, wet weekend.

There is something else I remember from that Saturday. Not with the same vividness, to be sure, but still with a certain clarity that time has not diminished. I recall that for a brief period on that November evening, when even thoughts of Christmas just a month away were forgotten in the feeling of sorrow, that I was transported from the aftermath of those events far across the Atlantic in the company of a mysterious, rather crochety old man with white hair who could apparently travel in space and time.

After twenty-four hours of almost non-stop coverage of the drama and anguish following the assassination, BBC television at last returned viewers to uninterrupted scheduled programmes. The first of these was the opening episode of a new series called *Doctor Who* – which, in hindsight, one might almost expected to have been cancelled. Instead, it

came on our screens at 5.25 p.m., ten minutes after the time advertised in the *Radio Times*.*

There were those who switched off their sets at that moment, of course. Saturated by television and drained by the Kennedy tragedy, they doubtless wanted time to think, to readjust. Those of us who stayed tuned in, young people mostly, were whisked off on a journey through time that, incredibly, has never ended. . .

Twenty years ago that was – and that self-same Doctor, regenerated four times since, is still with us, a phenomenon unmatched in television history. Yet could any of us have suspected that such was to be the destiny of a series born amidst one of the greatest personal tragedies of the twentieth century?

The murder in Dallas apart, 1963 had been an eventful year. Beatlemania was at its height and the headlines had also been full of the incredible Great Train Robbery in which over £2.5 million had been stolen. In Britain, too, there was horror at the unemployment figure of 815,000 – the highest since 1947. And on the world scene, Russian scientists had launched the first woman, Valentina Tereshkova, into space. . .

Space travel was, in fact, very much in the news that year and its topicality had generated in the minds of two BBC executives, Sydney Newman and Donald Wilson, the idea for a new series on that theme. How that idea became the longest-running science fiction/fantasy series in television history is what we are celebrating in this book to mark the twentieth anniversary of its first broadcast.

During the intervening years, the Doctor has become a national institution, as famous among the general public as that other great fictional character, Sherlock Holmes. Indeed, there are elements in the Doctor's story which match those of his detective predecessor, although our television hero has all of the galaxy and most of time to roam through, rather than just Victorian England. Like Holmes, the Doctor has in his companions a kind of multiple Watson, on whom he can sound off his ideas and plans, and in the Master a fiendish adversary every bit the equal of Moriarty. Like Holmes, too, the Doctor is now the subject of endless discussion and debate, as well as a popular and enduring misconception. Though Sherlock Holmes is forever associated with the phrase, 'Elementary, my dear Watson', *nowhere* in the adventures written by Sir Arthur Conan Doyle do these words appear. 'Elementary' certainly, and 'my dear Watson' frequently – but *never* together. Similarly, though many think of the Time Lord as Doctor Who, he has never been referred to as such.† He is 'the Doctor' – *Doctor Who* is the name of the series. Right from the very start of his wanderings, no one knew who the strange old man was – and even today there is still much we have to learn. A Doctor? Who?

* It is a curious fact, but that Saturday afternoon there was some horse racing televised from Doncaster. In the three o'clock race, there was a runner named Call Box which ran quickly but erratically and yet finished first. Surely a most appropriate omen for the Doctor!

† On the one occasion when it happened by mistake (in 'The War Machines') .there was a flood of mail pointing out the error, and it has never happened again.

Certain basic facts about the man are, though, fairly well established twenty years on. He is a Time Lord, one of the ageless guardians of peace in the galaxy. He possesses two hearts, a body temperature of sixty degrees Fahrenheit and is over 750 years old. He began his self-appointed mission helping to restore order in troubled worlds and vanquishing an unending stream of monsters and aliens after leaving the Time Lord's home planet of Gallifrey. He had become bored there with the routinised life of his fellows and sped off in a time machine called the TARDIS which he had purloined. (The word TARDIS stands for Time And Relative Dimensions In Space.) Part of the reason for the varying locations of the Doctor's adventures is the fact that this machine is temperamental and unreliable – as exemplified by its unlikely appearance as a police box. A chameleon circuit which controls the external appearance of the craft should enable it to change to blend in with each locality in which it materialises: in fact it stuck during the Doctor's very first visit to London and has defied correction ever since!

The Doctor himself has never claimed to be perfect and indeed part of his appeal lies in his fallibility. Another crucial element, of course, is his ability to regenerate.

Consider this. In any popular television series, the departure or death of the central character usually means the end – sooner or later – of the programme. Audiences find it extremely difficult to accept a new face in the role of an old favourite. This is not the case in *Doctor Who* – which makes the series unique among its kind. A new actor may take over as the Doctor and not a single viewer will find it anything other than perfectly acceptable.

This total flexibility of format has allowed five quite different actors to play the Doctor, each in his own particular way, developing and enlivening the series as they did so. The changing faces of the Doctors have, for many people, been the key to its continuing success. The transformation of the Doctor from one likeness to another – his regeneration, to give the process its correct title – has always been a very special moment in the series. For it represents far more than just the conclusion of one serial: a whole era is, in fact, coming to an end with all its particular idiosyncracies and mannerisms and leaving the door wide open for a completely new one. The five actors in question have all approached this challenge with verve and originality, giving the Doctor a kind of magnetism no other fictional character on television can match.

William Hartnell, the first actor to play the role, evolved him as a kind of eccentric Victorian gentleman with long white hair, frock coat and winged collar. Given to moments of intolerance, he could be irascible and petulant, but he also displayed great knowledge, a sense of justice and flashes of dry wit.

Patrick Troughton emphasised the humorous elements of the Doctor's character, though his jokes and apparently bungling manner disguised a deep wisdom. His appearance of a tramp-like magician – 'the cosmic hobo' – was underlined by his zany and extravagant behaviour, but his ability to improvise was invaluable when it came to defeating some of the evil aliens and monsters that crossed his path. Undoubtedly his off-beat humour was a comforting element to younger viewers during the more

'Doctor Who on the Web Planet', *TV Comic*, 27 March 1965

frightening moments.

Jon Pertwee was the Doctor who spent much of his residency in the role exiled on Earth, and he came across as a precise, confident figure, though given to moments of showmanship and flamboyance. He was very much a man of action, blessed with manual dexterity and addicted to gadgets and revolutionary forms of transport. A true humanitarian, outraged by injustice, he was an almost paternalistic figure and as such ideally suited to defend Earth from the various alien attacks directed towards it.

Tom Baker made the Doctor a galactic traveller once again, a man of unbounded energy, but subject to periods of wandering abstractness. His infectious smile ringed by a mop of unruly hair and enormous trailing scarf, made him an engaging anti-hero. Quick with the witty line and full of unashamed mannerisms, he nevertheless possessed the deep knowledge of a scientist and had a passionate concern for all forms of life. He was a resolute champion of good, with the naivity of a young boy.

Peter Davison has revealed in the personality of the latest Doctor a little of each of his predecessors. As the youngest of the five, there is something of the reckless innocent in his actions. Yet he combines a bit of William Hartnell's no-nonsense attitude with Troughton's impish sense of fun, Pertwee's outrage at injustice and Baker's moments of charm. There is also a solid, very English kind of resolve about him which inspires great trust in companions and viewers alike.

In each of the Doctor's 'lives' there has been a linking thread which stretches unbroken from Hartnell to Davison: a strong moral stance on every issue. The character represents a code of honour built on the universal wisdom of justice and fair play that humankind has itself for so long striven after. It is a code that the Doctor applies equally to humanoid or alien – hoping for the best until the worst is exposed, wanting to see good until the evil can no longer be denied.

The evil has, of course, often been represented in the most monstrous forms – and these monsters are undoubtedly another important element in the success of *Doctor Who*. Ever since the appearance of the first – and still most famous of the monsters – the Daleks, who brought the series fame and the producers the all-important audience ratings, the Doctor's

adventures have been inextricably linked with creatures often straight from the realms of nightmares. There are surely some viewers attracted just for the monsters and it says much for the creative minds behind the programme that the standard and imaginative excellence has been kept so high over twenty years. The Daleks have not been alone in finding public favour, of course, the Voords, Sensorites, Zarbi and Cybermen were early favourites in the Hartnell era, to be followed in Troughton's period by the Ice Warriors, the Yeti and the Krotons. Pertwee tangled with Autons, Draconians, Silurians, Sontarans and Sea Devils, while Baker had little

'Doctor Who', *TV Comic Holiday Special*, 1969

peace from Robots, Zygons, Mummies, as well as many of his predecessors' old adversaries who were often left for dead but would not lie down. Peter Davison has already encountered the Terileptils, the Cybermen, the Mara, the Urbankans, Omega – to name but a few – and doubtless still has many more unexpected pleasures to come!

Because one of the very basic objectives of *Doctor Who* is obviously to keep its audience engrossed, excited and occasionally a little frightened – on the edges of their chairs, if you like (even, sometimes, behind them) – and the showing of anything vaguely horrific on television can result in complaints, it is not surprising to find that the series has received more than its fair share of controversy over the years.

All the Doctors have strongly denied any accusations that the programme is unduly violent. Partick Troughton, for instance, was quite happy to concede that it might be frightening on occasions, but believed the Doctor represented reassurance to anyone who was worried, particularly children. 'It waters down the frightening bits if there is a chap who says, "It's all right. Don't worry." I always made the Doctor see the fun in situations, too' he said.

Jon Pertwee also felt strongly on this issue. 'The stories have got to be a bit scary,' he said. 'My son had a place under the table where he watched from. But he didn't have nightmares about it. He *liked* being scared by it. When parents wrote to me and said their kids were scared, I wrote back and said, "Well, it's very simple. You lean forward, put out your hand, and turn the switch to the off position."'

The major instances of complaint that made news began, predictably, with the Daleks, although the most vociferous attack on them was not launched until March 1975 when the National Viewers' and Listeners' Association accused 'The Genesis of the Daleks' of being 'too frightening'. The Cybermen, too, were criticised for violent behaviour in 'Tomb of the Cybermen' in September 1967 and there was an outcry from the RSPCA and even questions asked in the Houses of Parliament about the use of vampire bats ('they are just mice with wings' according to the RSPCA) in 'State of Decay' in 1980. Attitudes have changed over the years, to be sure, but the programme still attracts its critics.

Complaints such as these have naturally made the producers take infinite care with the material they use, and indeed several surveys have been conducted over the years to find out 'What makes *Doctor Who* frightening?' Without exception, the findings have shown that there is nothing basically wrong with the philosophy of introducing elements of fear into the programme – as long as those elements are of a suitably fantastic nature. It is *realistic* fear that is objectionable. Surely no one could argue that an impressionable child or viewer would be likely to find a Dalek under their bed or a Cyberman waiting for them down a dark alley?

Conversely, of course, strong reactions to anything seen on *Doctor Who* can be looked upon as a form of compliment to the skill of those who created the effect. For the very nature of the programme demands that the audience suspends their disbelief and allow themselves to see and hear things from the far worlds of imagination as if they were real. And, having once seen something scary, more than likely as a cliff-hanger at the end of an episode, *wanting* to watch when the next episode is screened.

'Doctor Who', *TV Action + Countdown* (front cover) 13 January 1973

That factor, known simply as human curiosity, is another part of what the appeal of the series is all about.

Even the most casual viewers of *Doctor Who* can hardly have failed to be impressed by the elaborate futuristic sets, the authentic-looking technological equipment and the splendid costumes and props which all add extra dimensions to the Doctor's adventures. The dedication and painstaking work that goes into the special effects of the series is of the highest order and sadly requires more space to be explained than can be allotted in a book such as this. (Fortunately, though, the whole business of producing a story from basic script to finished teleplay has already been documented in *The Making of Doctor Who* by Terrance Dicks and Malcolm Hulke (Target, 1976), and the interested reader is directed to this fascinating work.)

That the series is fabulously successful not only in Britain, but throughout a sizeable proportion of the rest of the world is now beyond question. Today the show is being televised in 39 countries with a viewing audience of 100 million people. It has several fan clubs in Britain, America, Canada and as far away as Australia, and has given its name to an almost uncountable number of items of merchandise from Doctor Who dolls to model Daleks, from TARDIS money boxes to monster soaps, as well as all manner of games, jigsaw puzzles, posters, cards, pencils, sweets, wallpapers, scarves, hats, underpants, bubble-baths, T-shirts, badges and records (the most extraordinary, surely, being a disc entitled 'I'm Going to Spend My Christmas with a Dalek' by the Go-Joes released in 1964!).

Many of the Doctor's adventures have, of course, been turned into a huge and ever-expanding library of novels (some translated into a score of languages from Spanish to Japanese) and he also has his own annuals. He has been a star of comic strips and magazines from the days of William Hartnell right through to Peter Davison.

The Doctor has been the subject of special programmes about his enduring appeal on radio and television, is featured in two exhibitions in England and draws thousands of fans to annual conventions held on either side of the Atlantic. It is true to say that even though this list barely scratches the surface of the *Doctor Who* spin-offs, it is easy to see why BBC Enterprises consider it one of their biggest selling programmes. (It should perhaps also just be added that apart from the countless fan letters received by the Doctors and the other leading characters, the *Doctor Who* production office in London receives over 150 pieces of mail every day: with everything from comments on past stories to ideas for further adventures.)

To maintain such a success has demanded great teamwork over the years and one of the pleasures for me while I was working on this book has been meeting and corresponding with the many people associated with *Doctor Who*. From the gracious Verity Lambert, the show's first producer and now the head of EMI Films, to John Nathan-Turner, the likeable present incumbent, and from the courteous Patrick Troughton to the unassuming Peter Davison, I have received nothing but kindness and enthusiasm for the project. Those who have shared in the making of the legend of *Doctor Who* have all retained a genuine affection for the series and, one might be tempted to conclude, become not only famous in their own right but richer for the experience. They are also quick to acknowledge the debt they all owe to the fans.

The key to this teamwork, it seems to me, was and is fun. Although creating the programme has always been exacting and enormously time-consuming, everyone associated with it enjoyed their work while giving it everything they had. Katy Manning, who played companion Jo Grant, summed up the feeling of most of her colleagues when she said, '*Doctor Who* was a fun thing. We joked all the time.' Caroline John (Liz Shaw) agreed with this, adding, 'The programme is a fabulous TV training ground, because there are so many different facets to it. It's technically so exciting, too.'

I believe the reader will find much of this sense of enjoyment in the

'Doctor Who–Timeslip', *Doctor Who Weekly*, 1979

essays by my various contributors, the men and women who were most directly involved in the success of *Doctor Who*. The Doctors need no introduction, of course, nor, surely does Terry Nation, the man who created the Daleks and is now one of the most sought-after script-writers in both Britain and America (where I finally managed to catch up with him in Hollywood!). Verity Lambert, the first producer, I have already mentioned, and Barry Letts, now producing family classic serials at the BBC, was associated with the series in just about every capacity, as writer, director, producer and executive producer and reflects this wide-ranging knowledge in his contribution. Terrance Dicks was the longest-serving script editor and writes of the pleasures and problems of this crucial job. Jeremy Bentham, who provides the unique story line and background details on every single adventure from the last twenty years, is a life-long fan of the series and former contributing editor of *Doctor Who Monthly*. The rest of the work is mine: thanks in very large measure to the many people quoted who gave their time and information so generously.

Mention should, I think, be properly made of those members of the *Doctor Who* team who are no longer with us, but nonetheless contributed immeasurably to the success story. Firstly, of course, the pioneer Doctor himself, William Hartnell, whose influence is still evident, but who died so tragically of multiple sclerosis in April 1975. Then, Anthony Coburn,

script-writer of the very first adventure, 'An Unearthy Child', who died in 1978, and David Whitaker, script editor of the programme from its inception to December 1964, whose death occurred in 1980. A year earlier, writer Malcolm Hulke (creator of the Silurians and the Sea Devils) had passed on and more recent loses have been Brian Hayles (who gave us the Ice Warriors) and Kit Pedler, co-deviser of the Cybermen and later creator of another famous television series, *Doomwatch*. Mervyn Pinfield, who was associate producer with Verity Lambert and also directed some of the earlier stories, has died and sadly Lennie Mayne, director of a number of Doctor Who stories, including 'The Three Doctors', died in a boating accident in 1976. And one must not forget the splendid Roger Delgado, the first Master, who was killed so tragically in 1973. This twentieth anniversary belongs as much to them as those of us – actors past and present, writers old and new, members of the production team yesterday and today and fans of all ages – who *will* be marking 23 November 1983.

It has been my pleasure to chronicle the extraordinary success story of *Doctor Who* and I trust that at the end of my bit of personal time-travelling that the book echoes something of the continuing appeal of the series. As John Nathan-Turner has so eloquently put it:

'It's a magic formula, from the start it was an original idea. Science fiction had become somewhat predictable, with rocket ships, spacemen and little green men from Mars. But here was a time traveller in human form whose machine was a police box that got much bigger once you got inside. Over the years the script-writing has been constantly inventive and the stories have never been predictable. We have a licence to do anything and that is the essence of good magic.'

Welcome, then, to the magic realms of *Doctor Who* . . .

'Doctor Who–The Tides of Time', *Doctor Who Monthly*

CHAPTER ONE

THE ARRIVAL OF A TIME LORD

The scene is the yard of a scrap-metal dealer, shrouded in darkness, silent and still. For a moment nothing disturbs this stillness, then in the shadows, away to the right, a figure is glimpsed, moving slowly. The figure coughs, clears his throat, and moves into a small pool of light.

Two other figures, a man and a woman, are standing close to what is evidently a police telephone box. At once their attention is drawn to the moving figure, who is now revealed as an ageing man dressed in curiously old-fashioned clothes. He has a scarf around his neck and long white hair tumbles from beneath an astrakhan hat. Despite the appearance of age, the man has alert, darting eyes and his face is registering an emotion midway between annoyance and haughty indifference.

For what seems like an eternity the couple, two schoolteachers named Ian Chesterton and Barbara Wright, stare in obvious amazement at discovering such an unusual figure in an unprepossessing place such as this. Clearly the man is no scrap-metal dealer, nor a tradesman of any sort. An eccentric? Certainly. A professor? Possibly. Their eyes meet those of the old man – and in that instant mirror an astonishment that we can still readily understand twenty years after the event occurred. For Ian and Barbara have just become the first human beings to clap eyes on the fabled time traveller, the Doctor.

And at that same moment, too, those television viewers fortunate enough to be tuned in to the BBC watched the arrival of a character destined to become one of the most famous TV figures of the second half of the twentieth century – a man whose name might be a mystery but who has become the favourite of generation after generation of viewers.

In the light of the legend which has subsequently grown up around the Doctor, it still comes as a surprise to many people to learn that he should have made his début in such an unlikely place and in such a mundane way. It seems scarcely credible that he did not sweep into our consciousness in a blaze of colour or a swirl of galactic pyrotechnics, but almost hesitantly, certainly unheralded and in a gloomy setting heightened by the fact that the television pictures were in black and white. No modern-day hero could have had a more inauspicious start.

Yet, on second thoughts, there was *something* very apposite about the

way in which the Doctor first appeared in the story of 'An Unearthly Child' back in November 1963. For somehow those shadowy moments in the junkyard were rich in mystery, intriguing with possibilities, and indeed when the strange old man began to talk he quickly started to create ideas in the minds of viewers about worlds beyond our vision and of knowledge beyond our understanding. And with the passing of time – which was, of course, to prove the key to the personality of this man – he has fulfilled those visions, taking us on journeys into the far reaches of the galaxy to meet all manner of life forms and tread on countless strange planets. On that day we began a journey into the worlds of imagination which has continued unbroken to this day – and still clearly has far to go. . .*

To return in time to see that meeting of Ian and Barbara with the Doctor when they are trying to find out about the background to the strange, wise-beyond-her-years new pupil at their school – the 'unearthly child' of the title, Susan, the Doctor's granddaughter – is rather like taking a trip in your own personal TARDIS.

It is particularly fascinating to compare the original 'pilot' film for the series against the later, televised version. This 'pilot' of the first episode was made by the first producer, Verity Lambert, and her team, to show BBC executives how the totally original and potentially expensive series might look. It is now arguably among the most important and certainly the rarest pieces of evidence in the story of the birth of the *Doctor Who* legend. (Verity Lambert's own account of these early days follows this section.)

Watching re-runs of both versions of 'An Unearthly Child' is a startling experience, viewing features that had never been tried on television before, yet have since become commonplace. My over-whelming impression of those twenty-five historic minutes is that the episode – indeed the whole first story – could be re-shot in colour today without a word or an action changed and its impact would be just as remarkable. Time has done nothing whatsoever to diminish this pioneer piece of television.

The 'pilot' does, however, differ from the televised version in a number of quite significant and interesting ways. The title music, for instance, is punctuated by thunder-clap sound effects which were deleted from the broadcast conventional arrangement. The TARDIS has a high-pitched engine whine sound which was changed to a low electrical hum, while a buzzing noise effect was added to the opening and closing of its doors. (It is amusing to note in the 'pilot' that the doors of the TARDIS actually refuse to close and the actors continue with their lines while hidden stage hands try desperately to get them shut!) In the climax to this episode when the TARDIS dematerialises, it is done to a mixture of oscillating bleeps with intermittent snatches of what was afterwards turned into the now-recognised sound effect.

As to the characters themselves, in the first trial, William Hartnell as

* It is an interesting fact to note that another of the BBC's most successful television series also had its beginnings in a scrapyard, the exploits of that remarkable pair of rag-and-bone men, *Steptoe and Son*!

DR. WHO

5.15

DR. WHO? That is just the point. Nobody knows precisely who he is, this mysterious exile from another world and a distant future whose adventures begin today. But this much is known: he has a ship in which he can travel through space and time—although, owing to a defect in its instruments he can never be sure where and when his 'landings' may take place. And he has a grand-daughter Susan, a strange amalgam of teenage normality and uncanny intelligence.

Playing the Doctor is the well-known film actor, **William Hartnell**, who has not appeared before on BBC-tv.

Each adventure in the series will cover several weekly episodes, and the first is by the Australian author **Anthony Coburn**. It begins by telling how the Doctor finds himself visiting the Britain of today: Susan (played by **Carole Ann Ford**) has become a pupil at an ordinary British school, where her incredible breadth of knowledge has whetted the curiosity of two of her teachers. These are the history teacher Barbara Wright (**Jacqueline Hill**), and the science master Ian Chesterton (**William Russell**), and their curiosity leads them to become inextricably involved in the Doctor's strange travels.

Because of the imperfections in the ship's navigation aids, the four travellers are liable in subsequent stories to find themselves absolutely anywhere in time—past, present, or future. They may visit a distant galaxy where civilisation has been devastated by the blast of a neutron bomb or they may find themselves journeying to far Cathay in the caravan of Marco Polo. The whole cosmos in fact is their oyster.

The announcement of the very first episode of *Doctor Who* – from the *Radio Times* of 21 November 1963

the Doctor is very malicious in his attitude towards the two teachers, declaring to Ian at one point: 'And I tell you this, school-master, before your ancestors turned the first wheel, the people of my civilisation had reduced travel in the fourth dimension to a game for children.' Carole Ann Ford, playing Susan, also looks very 'out-of-this-world' and informs us that she was 'born in the forty-ninth century' – a statement which is revised to being 'born in another time, another world' in the televised version, where she remains in her school dress instead of making a dramatic change into futuristic-looking garments.

Interestingly, too, in the 'pilot' all three companions, Susan, Ian and Barbara try to stop the Doctor from dematerialising the TARDIS, while in the later version it is only Susan who tries to prevent him. The closing shot of the episode – which very rightly remained unchanged in the finished programme – shows a misshapen shadow looming over the TARDIS which has now dematerialised from the junkyard on to a barren, savage-looking landscape. It is a cliff-hanging moment, stylish and replete with tension, which has since become one of the hallmarks of the series.

The 'pilot' was shot in a single day's filming at the BBC's Lime Grove studios in the late summer of 1963. The budget was £2,000, and allowed for six sets: a school classroom and corridor, Ian's laboratory, Totter's Lane where the junkyard is situated, and the interior of this yard, plus, of course, the control room of the TARDIS. Today we take the sight of this, the heart of the Doctor's world, quite for granted: in 1963 it was a mind-boggling concept that something resembling a phone box that was bigger on the inside than out could cross the barriers of space and time in the blink of an eye!

Although Verity Lambert and her script editor, David Whitaker, were

largely responsible for producing this remarkable teleplay, the contribution of the late Anthony Coburn who scripted the story is deserving of the highest praise. It was he who put the basic concept into a story form, only disagreeing with the idea of Susan being a mere travelling companion of the Doctor who had joined him from another time. Instead he turned her into the old man's granddaughter, feeling it would be easier for young viewers to relate better to this relationship. This idea of the Doctor having kin was the only major element of his original background which was to be revised to make way for his constantly changing groups of companions.

There was to be one hiccup before *Doctor Who* was given the go-ahead, however. The BBC executives were not happy with the general character of the Doctor in the 'pilot'. They envisaged the show having an early evening slot and as such appealing primarily to children. Hartnell was playing his role in a rather unsympathetic way: he should be mean and a little crochety, certainly, but he had to win the hearts of the viewers as well. Verity Lambert was asked to develop his character into one that was supercilious and condescending, rather than deliberately malign. This re-writing, along with small changes to the other characters and certain little alterations to the action, props and background sound effects which I have already detailed, were then implemented, the additions to the script being carried out by a BBC staff writer named C. E. Webber. Then the whole thing was re-recorded.

The screened version of 'An Unearthly Child' can be seen immediately to be that bit more polished and fluent. There are no fluffed lines, the TARDIS doors open and close properly and the Doctor is markedly less hostile and a little more eccentric. There is also a more general and easier-to-understand explanation of the amazing powers of the TARDIS – 'When the Red Indians saw the first steam train their savage minds thought it an illusion, too,' the Doctor observes with a hint of sarcasm in his voice.

The exchange between Ian and the Doctor about his name also proves a very significant moment. For, as the scrapyard in which the teachers meet him bears the name Foreman on the outside, Ian assumes there to be some relationship. He therefore addresses the time traveller for what has proved the first and only time in the entire series by a full name – Doctor Foreman.

'Doctor who?' Hartnell glares back at him. 'Who?'

At that moment, if in no other, the mystery and the magic of what was to come was crystallised for all time.

Stills taken from the pilot film for 'An Unearthly Child'

HOW WE CREATED DOCTOR WHO

by Verity Lambert

Before *Doctor Who* came into my life, I had been working at ABC Television as a production assistant. The head of drama there had been Sydney Newman and one day after he had left to join the BBC he rang me up.

'What do you know about children?' Sydney asked me. Nothing, was all I could honestly reply. 'Well,' he went on, 'there is a new children's serial we are planning and we're looking for a producer. Of course,' he added encouragingly, 'you won't get it – but you might as well come along and talk to Donald Wilson, the Head of the Department.'

So I went along – but I think Sydney must have given me a pretty good recommendation beforehand, because I *got* the job! It was, of course, as the first producer of *Doctor Who*.

The idea for the serial was already pretty well worked out and Sydney Newman was the main instigator. That is not meant to be in any way disrespectful to Donald Wilson, but later on, when working on the programme, it was apparent from Donald's reactions that the impetus came from Sydney and that he had enthused his colleague with the idea.

What I first saw of *Doctor Who* was – literally – just one page of notes. However, before I joined the BBC, David Whitaker, who was already working there, had commissioned the first serial from Anthony Coburn. David, of course, was my story editor on *Doctor Who* and we enjoyed a fruitful and harmonious relationship in the years which followed.

Before Tony started writing the script for 'An Unearthly Child', he, David and I had several discussions about it and we all made several changes to the original format.

I had been briefed that *Doctor Who* was to be aimed at children from the ages of nine to fourteen. The character and motivation of the Doctor himself was also clearly delineated in that original one-page concept. He was supposed to be something of a mystery. Nobody knew how old he was; nobody knew where he had come from. Nobody, in fact, really knew if he was a thief who had stolen the time machine, the TARDIS – he certainly didn't know how to operate it very well! I thought the mystery about his background was a very good thing.

There was also an unpredictable side of his character – although it was clear that he was much more knowledgeable than the humans he encountered, Ian and Barbara, and there were some areas where he could be totally unpredictable in his behaviour. He could be irascible, difficult, sometimes involving his companions quite unnecessarily in dangerous situations. He also had a volatile temper which, of course, is how they all

started off on their journey to begin with!

All four of the main characters had been clearly defined in that original outline. It was interesting to find that whereas sometimes when things are worked out in theory they don't work in practice, but in this case they did – superbly. I remember, too, that all the characters were designed to have different impacts on the audience.

The Doctor was there to be a bit of a mystery, anti-establishment, not part of authority. And if the serial got boring because there wasn't enough incident, he could always be relied upon to do something idiotic and get the story moving again.

Susan, in the first format, was just a child. But Tony Coburn very much wanted her to be the Doctor's granddaughter – he thought that would be a more logical reason for her travelling with him. She was supposed to represent the adolescent – again very knowledgeable about some things but with a total lack of knowledge about other more everyday matters.

Ian and Barbara were the voice of Earth people – the people who questioned, who knew only what we know, who reacted to strange and bizarre situations as we would and asked the kind of questions that we might ask of such extraordinary beings as the Doctor and Susan.

When it came to casting actors to play these characters, the role of the Doctor was naturally of the greatest importance. William Hartnell was not the only person we had in mind. We thought about other actors including Cyril Cusack.

Yet, all along, I was very keen on Bill Hartnell because I had seen him do two very different things. One was the irascible sergeant in *The Army Game* and the other the talent scout in *This Sporting Life* where he was on the fringes of the Rugby set trying very hard to cling on. He was very touching and it seemed to me that if he could play both those roles he had the right range for the part.

There were suggestions at the time that the Doctor should be played by a young man. Making a weekly show can be onerous and it was felt that it might be easier for a young actor made up to look like an old man to cope. At that time the character of the Doctor was conceived of as an old man – not a young man as he is today.

Working on the programmes in those early days was immensely stimulating due to the constant changes in style each new story brought. We also had to contend with creating all the special effects and technical equipment for the stories, like the TARDIS, alien cities, jungle sets and various monsters – all on a budget of £2,500, sometimes £2,400! Some people might say that was a lot at that time, but take it from me it was absolutely nothing!

Strange as it may seem, I remember the night *before* the first transmission of 'An Unearthly Child', rather than that first Saturday night itself. For it was on the Friday that President Kennedy was shot.

We were actually recording another episode of *Doctor Who* in the studios at Lime Grove – where they did most of the news programmes – when the news of Kennedy's assassination came through. At first we didn't believe it. Everyone was terribly upset. We went on to finish the recording: there was no alternative.

The details which kept flooding in about the assassination delayed the first *Doctor Who* on the Saturday evening and so it was decided to show it again. The feeling of people at the BBC was that this was the first episode of a series that everyone hoped would run for a very long time, that probably a lot of people *hadn't* watched it because of the Kennedy tragedy – so it wouldn't do any harm to put it on again the next week.

Looking back, I think there were a number of factors that helped make *Doctor Who* the success it became, some of which had amusing stories behind them.

For instance, Ron Grainer's title music – which I think is absolutely wonderful and which I am not at all surprised to see has been retained ever since. I also thought the titles themselves were excellent, too. Sydney Newman, though, didn't like the music *or* the titles when he first saw them! But I insisted on keeping them. Afterwards he changed his mind – he was terrific to work for.

The Daleks, of course, are imprinted on everyone's mind and I remember when we got in the first serial featuring them from Terry Nation. Both David Whitaker and I thought it was very good – but Donald Wilson hated it! In fact, he didn't want us to do it. And the only reason we did it was because we didn't have another serial to replace it! We had only just commissioned a new one which obviously wasn't ready – so we were stuck with it. That's how close we came to never seeing the Daleks!

Afterwards, Donald was marvellous about it. And it's another reason why I think the impetus for the whole series came from Sydney – for after the success of the Daleks with viewers he said to me, 'I clearly don't understand this idea at all and you do. I shall leave you alone to get on with it!'

Although it is true that the Daleks brought the show to the public's attention, they were not the reason why it has continued for twenty years. If you consider the facts, there have not been many stories featuring them during this time – which I think proves the point that the series has a life very much of its own.

Doctor Who has been very important to me. Firstly, from the point of view of my career. And, secondly, it was so enjoyable. I was perhaps luckier than any of the producers in that I was in at the very beginning, starting it. There were no rules laid down and consequently I could do almost anything I wanted.

When I came to move on, the show had been on the air for about eighteen months I suppose. I felt that the stage had been reached where it would be an advantage to have a new person, a new viewpoint, so that it didn't get stale.

A great reason for the programme's continuing success has to be the fact that every four or five years you have a new generation of kids growing up. I also think that from time to time there has been a certain anarchic feel about the stories which appeals to people. The time I liked least was when the Doctor became the person the establishment rang up and said, 'Help us out, Doctor!'

This is nothing against Jon Pertwee – who played the part extremely well – but somehow the character had become earthbound. One of the reasons why children and older people liked the Doctor was because he

A celebration for Verity with the stars to mark 52 programmes and sale of the series to Canada, October 1964 (It had already been sold to Australia and New Zealand)

took on the establishment, he wasn't a member *of* the establishment. Once he became a member of the establishment that, for me, was a mistake.

I can honestly say that *Doctor Who* will always have a corner of my heart. I have been grateful, too, for the fans – the really devoted fans who have followed it through the years and now continue to make it something of a legend. They are marvellous and absolutely committed to it as a programme. I shall never forget going to one of their conventions and finding it such a heart-warming experience to think that something could gain such a place in people's lives.

I wish them – and *Doctor Who* – a long and happy future.

January 1983

The Daleks 'conquer' the front page of the *Radio Times* as their popularity soars

CHAPTER TWO

THE COMING OF THE DALEKS!

The Doctor and the Daleks are virtually inseparable in the general public's mind and have been so throughout the entire growth of the legend of *Doctor Who*. Though, in fact, they have only appeared very occasionally in the Time Lord's many adventures, the fame of these strange, evil machines with their blood-curdling cry of 'Ex-ter-min-ate, ex-ter-min-ate!' is second only to his and far outstrips that of any other monster or adversary that he has confronted over the whole period.

The marauding, cone-shaped Daleks first appeared in the series on 28 December 1963 in the second episode of the Doctor's second adventure, which was entitled simply, 'The Daleks'. (An arm of one Dalek had actually been seen in the first episode of this story – of which more in a moment.) The story had been written by Terry Nation, a young script-writer who only took on the assignment for the programme when his current work with the comedian Tony Hancock was suddenly curtailed. (See Terry's own exposition of this extraordinary twist of fate in the following article.) What, though, he gave the series at a stroke was its most famous villains and an audience rating which immediately soared up to the eight million mark! The advent of the Daleks undoubtedly ensured the success of the embryo programme and also gave birth to what became known as 'Dalek mania'.

In the months and years which followed, the Daleks became an integral part of the *Doctor Who* story – the mere mention of them drawing children of all ages to sit glued to their television screens every Saturday evening with a mixture of delight and apprehension mirrored on their faces.

Barry Norman, the television and film critic, and a long-time admirer of the series, well remembers what it was like in his own home at that time. And it was doubtless little different from millions of others, he believes.

'My little girl had her own particular method of watching the Daleks on TV,' he recalls. 'She would sit on my lap, clutching my hand and demanding constant reassurances from my fixed grin that the whole thing was strictly for laughs. "They are funny, aren't they?" she would say, anxiously. "Yes, they are," I would reply, ho-ho-hoing like a chain-store Santa Claus. "No, they aren't," she would add. And around

about Wednesday breakfast time, she would pause in the act of dismantling an egg to remark thoughtfully, ''Daleks frighten me.'' Nor was she alone, for I knew of other children who would only watch them with the sound turned off or by peering through a crack of a door from the safety of another room.'

Her reaction did not make her any the less of a fan, Barry adds, she was too taken up with 'Dalek Worship', a phrase coined by columnist Felix Barker, who wrote in his best purple prose in June 1965:

'You will have noticed how the bedlam of Saturday afternoon subsides at exactly five-forty. Not a child is to be seen in street or garden. Swing parks clear as if by magic. This is the time for Dalek Worship, and I have heard of parents being torn to pieces by furious offspring for trying to deny them their TV sets during the next sacred half hour.'

And another critic, Ewan Ross, went perhaps even further by declaring that the Daleks were 'one of the finest creations for children since Bambi'.

The build-up to the first appearance of the Daleks was indeed beautifully stage-managed. In the first episode of 'The Daleks', 'The Dead Planet', the Doctor and his companions find themselves on the mysterious world of Skaro. They begin to explore and discover a stark but impressive-looking city. The rather sombre background music helps generate an eerie atmosphere which changes to a feeling of claustrophobia once the little party enters the buildings of the city.

Barbara, separated from the others, wanders from one room to another, her anxiety mounting. Soon we find ourselves sharing this anxiety. Then, suddenly, a rod-like arm with what appears to be a suction pad on the end, shoots into view and blocks her progress. Her instinctive fright is shared by every viewer. What on earth could it be? – and we were left to wonder just that over the closing credits.

There is no more subterfuge in the next episode. We see *exactly* what has horrified Barbara when a group of Daleks round up her and the others. And from then on neither those intrepid adventurers, ourselves the viewers, nor even the programme itself will ever be quite the same after that dramatic entrance.

The immediate impact of the Daleks came as big a surprise to their creator Terry Nation as it did to Verity Lambert and the rest of the actors and production team. Terry readily admits his amazement, as well as the fact that he had no sudden flash of genius in devising what have become his most enduring creations in a long and inventive career writing science-fiction and fantasy scripts.

'My only source of inspiration came from the television,' he says. 'It was a wholesome case of the medium creating its own new image. I'd been watching a performance of the Georgian state dancers and they seemed to me to be gliding across the floor, their feet invisible under their long costumes. It was the strangeness of this movement I wanted to recapture in the Daleks: creatures with no apparent motive power.

'As for the name, it simply rolled off the typewriter. Once the blueprint for the Daleks – ''hideous machine like creatures . . . legless . . . with no human features'' had appeared on paper, Ray Cusick, the programme designer, took over and he was the man who must take the

A rehearsal shot taken in December 1963 of one of the most famous encounters on television –
the Doctor (William Hartnell) first meets the Daleks in 'The Survivors'

credit for the Daleks' startling pepper-pot design. It wasn't until I saw them that I realised they were just what I'd had in mind from the start.'

Terry, of course, helped generate the very beginnings of the Dalek legend when he told writers and journalists seeking for a profound reason for the success of the machines and the singularly appropriate name he had given them – that he had actually seen it on the spine of an encyclopedia volume covering the words DAL to LEK. It was a piece of sheer invention to satisfy the insistent demands of the press, he now readily admits: 'And in fact anyone checking the encyclopedias would have found that there has never been one covering those particular letters!'

The amazing popularity of the Daleks brought fame and fortune to Terry Nation (he retained part copyright in his creation and has shared in all the many and varied kinds of merchandising which followed). But success also brought its problems, as he recalls:

'In that first series I killed them off completely, having no idea popular demand would insist on their return. Nobody has ever killed off their brainchild as thoroughly as I annihilated mine – with the possible exception of Sir Arthur Conan Doyle trying to rid himself of Sherlock Holmes.

'Fortunately, though, the trusty TARDIS came to my rescue – I was able to bring the Daleks back in a time era *before* the date they were exterminated!'

Terry has paid generous tribute to Ray Cusick who gave the idea of the

Daleks a tangible shape, but believes the reason for their success to be basically a very simple one: fear. He explains:

'I have been asked more times than I can count to explain their success. I think it's this – that kids love to be frightened. To them it's like creeping up to the top of the stairs in the dark, which is surely a healthy emotion.'

Another aspect of the Daleks which caught the imagination of viewers was their harsh, metallic voices, screaming 'Ex-ter-min-ate! Ex-ter-min-ate!' – cries that were soon being imitated all over the country by young fans. These voices were, in fact, the joint efforts of radiophonic sound-engineer Brian Hodgson and actors, Peter Hawkins and David Graham.

Initially, it had been planned that the Daleks would have voices virtually the same as humans, but Hodgson and the production team came up with the peculiar metallic tones by speaking through a ring modulator. Hawkins and Graham then made them unforgettable. Both men continued in their 'roles' until 'The Dalek Master Plan', when David Graham left. Peter Hawkins remained with the series until 'The Evil of the Daleks', and extended his contribution to the programme by providing the voices of the Cybermen in 'The Moonbase', 'Tomb of the Cyberman' and 'The Wheel in Space'. (Both men, incidentally, have also provided memorable voice-overs in other programmes: Peter in *Captain Pugwash* and David in *Thunderbirds*; while David has been seen in person in two *Doctor Who* stories, as the barman Charlie in 'The Gun Fighters' and Professor Kerensky in 'City of Death'.) Although a number of other character actors have made one-off appearances as Dalek voices, mention should also be made of Michael Wisher and Roy Skelton for their contributions.

The combination of the grating voices, violent actions and generally hostile appearance has on occasions brought the Daleks into trouble with certain sections of the viewing public. 'Genesis of the Daleks' in 1975 is perhaps the most frequently cited example of this, when the scenes of 'Nazi-style cruelty' – as they were called by protestors – and graphic violence caused the programme to be widely condemned by parents and viewers' associations. Terry Nation, though, strongly defended his script as being 'a modern-day morality play which also just happens to feature the origins of the Doctor's oldest and most popular foes'.

Despite all their fame, however, the mythology of the Daleks still remains confusing. Did they evolve from a race of blue-skinned intellectuals as speculated by Terry Nation in his fondly remembered 'Dalek Chronicles' of the mid-sixties? Or were their cone-shaped life-support machines the end product of a genetically crippled race of Kaled warriors struggling for survival in the 1975 serial, 'Genesis of the Daleks'? Whichever the case, these evil mutations bent on destroying all other life forms are 'too terrible to look upon' in a visible state.

Such a view has naturally only quickened the interest as to just *what* might be concealed inside the casings. Stories that *something* has been glimpsed from time to time have persisted over the years, typified by the remark of Gavin Scott in his TV programme *Did You See?* In March 1982 when he said, 'I remember being enthralled as a child when a Dalek was opened up and something slithery fell out! That must have been one of the best moments of television fiction.'

The *facts* about the sightings are these. In the 1966 serial, 'The Dalek Master Plan', there was a climatic scene where the Doctor (William Hartnell) examined an octopoid-shaped husk and pondered whether it might be the ultimate development of the Daleks. During Patrick Troughton's regeneration, in the course of 'Power of the Daleks' (1966) a tentacled creature was briefly glimpsed, but this was no more than an infant form of what would ultimately grow into a Dalek. This same form was also seen briefly during Tom Baker's period as the Doctor in what was called 'the embryo room' in 'Genesis of the Daleks' (1975). (Baker, incidentally, delivered this verdict on the Daleks. 'They're terrible,' he said. 'No humour, no jokes. And without jokes, there's no optimism!')

But the most positive revelation in fact occurred in the first Dalek story, 'The Daleks' (December 1963–February 1964), when the Doctor and his companions captured a Dalek in their cell, forced off the top cone, pulled out a squirming mass about the size of a football and wrapped it up in a cloak. At the end of the episode we see a three-clawed talon start to edge out from under the cloak. *That* is a Dalek.

Mythology apart, what goes on inside the metal casings constitutes very hard work for the various actors who have operated the Daleks over the years. Principal among these has been character actor John Scott Martin who, in thirteen years associated with the programme, has played a whole variety of roles from a Zarbi to a Mutant, as well as various Daleks.

'For all these sorts of parts you need to believe in what you are doing, as they are very physically demanding,' he says. 'The costumes are hot to work in and often heavy, and you might spend two hours in make-up beforehand.

'A Dalek is fun, though. It's like a bubble-car on castors and you sit inside and trundle it along with your feet. It gets a bit hot and claustrophobic at times, but at least you can sit down. Inside there's a bit of gadgetry to work to operate the lights, the eye-stick and the gun.

'We don't say the lines, of course, but we do have to learn them. We press a button inside the Dalek to cue in the lines from the control room. Anyway, you need to know the lines at rehearsal so that the other actors can react to you and you don't just stand around like a pepper-pot.

'Being a Dalek can be a bit dangerous. Once my Dalek was supposed

The day the Daleks were born

SCRIPT - WRITER Terry Nation stared at a blank sheet of paper and racked his brains, writes CHARLES CATCHPOLE.

He needed a villain for a new children's series he was writing for BBC TV—something impersonal, and irredeemably evil. Suddenly, inspiration dawned. A metallic robot, shaped like a pepper pot, gliding silently and menacingly on invisible wheels.

Nation passed his idea to BBC de-

signer Ray Cusick, who made a few sketches—and the Daleks were born.

That was 16 years ago. Today Nation, who owns the rights to the Dalek name and splits royalties with the BBC, is a rich man. He lives in a 15-room Elizabethan house in Kent which he bought for cash.

And tonight, as the Daleks emerge from the North London depot where they have been gathering dust for four years, Terry Nation's six-year-old son

Joel will get his first sight of daddy's evil inventions.

But who remembers Ray Cusick, who actually designed the creatures? For him there has been no windfall. He still works as a staff designer at the TV Centre.

'I didn't get much out of it,' he says. 'I'm an employee of the BBC and whatever I do is their copyright, although I did get an ex-gratia payment.'

From *Daily Mail*, 1 September 1979

to blow up, but things went wrong and it caught fire. I had to be hauled out quick!'

A more happy memory for John was appearing on Jimmy Savile's show, *Jim'll Fix It*, when a young viewer asked to be able to meet a Dalek. 'I was happy to oblige,' he says, 'though I'm not sure I was quite what the boy expected to find inside!'

One of the Doctor's companions, Anneke Wills, who played Polly, recalls a similar amusing moment with the Daleks. 'A photographer was taking some shots on the set and took this picture of a group of Daleks with their cones off. The operators were still sitting inside them, some puffing away on cigarettes. The picture caused quite a fuss. It was thought it ruined the illusion!'

Illusion or fantasy, the Daleks are now not only a major part of the *Doctor Who* legend but have a place in the folklore of our times. For the name Dalek is often to be found in newspaper headlines, while their image has provided a rich source of inspiration for cartoonists – as the recent examples of both clearly demonstrate.

The Daleks become a part of the language: in comic strips, advertisements, newspaper headlines and even political cartoons: *Daily Mail*, 16 October 1981

This said, can there remain any doubt that Terry Nation – almost despite himself – has created one of the most enduring symbols of this century?

'MY GOD, WHAT IS IT?'

The Daleks and Me

by Terry Nation

I think that a book to mark the twentieth anniversary of *Doctor Who* is a splendid idea. I have a great affection for the series and many happy memories of those very first Dalek episodes.

However, I must tell you in all honesty that I had very little faith that the series would ever continue past the original thirteen shows. I was working with Tony Hancock at the time, moving around theatres all over the country trying out material for a new stage act. We were in Nottingham when my agent called and said the BBC had asked if I would write some episodes for a new children's series. I remember feeling vaguely insulted at being asked to write for 'children's hour'. As Hancock said, 'A writer of your calibre being asked to work for flippin' kids!' I turned the job down immediately.

That night Tony and I got into a dispute about a piece of material. I can't remember if he fired me or if I walked out in high dudgeon. Anyway, I was on a train back to London and realised I was unemployed. I called my agent and said I'd do the show. I met with Verity Lambert and outlined a story. I got the go-ahead to get started and at the same time was asked by Eric Sykes if I would go with him to Sweden to do a series of shows on a luxury liner. That was something I wasn't about to miss. So I started writing *Doctor Who* very quickly. Indeed, I wrote one episode per day, completing the serial in a week. I did the Swedish stint and then moved on to write episodes for Roger Moore in *The Saint*.

Some months later I watched my first episode as it was broadcast. To my surprise it was rather good. In the very final frames of that episode we saw only the 'arm' of a Dalek and heard its voice. Then as the credits began to roll my telephone started to ring. Friends asking, 'My God, what is it?'

In the next episode the Daleks really came into their own and children all over the country were putting cardboard boxes over their heads, sticking their arms out and shouting, 'Exterminate.' Before the Dalek segment ended, I was receiving literally vans full of mail. Thousands of letters. The Daleks were on their way to becoming a folk hero to English children.

There were many rewards and pleasures to come from the Daleks, but the one I treasure most was when I learned the word Dalek had been

included in a new edition of the *Oxford English Dictionary*. Not only had I created a monster, I had created a word. What writer could ask for more?

Terry Nation

November 1982

Terry Nation with some of the monsters who made him famous, *Doctor Who Radio Times Special,* 1973

CHAPTER THREE

THE DOCTOR WHO FILE

WILLIAM HARTNELL

'A Time Traveller with Long White Hair and Eccentric Clothes'

The man who first brought the Doctor to the screen and thereby secured himself a place in television history was William 'Bill' Hartnell, a veteran actor who thereby achieved fame after a lifetime of endeavour in the acting profession. As a young man he had run away from school, later worked through a variety of jobs in the theatre and in films, before finally – perhaps appropriately for such a restless soul – finding stardom as the first incarnation of the Time Lord with all of space and time to roam through!

For a man who was to have the galaxy at his finger-tips, William Hartnell was born on a very down-to-earth farm in the village of Seaton in Devon on 8 January 1908. He was the only child of a dairy farmer whose family could trace their ancestry back for over three hundred years: perhaps another suitable attribute for a man destined to play the almost ageless Doctor.

Life on the farm was, however, extremely harsh; early rising, endless work and little free time. In 1924, young Bill ran away to London. Because of his country upbringing he tried his hand as a stable lad and apprentice jockey to trainer Stanley Wootton – but unfortunately he put on too much weight! A period as a flyweight boxer developed his strength, but did not hold out the prospect of a lucrative career.

From his very earliest days, Bill had apparently dreamed of being a Shakespearian actor, so when his other attempts to find a career failed he decided to give this a try.

'All my spare coppers were spent on visits to the cinema,' he recalled

later. 'I revelled in the serials of Pearl White and the exploits of Tarzan. But my real guiding star was Charlie Chaplin. He influenced me more than any other factor in taking up acting as a career.'

He secured an introduction to Sir Frank Benson, whose Shakespearian company were occasionally interested in new recruits and much to his delight he was taken on. But to earn his meagre thirty shillings a week salary, Bill was called upon to act as call-boy, assistant stage manager, property manager, even assistant lighting director. He was, he remembers, a general dogsbody, but he did get the occasional small walk-on part.

'It was good training,' he said. 'Not only in Shakespeare, but in keeping fit! Sir Frank Benson believed in keeping his actors in good health and we were organised into hockey teams and cricket sides.'

For two years, Bill learned all about the theatre, but his attempts to emulate Chaplin and become a comedian were generally frustrated, so at eighteen he left the company and for the next six years toured the country playing in comedies and song-and-dance shows. He worked for a time for the great C. B. Cochran and understudied Bud Flanagan and Lawrence Grossmith. He then spent a period with a touring company, appearing in farces, often taking the roles which had been made popular by one of the stars of the time, Ralph Lynn.

Success at last seemed to be beckoning when he enjoyed a protracted run in the lead role in *Charley's Aunt* during a tour of the London suburbs.

However, in 1928 he was engaged to go abroad for a tour of North America – and there across the Atlantic he found himself faced with a dilemma. It was quite obvious from what he could see and hear that films were the up-and-coming form of entertainment. So should he try his luck in Hollywood – or return to Britain?

'I reasoned that my light comedy style was much more fitted for British talkies than their American counterparts, so I returned to England,' Bill said years later. 'But I now think that decision was completely wrong.'

On his return, Bill found that parts in British films were hard to come by and, even when he managed to secure the lead role in one comedy short entitled *I'm an Explosive*, his total earnings were just £60! Though by now he was somewhat disheartened, he put his time in the studios to good use, often hovering near the director so that he could learn the business of film-making. He was always on hand, too, in case another actor was suddenly needed for a scene.

'Although this strategy worked on occasions', he recalled later, 'and I did get bigger "bit" parts, it did not lead to stardom. In fact, after crowd work for two years I was told by a casting director that I had not got a "film face". I remember, incidentally, that Laurence Olivier was also a neighbour at the film casting offices as we all sought vainly for work!'

Then, quite out of the blue, Bill enjoyed a sudden change of fortune when he was cast for a picture called *Sabotage at Sea*. But not as a comic – rather as a villain, complete with thick glasses and a dark moustache! His performance, though, earned him qualified praise – though he vowed never to use heavy make-up again. He came to the conclusion he could have just as strong an impact on the screen without it: making the most of

William Hartnell as the Doctor in the first of the 'historical' stories, 'Marco Polo', with Mark Eden in the title role and Martin Miller as the aged Kublai Khan (1964)

his expressive features and darting, hazel-brown eyes.

'Anyone can be horrific by gumming on lumps of hair and wax and by putting cotton wool up their nostrils to look like an ape,' he said, 'but I think the real shudder-creating villain is the one who looks the same as other men, except for the eyes, and the eyes ought to reveal just how rotten to the core the heavy is, with subtle graduations such as ''forced into crime by mental instability'' or ''gone to the bad through evil surroundings'' or ''not a bad chap at heart but just lacking in strength of character''. It's a fascinating study.'

The advent just then of the Second World War, however, proved an unhappy time for Bill. He was drafted into the Tank Corps, but suffered a nervous breakdown and had to be invalided out after fifteen months.

'The strain of training was too much,' he recalled later. 'I spent twelve weeks in an Army hospital and came out with a terrible stutter. The colonel said, ''Better get back to the theatre. You're no bloody good here!''

'I had to start all over again. I was still only a spit and cough in the profession and now I had a stutter which scared the life out of me.'

Bill set about rebuilding his career with iron-willed determination and in 1943 by one of those remarkable twists of fate that sometimes change people's destinies (considering what had happened to him in the Army) he at last made his mark as an actor playing a tough sergeant named Fletcher in Sir Carol Reed's very popular film *The Way Ahead*!

This success, not surprisingly, lead to a succession of similar army roles, as well as playing tough guys, criminals and even the occasional

detective in more than sixty films, including such notable pictures as *Private's Progress* and *Brighton Rock*. He also began to secure work on television, appearing as Sergeant-Major Bullimore in the long-running series *The Army Game*.

It was not until 1963, however, when he was fifty-five, that *the* highlight of his career arrived. The first step was being cast in Lindsay Anderson's marvellous film about Rugby League football, *This Sporting Life*, in which he played a tough old talent scout. His acting so impressed one member of his audience, Verity Lambert, that when she was later looking for an actor to play in her new series, *Doctor Who*, she offered him the role of the time traveller. Despite some initial reservations he agreed to launch the series – and by so doing began what has now become a twenty-year legend. (See William Hartnell's own comments in the following item.)

'It was like manna from heaven getting right away from all those barrack rooms,' he recalled ten years later. 'The original Doctor was pig-headed and irascible, certainly, but there was also an element of magic in him – and that was what I tried to bring out.'

No less a newspaper than *The Times* has chronicled Bill's début as the Doctor:

'It was as a result of his part in *This Sporting Life* that he was offered the part of Doctor Who, a time traveller with long white hair and eccentric clothes, in a new television programme.

'*Doctor Who* was originally expected to run for about six weeks, but Hartnell went on to play the part for three years, becoming a national celebrity and attracting a huge personal fan mail from grown-ups as well as children.'

This enormous regular audience was the first that Bill had enjoyed in all his career and his acceptance – in particular by children for whom he had not worked before – delighted him.

'Everyone calls me Doctor Who and I feel like him,' he told a reporter in 1965. 'I get letters addressed to me as "Mr Who" and even "Uncle Who". But I love being this eccentric old man. I love it when my granddaughter Judith calls me "barmy old grandad".'

As to the character of the Doctor, he explained to another journalist, 'I'm the High Lama of the Planet. Although I portray a mixed-up old man, I have discovered I can hypnotise children. Hypnosis goes with fear of the unknown. I communicate fear to children because they don't know where I'm going to lead them. This frightens them and is the attraction of the series.

'I'm hypnotised by *Doctor Who*,' he added. 'When I look at a script I find it unbelievable, so I allow myself to be hypnotised by it. Otherwise I would have nothing to do with it.'

Undoubtedly Bill's special attitude to the role helped enormously in the development of the character of the Doctor from a cranky old man into a magical figure still remembered with great affection today. While playing the part on one occasion he remarked revealingly, 'I think I represent a cross between the Wizard of Oz and Father Christmas. Yet I am always adding fragments to the part, always trying to expand it.'

Some of those who worked with William Hartnell recall that at times

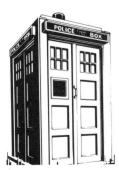

he could be as irascible and cranky as the character he played and he was always a stickler for detail in his search for perfection. Yet when he argued over aspects of the character with new members of the production team, it was from a deep-seated knowledge of the Doctor and what he stood for and the way he would react to a given situation.

Bill had every intention of continuing with the character as long as the BBC wanted the series to run – but fate frustrated this wish. He contracted multiple sclerosis and in 1966 the crippling disease finally forced him to relinquish what had become a much-loved role.*

He retired to a country cottage in Mayfield, Sussex (later moving to Marden in Kent), with his wife, Heather McIntyre, a former actress herself and also a playwright. (The couple had one daughter, Anne, who was married in 1952.) There he was happy to see young enthusiasts who still called him the Doctor, reply to a scarcely diminishing fan mail and, of course, made a brief reappearance in the series in 1973 to celebrate the tenth anniversary of the programme in 'The Three Doctors'. Unfortunately, his condition made it impossible for him to appear live with his successors, Patrick Troughton and Jon Pertwee, and his part had to be pre-recorded and cleverly interlinked to the story through the medium of a television console.

The first Doctor with two of his successors in a publicity photograph for 'The Three Doctors' (1973)

* Although there is no doubt that his illness would have ultimately prevented William Hartnell from continuing to play the part of the Doctor, he did write in a letter to a fan, Ian McLachlan, in 1968, that he actually parted company with the series after a disagreement over policy. Writing in August 1968, he said, 'I left because we did not see eye to eye over the stories and too much evil entered into the spirit of the thing. It was noted and spelled out to me as a children's programme, and I wanted it to stay as such; but, I'm afraid, the BBC had other ideas. So did I, so I left.'

William Hartnell, 'the man the Daleks could not kill' according to the *Daily Mirror*, died on 24 April 1975, aged sixty-seven, much mourned by his fans, yet happy in the knowledge he had played a crucial part in launching what has become the most successful of all BBC series. Terry Nation, the man who created his arch-enemies, the Daleks, put the thoughts of millions of people into words when he said on the following day, 'The biggest tribute to William Hartnell is that he started a show which is still going on with huge audiences.'

And how true those words still remain today.

I FELT LIKE THE PIED PIPER

by William Hartnell

I was so pleased to be offered *Doctor Who*. To me kids are the greatest audience – and the greatest critics – in the world.

It may seem like hindsight now, but I just *knew* that *Doctor Who* was going to be an enormous success. Don't ask me how. Not everybody thought as I did. I was universally scoffed at for my initial faith in the series, but I believed in it. It *was* magical.

Before the part came along I'd been playing a bunch of crooks, sergeants, prison warders and detectives. Then, after appearing in *This Sporting Life*, I got a phone call from my agent. He said, 'I wouldn't normally have suggested you work in children's television, Bill, but there's a sort of character part come up that I think you'd just love to play.'

My agent said the part was that of an eccentric old grandfather-cum-professor type who travels in space and time. Well, I wasn't that keen, but I agreed to meet the producer.

Then, the moment this brilliant young producer Miss Verity Lambert started telling me about *Doctor Who*, I was hooked. I remember telling her, 'This is going to run for five years.' And look what's happened!

We did it forty-eight weeks a year in those days and it was very hard work. But I loved every minute.

You know, I couldn't go out into the high street without a bunch of kids following me. I felt like the Pied Piper.

People really used to take it literally. I'd get letters from boys swotting for O-levels asking complicated questions about time-ratio and the TARDIS. The Doctor might have been able to answer them – I'm afraid I couldn't! But I *do* believe there is life on other planets – and they know there's life here but don't have the technology to get through.

Doctor Who is certainly a test for any actor. Animals and children are

A hint of a smile from the 'cranky old man'

renowned scene-stealers and we had both – plus an assortment of monsters that became popular in their own right. Look at the Daleks. They started in the second series and were an immediate success.

At one time (in late 1964) I thought we might extend the series and I suggested giving the Doctor a son and calling the programme *The Son of Doctor Who*. The idea was for me to have a wicked son. We would both look alike, each have a TARDIS and travel in outer space. In actual fact, it would have meant that I had to play a dual role whenever I 'met' my son.

But the idea was not taken up by the BBC so I dropped it. I still think it would have worked and been exciting to children.

Memories? There are so many. There was the occasion when I arrived at an air display in the TARDIS and the kids were convinced I had flown it there! On another occasion I went by limousine to open a local fête. When we got there the children just converged on the car cheering and shouting, their faces all lit up. I knew then just how much the Doctor really meant to them.

I think that if I live to be ninety, a little bit of the magic of *Doctor Who* will still cling to me!

William Hartnell

(Quotes given by the actor between 1965 and 1975)

PATRICK TROUGHTON

'The Cosmic Hobo'

When Patrick Troughton agreed to take over the role of the Doctor from William Hartnell in 1966, there was one immediate question to be resolved. *How* should this new regeneration of the Time Lord be played?

Fortunately, a famous actor's name on whom the part might be modelled almost immediately came to mind – and, curiously, it was one that had links with Bill Hartnell, though he had never been able to utilise the character. The name was Charlie Chaplin. And that, in a nutshell, is how Patrick Troughton came to develop his 'cosmic hobo' Doctor, complete with baggy clothes and air of injured innocence.

There were other suggestions, to be sure. Indeed, because of his initial reluctance to play the part – shades of Hartnell yet again! – through an understandable fear of becoming type-cast, Patrick insisted on making his Doctor 'different' from his predecessor. He recalls vividly how the character as it eventually became familiar to millions of viewers was evolved.

'Sydney Newman, who was then head of BBC TV Drama, said, "All right. Do what you like with him. Play him like Charlie Chaplin if you want to." But we still went through a lot of costume ideas, like making him a rather tough, seafaring man, or something like that.' (Troughton, in fact, has a strong affinity with the sea.)

'But,' Patrick continues, 'Sydney obviously had the Chaplin idea well in mind. In the end he said, "But whatever happened to the cosmic hobo?" So we compromised. In the beginning I played him very clownish. But I mellowed him as the series progressed. He was always off-beat, but I tried to make him human.'

Patrick also found the idea of the Doctor being able to change his appearance and personality perfectly feasible. Speaking at the time of the tenth anniversary of the series in 1973, when three actors had already played the part, he said, 'We are all different aspects of the same character. Of course it's bound to be a bit of a mystery to us, but in the Doctor's space–time machine the so-called past just doesn't exist.'

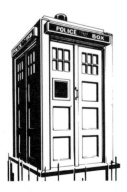

Patrick Troughton has not earned his reputation as one of today's most diverse and accomplished actors for nothing. It is a fact that from his teens he set his heart on just such a goal and he has achieved it with single-minded determination and a dedication to each and every one of his roles which makes him reject any form of gimmicky publicity to promote either himself or his work. Indeed, Patrick rarely gives interviews, preferring to let his performances speak for themselves and insisting on his privacy when he is not acting. Piecing together the facts of his career is not, therefore, the easiest of matters.

He was born on 25 March 1920 in Mill Hill, London, and grew up a fairly average child, he says. He went to Mill Hill Public School, and it was when he was sixteen that he felt the impetus to make acting his career.

'I heard a radio programme about Fay Compton,' he recalls, 'and I was interested in what she had to say. The life she described appealed to me, and I felt that I'd like that kind of life for myself. We actually met for the first time about seven years ago and I told Fay she was to blame for influencing me into the acting profession.'

Patrick's first step towards achieving his objective was to enrol at the Embassy School of Acting in Swiss Cottage, London, which was then run by Eileen Thorndyke, sister of the actor/writer Russell Thorndyke and the famous Dame Sybil Thorndyke. His hard work and dedication won him a scholarship to the prestigious Leighton Rollins Studios at the John Drew Theatre at Easthampton, on Long Island, New York.

After his sojourn across the Atlantic to complete his studies, Patrick returned to England and joined the Tonbridge Repertory Company. However, the outbreak of the Second World War cut short his embryo career. He was called up to serve in the Royal Navy and was first posted in destroyers patrolling the east coast.

Those who have worked with Patrick and become aware of his strong, assertive personality can well understand how he was quickly singled out for leadership by the Royal Navy and how, by the middle of the war, he

The Doctor helps a Yeti learn his lines – an amusing location shot taken while filming 'The Abominable Snowmen' (1967)

had been transferred to motor gun boats and was captain of his own craft on duty in the North Sea. He continued in the service until the end of hostilities in 1945.

Not surprisingly, Patrick went straight back into the theatre after he was demobbed in March 1945 and joined the Amersham Repertory Company. Not long after, he was asked to join the famous Bristol Old Vic Company and later spent two years with the Pilgrim Players doing T. S. Eliot's plays at the Mercury Theatre Nottingham

'I like to play all kinds of people in all kinds of plays,' he said recently. 'I've got a special liking for fantasy and for rip-roaring adventures with plenty of action such as *Robin Hood* and *Kidnapped*.'

Kenneth Bailey, the film and TV critic and an admirer of Patrick's work, has written of his talent, 'In the studio he electrifies his fellow actors. In the early days of TV, playing the first-ever Robin Hood, he really became to the other actors the leader of a gang.

'In the small pioneer studio, he had them rampaging with blood-racing fervour under his outlaw leadership.'

This kind of commitment naturally made him one of the most in-demand actors and his notable performances include Hitler, Disraeli, St Paul, the Dickens character Quilp, along with appearances in such perennial favourites as *Dr Finlay's Casebook* and *Coronation Street*.

It was while he was working on a feature film called *The Viking Queen* in 1966 that he was offered what he has since called 'one of the happiest things I've done' – the part of the Doctor. Initially, though, he was very dubious about taking it on, he admits.

'To be quite honest,' he says, 'I had a feeling that it had perhaps been done to death and that it wouldn't last.' He had often watched the series at home with his own children and did not see how William Hartnell's role could be bettered.

Finally, Innes Lloyd, the producer who had taken over from Verity Lambert, talked him into playing the role by giving full vent to his love of clowning. In typical Troughton style he absorbed himself totally in the part.

'When you're playing a part for a long time you certainly take on some of the mental attitudes of the fellow you're playing,' he says. 'Luckily the Doctor was a very jolly fellow and I just bubbled along.'

It has to be said that Patrick Troughton's reputation as a fun-loving, practical joker is legendary around the television studios.

'He's great fun . . . pure joy to work with,' Innes Lloyd said later, adding that he was also serious-minded, often intense, but always charming, particularly to women. Yet he can swear mightily and be very scathing about a script he dislikes. And it is not unknown for him to leave the studios after a day's work roaring with laughter over some bawdy crack he's made at the cast – though they all love him the more for it!

When Patrick joined the cast of *Doctor Who* his reputation went ahead of him as Anneke Wills, who played his first companion, Polly, recalls: 'We played our own little joke on Patrick the first day he started. Michael Craze and I ordered some special T-shirts and we greeted our new Doctor with the words "Come Back, Bill Hartnel" blazoned across our chests!'

Patrick took the joke in the spirit it was intended and remembers his

The clownish, fun-loving Doctor, Patrick Troughton

co-stars with great affection. 'It was such fun and the people were so nice. Michael and Anneke were marvellous to me when I first started. It must have been extremely difficult for them, being used to William Hartnell's Doctor.

'And then I was very lucky having Frazer Hines, Deborah Watling and Wendy Padbury with me for so long. Somehow, I always used to find myself running with Frazer and Debbie. As I was the Doctor I felt I had to outrun them, but they were young and I was old and it was difficult!'

He remembers that he couldn't resist a joke at the expense of the hapless Deborah Watling on one occasion. While filming an episode he suddenly produced from his pocket not a handkerchief, but a pair of very pretty woman's knickers. As the rest of the cast collapsed in laughter, poor Debbie could only protest vainly, 'But they're not *mine!*'

Patrick Troughton played the part of the Doctor for three years and then decided it was time to move on. There were other roles, both serious and comic, awaiting his highly professional approach and he felt the tug unmistakably.

Memories of the series remain with him – and indeed one particular part of his character is rather like that of the Doctor: his ability to disappear into his own private world when he is away from the studios. Patrick now lives near Hampton, Middlesex, and is married with six children, four boys and two girls. (His sons, Michael and David, are, incidentally, following in his footsteps as actors.) He likes to relax by reading books on philosophy and comparative religion, as well as painting, fishing, playing golf and gardening.

Patrick remains totally committed to the belief that he is an actor and not a personality. Yet, as Innes Lloyd says of him, 'You never forget working with Pat. He etches himself on your brain.'

The same comment could also be applied just as emphatically to his unique portrayal of the second regeneration of the Doctor. . .

Patrick Troughton as the Doctor with Nicholas Courtney as the Brigadier in 'The Three Doctors' (1973)

DOCTOR WHO INDULGED MY PASSION FOR CLOWNING

by Patrick Troughton

It now seems so long ago that I played the part of the Doctor that there is really very little I can add to what has already been written. And, of course, I've played so many different parts in the last forty years.

How did I feel about taking on the role? To begin with, I thought it would last about six weeks after Billy Hartnell had finished. My children and I had been fans of the programme and I loved the way he had played the Doctor. But I knew I couldn't possibly do it like that.

At one point in my discussions with the producer, he was going to become an old-fashioned wind-jammer captain – imagine the problems *that* would have caused in space! I even suggested he might be blacked up and turned into something out of the *Arabian Nights*!

However, my contribution lasted three years as it turned out – and that was a show every Saturday each year, except for August. They only do a few each year now. So it was very hard work.

Nevertheless, it was the happiest time of my professional life – except perhaps for one play which I've just done with Gwen Watford on BBC TV.

Doctor Who gave me a chance to indulge my passion for dressing up and being able to have some sly fun as well as a bit of clowning.

It also gave me great pleasure coming into contact with children, for if I had not been an actor I would quite like to have been a teacher. Children keep one young.

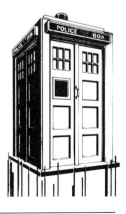

I believed totally in the possibilities implied in the series. I never thought of it as fantasy. Far from it – it's all happening. I think space will be conquered through the mind rather than the clumsy medium of space travel.

I have been asked what impact the part of the Doctor had on my career and I can honestly say none. For, luckily, I got out in time before I was too type-cast. And when I'm asked if I have any anecdotes of those years, I'm afraid to say that there are none that could be printed!

Why has the programme proved such a continuing success? I think the simple answer to that is because new children keep on being born!

Patrick Troughton

October 1982

JON PERTWEE

'The Man of Action'

Jon Pertwee continued the same sense of fun in the third regeneration of the Time Lord when he took over from Patrick Troughton in 1970. As a man with a very independent mind and love of humour, he knew from the start he had to be allowed to work in his own particular way to succeed in the role and keep the series successful after his two very different predecessors.

'I didn't see Doctor Who as such a clown, as a pixilated character,' he recalled later. 'More as a folk hero, I suppose. In a way he became very much what I'm really like. In my time I've done water-skiing and skin-diving, I've raced cars and boats. I've worked in a circus on a Wall of Death, as a bare-back rider, Madame Pertweeova, even once with a flock of performing geese!'

This said, it was no surprise to those close to the programme when Jon told reporters after the announcement of his casting, 'Doctor Who is me – or I am Doctor Who. I play him straight from me.' Just how closely the man and the character he brought to the screen *were* alike was emphasised by television and theatre critic Sheridan Morley writing in *The Times* in June 1976:

'Jon Pertwee's career in show business has not been so much eclectic as purely eccentric and, irritating though it must be for an actor and comedian of his experience to be chiefly known as the hero of the children's television serial, *Doctor Who* (a part he played for four years and gave up two years ago), there is a kind of rough justice in that Pertwee, like the celebrated Doctor, is apparently incapable of remaining in any one place for more than a moment or two.'

Though Morley is wrong to think that Jon is in any way irritated to be known for having played the Doctor, he is right in declaring his career to have been eccentric, as a run through the facts soon reveals . . .

Jon was born on 7 July 1919 into a family with the strongest possible theatre connections, thereby – as he says – making a career in acting almost a foregone conclusion. His father was Roland Pertwee, the author of several successful stage dramas; his aunt Eva Moore, was a celebrated actress whose daughter Jill was Laurence Olivier's first wife; his grandmother Emily an opera singer; while his brother Michael became a playwright; and his cousin Bill was destined to become an actor and comedian like himself. Jon recalls his youth vividly:

'I suppose anyone named Pertwee has to be an actor or a corn merchant, which is more or less the same thing, though I did have an uncle who was the head of the Poetry Society so that adds a touch of class.

'I started in the usual way – family concerts at Christmas – but in a house in Drayton Gardens which is now a kindergarten where I watched my daughter forty-five years later dancing in a Christmas play, so you never really get away from anywhere for long.

'I was the youngest of my lot and a hopeless child: the theatre seemed such an obvious thing to do that I started rebelling before I'd even joined it. Because it was the family business I never had to struggle to join in – I took it for granted, which is maybe why some people say I've never taken it seriously enough.'

Jon Pertwee as the Doctor and Katy Manning as Jo Grant penetrate Dalek headquarters in 'Planet of the Daleks', 1973

Jon started his career at RADA in the 1930s and remembers with a wry smile that the principal, Kenneth Barnes, soon told him he had no talent and should choose another career. However, just before he was due to leave, he took two small parts in an end-of-term mystery play – appearing as the murder victim in act one, and a police inspector in the last act. Noel Coward, who was adjudicating on the production, announced at the end that he had only seen two actors during the entire performance who might *just* make professionals . . . the murder victim and the police inspector!

Jon, barely able to restrain his mirth, decided there and then that acting must, after all, be the profession for him!

After that he spent years working in repertory companies around the country – years in which his sense of humour frequently got him into trouble.

Still, his humour stood him in good stead during hard times and he was encouraged by a chance meeting with the great Charles Laughton who told him that being expelled from RADA, as he himself had been, was guaranteed to bring success! Jobs followed, including the last tour of the Arts League of Service Travelling Theatre directed by the redoubtable Sir Donald Wolfit, spells in a circus and an ice show and then repertory on Jersey where he was once again sacked on the instigation of the leading man who claimed Jon was not taking the job seriously. There was another minor disaster during his time with a company in Brighton when he marched on stage dressed in the costume from the previous production. He had completely forgotten that the programme had changed!

The Second World War intervened and Jon spent five years in the Navy, narrowly avoiding losing his life when HMS *Hood*, on which he was serving, was sunk. It was while he was deskbound working for the Admiralty that he met the radio comedian Eric Barker and began to wonder if he might have more of a penchant for comedy than straight acting.

The two men, who became firm friends, appeared for five years in the popular *Waterlogged Spa*. This led to *The Navy Lark* in which Jon was one of the original participants and it became the longest-running radio comedy series of all time – eighteen and a half years. During the show's run, he earned his reputation as 'The Man of a Thousand Voices', demonstrating a quite phenomenal range of accents which he has since put to good use in his cabaret acts, music hall appearances, in films and, of course, in his television roles. (Notable among his stage performances have been comedies such as *A Funny Thing Happened on the Way to the Forum* and *There's a Girl in My Soup*, and movies such as *The House That Dripped Blood*, in which he played a hilarious vampire, Walt Disney's *One of Our Dinosaurs Is Missing*, and in 1983, *The Curious Case of Santa Claus* with James Coco.

When Jon came to be offered the part of Doctor Who in 1970 while he was busy in *The Navy Lark*, he was completely amazed, as he explains in the accompanying essay. However, once he had overcome his shock and begun work on the part, he determined to make his Doctor more a man of action than a thinker as his two predecessors had done. This, of course, was very much an extension of his own character and also gave him the chance to indulge his love of all things mechanical during his various battles with fiendish enemies of one kind or another. Being the most earthbound of the Doctors proved no draw-back at all!

Jon admits he is fascinated by motorbikes, cars, speed-boats and even aeroplanes and despite his often comic demeanour is actually a very good mechanic. He spends hours tinkering with gadgets of all kinds and was directly responsible for the introduction of several of them into the series. He took special delight in 'Bessie', the yellow Edwardian roadster he was given at the start of his period as the Doctor, and actually helped design the remarkable two-seater, flying-saucer-shaped 'Whomobile', complete with its 'pepped-up' engine, TV, stereo, telephone and special computer bank to enable it fictitiously to take to the air in an emergency!

'I'm a gadget lunatic,' he confesses unashamedly, 'and I'm mad for speed. Give me a car, a motorbike or a boat – and I'm happy.'

This love of fast machines and adventure in general has often caused Jon to play the dare-devil when off-screen – when relaxing at his holiday home on the Spanish island of Ibiza, with his wife, Ingeborg, and two children, Daniel now aged twenty-one and Sean eighteen, he liked nothing better than to go skin-diving or water-skiing, not to mention roaring a tiny motorbike over the local mountains! He prides himself on keeping fit and, during his time as the Doctor, undertook many of his own stunts – mostly successfully, but occasionally with quite painful results!

One of Jon's few dislikes about the series was the Daleks. 'I think they're boring,' he declared when working on one story, 'but people love them, so I suppose I'm wrong.'

His favourite adversaries were the Draconians and he remembers one incident vividly. 'We were on location once and I was talking to an actor dressed as a Draconian during a break in shooting. There we were, sitting on top of a gravel pit in Reigate talking about outer space and life on other planets. I became completely engrossed in the conversation and suddenly realised that, quite unconsciously, I was talking to the man as though he really *were* a creature from another world! A most weird experience. It just goes to show how *Doctor Who* gets into your blood.'

The Doctor did indeed get into Jon Pertwee's blood and he played the role for five years, before deciding it was time for a change. He explained his decision thus to Margaret Forwood of the *Sun* in June 1974:

'For one thing, Roger Delgado, who played the Master, was a very dear friend of mine. When he died, I was terribly upset. Then the producer, Barry Letts, decided to leave. So did the script editor. . . It was the end of an era.'

From playing the Doctor, Jon went back onto the stage in a comedy, *The Bedwinner*, starred for two years in the musical *Irene*, and became chairman of the TV quiz show *Whodunnit*. He also began to develop a part that had actually been offered to him while he was still in *Doctor Who* – that of the tatty old scarecrow, Worzel Gummidge. Jon had loved the books about this character when he was a child and enthusiastically threw himself into getting the programme on to the screen. That was in the mid-seventies – today Jon Pertwee has become famous all over again in this very different role from that of the Doctor.

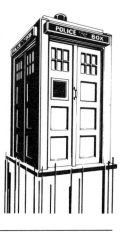

Jon hopes that *Worzel Gummidge* will capture the heart of American viewers just the way *Doctor Who* has done. 'Some American TV tycoons have called it gobbledegook,' he says, 'but at the *Doctor Who* conventions they play the programmes and the *Doctor Who aficionados* have no trouble keeping abreast of the words.'

For a man who has been a Time Lord, obviously no challenge is going to prove too much!

I SAW THE DOCTOR AS AN INTERPLANETARY CRUSADER

by Jon Pertwee

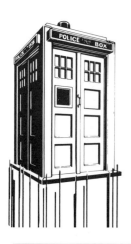

It never occurred to me that I could ever be remotely considered for the part of the Doctor. When Tenniel Evans, with whom I was playing in *The Navy Lark*, suggested I put myself up for the part, I thought it was an absurd idea. I was widely known as a radio and stage comedy actor and they would never take the suggestion seriously.

What then followed was quite extraordinary. When my agent approached the BBC and that long silence on the phone was over, we were told that I was on their short list and had been ever since they wanted a replacement for Patrick Troughton.

When I was finally offered the part I said to Shaun Sutton, then head of drama, 'How do you want me to play it?' 'As Jon Pertwee,' he said, 'just play it as yourself.'

I then began to worry a little. The problem was, I didn't know who 'me' was. It was quite a frightening experience. There was I in my fiftieth year and I'd never really found myself in life. I'd always used another identity in every part I'd played, whether it be by the use of a funny voice or by hiding behind a pair of spectacles. Consequently I found it difficult at first and we were well into the first season before I really started to relax. So, for helping me to realise who Jon Pertwee is, I owe a lot to *Doctor Who*.

The impact it made on my career was immense. I saw the Doctor as an interplanetary crusader and it was this dashing Pied Piper image that appealed to me. I could spread my cloak, take the Earth under my wing and say, 'It's all right now . . . I'll deal with this.' The basic key to the programme's success is that it is pure escapism. What can be better than to drift away to another world in another time and forget about the pressures of everyday life?

We were such a happy team. I'm a great believer in making people feel at home, and we sometimes behaved outrageously on the set. In fact, during my first season, I was taken quietly to one side by the producer who was under the impression I wasn't taking the job seriously. But, of course, I was. It was just my way of working.

In a technical show like *Doctor Who*, things can frequently go wrong during a recording, whereupon I would usually stop immediately. But I remember one marvellous scene from 'The Mind of Evil' when Roger Delgado pulled a gun on me and, in the struggle that followed, we accidentally knocked a jug of water on to the studio floor. It practically turned into a sheet of ice. Roger and I both fell over. Neither of us could stay perpendicular and we kept scrambling for the gun. I was about to stop then I imagined the producer up in the box saying, 'Go on! Don't stop!' So we carried on, and apparently the whole scene looked superb.

Jon Pertwee

November 1982

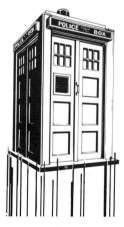

The Doctor in his Whomobile in 'Planet of the Spiders', 1974

TOM BAKER

'Hello, I am the Doctor – have a jelly baby'

The flamboyant Tom Baker who took over the role of the fourth Doctor not only enhanced the character's eccentricity, but secured more publicity for the series than any of his predecessors. He also became something of a cult figure – which was not altogether surprising, for at six foot three inches tall, garbed in frock coat, floppy hat and a seventeen-foot-long striped scarf, Tom came across the screen as very much a larger-than-life personality.

A primary reason for casting Tom in the role had been to try and get back some of the eccentricity of the first Doctor and he himself was never in any doubt of the challenge that faced him. 'It's a fascinating part,' he told the press in February 1974 before beginning work on the new season. 'Probably as interesting to an actor as Macbeth, which I have also played. You have to suggest somebody who is from another world, but has human characteristics. I'm really quite fascinated by science fiction and I'm working on ways of bringing my own interpretation and identity to the part.'

The newspapers, naturally enough, made a point of reporting that Tom had previously played the mad monk Rasputin in the film, *Nicholas and Alexandra* – but two years on, in September 1976, the *Guardian* among others was voicing the general opinion that he was 'an inspired choice' in the part of the Doctor.

'He has turned the character into a cult figure,' said the paper, 'replete with fan clubs and *Doctor Who* societies all over Britain. It is even rumoured that a university administrator recently broke up a student demonstration by announcing that *Doctor Who* was on the television. By the time they realised it was only Tuesday, it was too late!'

Tom's own life and personality are, in fact, every bit as surprising as the events which the Doctor himself has encountered. That same year of 1976, *The Times* caught something of the mercurial side to his nature by declaring that he had 'a range of expressions from the nobly heroic to a fleeting resemblance to Harpo Marx!'

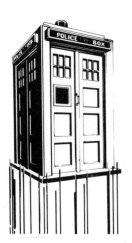

Tom was born 20 January 1934 in Fountains Road in the tough Scotland Road area of Liverpool. His mother was a very religious woman, and he remembers going to Mass many times every week, as well as serving as an altar boy. In this capacity he had to attend many funerals, as he recalled recently:

'Of course, one never had breakfast because one wasn't allowed to eat before communion, and I was standing by the graveside and it was so cold I began to weep as the old lady was lowered. We used to get a threepenny bit afterwards, but a man came over, squeezed my arm, and gave me a two-shilling piece, which confounded me. And it suddenly clanged in my little head – already rapacity was rearing at the age of eight – that he thought I was crying for his mother.'

The young Baker grew up during the years of the Second World War 'when you didn't have to go to school and planes fell out of the sky and the city was bombed almost every day'. He recalls vividly being upset that his was one of the few houses *not* to be hit by a bomb:

'All the children whose houses had been bombed were getting games from America with greetings from the President. I prayed that my mother would be murdered on her way back from the pub where she worked. They'd have noticed me then. Odd, really, considering how much I loved her.'

It comes as no surprise in the light of such remarks to learn that Tom quickly developed a desire to escape from his environment.

'I was always looking for a way out, but how was I to manage it?' he says. 'I was from a poor background: from a house with no books and parents with no experience of how to form one's life.

'Here was a young man desperate to make his mark, fantasising and dreaming. Not clever at school. Rather overgrown and therefore odd to look at. "Good heavens! Is he only eleven? But he's six foot one!" people said. I was skinny and had a curved back because I could hardly ever stand up straight.'

However, the chance to break away finally presented itself when a group of careers officers came to give talks at Tom's school. But it was not an office or factory job that attracted him – instead, the thought of becoming a *monk*! Again, he remembers his feelings at this time very clearly:

'I was interested because, having been brought up by a very devout Roman Catholic mother – my father was away at sea all the time – I was very preoccupied with religion. The man who gave the talk warned us that we would have to take a vow of chastity, poverty and obedience – but that didn't matter to me.

'The chastity was enforced by my age, the poverty was understood and as far as obedience went – well, everybody kicked my backside. And it appeared they fed you as well and you had sheets on your bed. So at fifteen I went into a monastery in Jersey as a noviciate. But I must admit that I only did it to get away from my background.'

For almost six years Tom lived the monastic life with the Order of Ploermel in Jersey, rising early, working hard, praying earnestly. He was, he says, on the verge of a nervous breakdown when he finally realised he would never make a priest. Much to his relief, the Order allowed him to renounce his vows.

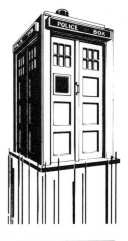

No sooner was he back in civilian life, however, than he was called up to do his National Service in the Army Medical Corps. Curiously, this was to prove the turning point of his life.

Tom explains, 'It was in the Army that I gained the conviction that I could act and enjoy it. I had acted at school and had been offered a job at the Abbey Theatre in Dublin when I was fifteen, but my mother wouldn't let me go.

'I was a terribly withdrawn, pained, skinny man and the Army released me. I loathed Queen's Regulations. It was the enforced contact with people of disparate backgrounds that did it. I was coerced into a unit show. When I discovered I could make people laugh it gave me a new strength.

'It was then I decided: "This is what I want to do." I've had some terrible moments of depression since and sometimes I felt really isolated and lost – but I've never wavered from that feeling.'

Completing his National Service, Tom followed his instinct to become an actor by enrolling himself in a London drama school – filling in the seven-month gap before the term began with a stint in the Merchant Navy which, he says, gave him a loathing of rough seas and opened his eyes to the strangeness of the world when he encountered a burly stoker on the ship who spent his off-duty hours dressed in an evening gown!

Tom studied hard at drama school and then followed a fairly humdrum period working in repertory.

'Nothing really happened to me of any significance until I went to the National Theatre,' he says. 'I was playing a dog in a revue at York – the other man was Professor Laurie Taylor. I was seen and invited to go to the National Theatre. And I played a *horse* – perhaps the most famous horse, apart from Bucephalus – in *The Trials of Sancho Panza*. Things began to look up after that, they let me play human beings. I was happy at the National. I liked being part of a company and Lord Olivier encouraged me and helped me a lot. He was responsible for me getting the part of Rasputin.'

Tom tackled the role of the mad Russian monk with considerable relish and with his piercing blue eyes and powerful voice made a considerable impact on critics and cinema audiences alike. This was followed by other film roles and a number of stage productions including a memorable appearance in *Macbeth* at the Shaw Theatre in London in 1973. Again, Tom has a funny story to relate about this production:

'I was waiting in the wings one night when someone offered me a peanut,' he remembers. 'Without thinking, I took it and put it in my mouth. Then as I went on, a bit of the peanut got stuck in my throat, it stuck on my vocal chords and I was terrified I was about to choke. So I went to the front of the stage and hissed and whispered my soliloquy to the audience.

'Afterwards all the actors crowded around me and congratulated me on what they thought had been a master stroke. Even the director asked, "How did you think of it?" I replied that it hadn't been easy – and then did the same every night after!'

However, in 1974 immediately after playing an evil magician named Prince Koura in the film *The Golden Voyage of Sinbad*, Tom suddenly found himself out of work. To keep the wolf from the door he was forced to seek casual employment – and it was while he was working as a builder's labourer that Barry Letts, on the look-out for a replacement for Jon Pertwee, saw his performance as Prince Koura.

'When they offered me *Doctor Who* I said yes like a shot,' Tom recalls, 'I was on a building site at the time and I handed in my hod with alacrity!'

He threw himself into the role of the Time Lord with unbounded enthusiasm and had soon made the fourth regeneration of the Doctor every bit as popular with fans as the predecessors. Playing the part also

Standing in Bessie, a pensive fourth Doctor ponders a problem in 'Robot' (1974)

worked wonders for Tom himself as he revealed early in 1976:

'Everyone who has played the Doctor seems to have enjoyed it,' he said. 'I find that my face is associated with something very nice and very charming and great fun. It is certainly delightful to see the effect it has on children. I have enjoyed my life much more since I became the Doctor – I used to get terribly tired of Tom Baker.'

And two years later he was still enthusing. 'Some actors get a bit neurotic when they are approached by people and called by the name of the character they play. But I don't mind being called Doctor Who – which I am all the time. I can't tell you just how dull life was when I was just Tom Baker. Simply nobody recognised me.'

This public recognition naturally made Tom a constant source of interest to the press, and his outspoken and occasionally outlandish comments gained him many inches in the gossip columns. But believing strongly in the privacy of his private life, Tom would not discuss his former wife, Anne Wheatcroft, whom he had married in 1960, and by whom he had two sons, Daniel, now twenty-one, and Piers, eighteen. (Tom has, of course, been married a second time to Lalla Ward, who played his companion Romana in the series, but they separated.)

One feature of his success as the Doctor which particularly delighted Tom was his appeal to children. In 1976 he told the *Guardian*, 'A child came up to me the other day and said, "You know, Doctor, you're my hero." And my heart contracted. He felt he knew me. I feel I have a great responsibility to youngsters.'

Later, he expounded further on this theme to another journalist: 'There is a marvellous feeling of intimacy with children, even though they are responding to a fiction. The small ones are not interested in Tom Baker's anxieties, only in the Doctor. They're utterly reliable and rather amusing. I aways try to put them at their ease. I get in first and say, "Haven't we met before? I know! I've seen you watching television." Or if they're very young, "I've seen you hiding behind the sofa." And that slays them, and they just gurgle.'

Tom has always been generous with his time for charity work, in particular visiting sick children in hospital. '*Doctor Who* has brought me so much, the least I can do is make this romantic hero useful where it really matters. With less fortunate kids,' he told Liz Prosser of the *Sun* in 1977.

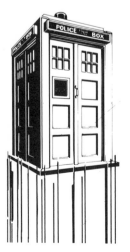

He once boasted that he could sign a hundred autographs an hour. 'But I like to talk to the children as well,' he said. 'They like little gags, too – like signing "To Paul. Who on earth is Tom Baker?"'

Adults, however, have a different attitude towards him, he says. 'Unlike children who are watching the Doctor, adults and older children are watching Tom Baker playing the Doctor and so when they see me in person they will often use me as a springboard to voice their protests about certain aspects of the programme as though it were my fault for playing the Doctor in a way that did not appeal to them. It can be very tedious.'

As with all his predecessors, the moment eventually arrived when Tom Baker decided it was time for him to quit the role. In October 1980 he announced, 'I've been seen by 100 million viewers in 37 countries and got recognised all over the world. There's nothing more I can do but repetition. Finishing with the programme is a great emotional jolt after playing it so long, but we need these emotional jolts in our lives, they are good for us.'

Since putting off his floppy hat and flowing scarf, Tom has demonstrated once again his ability as a versatile actor with fine performances as Oscar Wilde in Peter Coe's play *Feasting with Panthers* and on television as the redoubtable Sherlock Holmes in *The Hound of the Baskervilles*. But having had one taste of journeying into the unknown as he did as the Time Lord, Tom has every intention of trying something similar in the future.

'I look forward to the unknown,' he said recently, 'the wonderful idea that anything or nothing could happen to me. Who knows? Maybe I'll end up digging ditches or working behind a bar, even heaving coal. I wouldn't mind a bit. Anyway, I've been a nomad all my life and always will be.'

There, indeed, speaks a man who, just like the character he so compellingly brought to the screen in his fourth regeneration, stands ready to journey once again to places beyond our imaginings.

I LIKED DOCTOR WHO BECAUSE IT WAS ALL FUN, FUN, FUN!

by Tom Baker

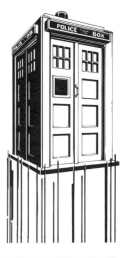

I was terribly out of work when I got the *Doctor Who* job. I was temporarily on a building site when the BBC asked me. A few weeks later some of the men went out to buy the racing edition of the *Standard* and there was my picture on the front page. The BBC had told me not to tell anyone. Those men couldn't believe it – their cement mixer becoming Doctor Who.

Adjusting to the role was not easy to begin with. I had to remember that I did not have an existence as Tom Baker. Apart from my close friends and colleagues, everybody called me the Doctor. Even children in push-chairs pointed at me in the street. I became very aware that they were not looking at Tom Baker, but at this image they had of the character. It was important to me, therefore, that I never disappoint people, especially children. I would never be seen being raucous in the

Tom Baker signing autographs for young fans, 1975

streets or smoking cigars.

One of the surprising things about playing the Doctor was the range of the audience. Although I first thought of it as a children's programme, not a childish programme I hasten to add, there was also a big adult audience. I was astonished to be invited to places like St John's and Somerville Colleges at Oxford and I spoke to absolutely packed halls. If I had accepted all the invitations I received I could have been going to universities three or four times a week!

I went to one of the *Doctor Who* conventions in Los Angeles. These people were coming up with theories about the Doctor I could not understand. I asked them what they wanted and they all wanted the same thing. Would I take them with me in the TARDIS? It was very strange.

Another occasion, I remember, I was returning with a colleague from Blackpool on a Saturday afternoon and I wanted to see the episode being shown that day. So we stopped at a television shop and asked if we could watch the programme. The assistant said she was just closing, but we could go to her house nearby and see it. When we got there we found her two children glued to the programme which had just started. I sat down quietly. Suddenly one of the children looked across at me. Then he looked back at the set. Then he looked back at me again. He couldn't believe his eyes!

The Doctor isn't really an acting part. It's a matter of being inventive enough to project credibility to scenes which aren't credible. The programme is like a hovercraft – on a fine line all the time. You don't dare touch the ground. I think it must have been the part of the Doctor that kept me fresh and young. All that fantasy is good for the mind, you know.

In the end it was not hard to leave the programme. I felt it in my finger-tips that the time had come to move over and give someone else a chance. There was nothing more I could do with it. I really liked *Doctor Who* because it was all fun, fun, fun! There's so much nastiness in the world, so much violence and horror, I want to keep away from it, bury myself in make-believe.

I think the biggest bores in the hero business are James Bond, Kojak, Callan and footballers. They're non-people who do nothing but kick other people. One wouldn't want to have them round for tea. The Doctor doesn't shoot anybody, drink, beat up women, but somehow he has a heroic appeal to children.

I am very pleased and proud to have been a little part of history.

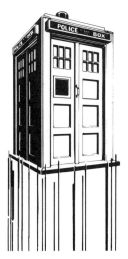

Tom Baker

January 1983

PETER DAVISON

'A Sort of Reckless Innocent'

The arrival of Peter Davison to play the latest regeneration of the Time Lord has in a strange kind of way somehow brought the programme full circle. For, as Peter is happy to admit, he was a fan of the first Doctor, William Hartnell, and one of the series' keenest viewers over eighteen years ago. Then, as a young teenager, he watched with bated breath as the Time Lord faced his latest enemy – and now the passage of time has placed *him* in that self-same position!

Peter is also the first young actor to have played the Doctor – a change that represented a tremendous gamble on the part of both the makers of the series as well as the actor himself. For would audiences brought up to think of the Time Lord as an older man accept this new regeneration in his youthful (albeit Victorian-style) clothes, and frequently reckless, if innocent, manner? That he has been enthusiastically received and the show continued to enjoy some of its highest ratings is a triumphant vindication of both.

As Peter reveals in his accompanying message, he was not immediately sure he *should* take the role when it was offered to him by the current producer, John Nathan-Turner. He asked for time to consider the idea – and found himself being encouraged to do it by his beautiful wife, Sandra Dickinson, who jokingly suggested she should have the part of one of his companions!

John Nathan-Turner, however, was in absolutely no doubt that Peter was the right man for the role. 'He was my first choice,' John said when making the announcement after Peter's agreement. 'I worked with him on *All Creatures Great and Small* and he is a very talented and capable actor. He has everything I am looking for in the new Doctor.'

Although Peter already had several enormously popular TV series behind him, he was quite unprepared for the furore which greeted the news that he was to be the fifth Doctor. He knew that there was always speculation and a bit of excitement surrounding the selection of a new actor to play the part of a character who had now become something of a popular legend. But what actually happened amazed him.

The announcement was made on the evening of 4 November 1980, on BBC's *Nine O'Clock News* and Peter found himself sharing the headlines with the newly elected American President, Ronald Reagan.

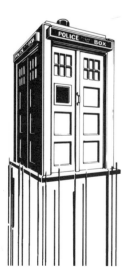

'I was absolutely staggered to see it announced on the news,' he said later, still somewhat shaken. 'I really had no idea that *Doctor Who* was so important. Some of my friends thought I'd died when they saw my picture!'

Being such an obvious contrast to his predecessors, Peter was naturally asked by the journalists who came clamouring after him just how he saw himself in the role. His answer demonstrated both his lively

The young cricket-loving fifth Doctor, Peter Davison

intelligence and his very real determination to create his own version of the character.

'For a start,' he said, 'I will be a much younger Doctor and I'll be wearing a kind of Victorian cricketing outfit to accentuate my youth. I would like him to be heroic and resourceful. I feel that, over the years, the Doctor has become less vital, no longer struggling for survival, depending on instant, miraculous solutions to problems.

'The suspense of "Now how is he going to get out of this tight corner?" has been missing. I want to restore that. My Doctor will be flawed. He will have the best intentions and he will in the end win through, but he will not always act for the best. Sometimes, he will even endanger his companions. But I want him to have a sort of reckless innocence.'

A 'reckless innocent' might almost describe Peter Davison's own childhood, the formative years which lead up to his very successful entry into the world of television. Born in Streatham on Friday, 13 April 1951, his schooldays at the Winston Churchill School in Woking were marked by a disinclination for homework and a fascination with song-writing and playing with tape recorders. His interest in such things had been fostered by the fact that his father worked in electronics – although his parents were more anxious that he should follow a career in banking when he left school.

Out of the jungle into even more trouble – a scene from 'Kinda' (1982)

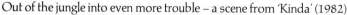

Whether his delight in the *Doctor Who* programme which he watched unfailingly for five or six years from the age of twelve had anything to do with fomenting Peter's restlessness is debatable, but he resolutely turned his back on a career in finance and plumped instead for the uncertain world of acting.

He enrolled at the Central School of Speech and Drama and is the first to admit he did not at first set the world of entertainment on fire with his potential as an actor. He remembers, too, that among the other young hopefuls he worked with, there were two now well-known celebrities, Kate Nelligan and Christopher Blake.

Peter's earliest stage work was in repertory at the Nottingham Playhouse where he spent a year and this was followed by a season with the Edinburgh Young Lyceum Company. He then toured in a highly eccentric version of *The Taming of the Shrew*, produced by Charles Marowitz, but reverted to more conventional interpretations of Shakespearian roles as Speed in *Two Gentlemen of Verona*, Osric in *Hamlet* and Lysander in *A Midsummer Night's Dream*.

Television, though, was already beckoning him. 'It is an ideal medium for good acting,' he declares emphatically, 'and it is every bit as taxing and rewarding as the live theatre.'

Driven by such a strong conviction, it was perhaps no surprise that he should make a success of his first TV appearance, playing in Independent Television's series *The Tomorrow People*. This was followed by an important role as Tom Holland in H. E. Bates' delightful story *Love for Lydia*.

Undoubtedly, though, it was being cast as the young, veterinary surgeon Tristan Farnon in BBC's hugely successful series, *All Creatures Great and Small*, that made him a household favourite. He enhanced his reputation further when he took the lead in two situation comedies, *Holding the Fort* and *Sink or Swim*. Peter particularly enjoyed playing the bespectacled and much-put-upon Brian. His establishment as a major television personality was assured in March 1982 when he was the subject of a *This Is Your Life* programme hosted by Eamon Andrews.

Despite his fame, Peter remains modest and friendly, and despite being cast in what is now undeniably Britain's most popular science-fiction/fantasy series, this has not affected his natural diffidence. Away from the cameras he lives in Surrey with his wife Sandra, their four cats and a mongrel dog called Spot. He is no mean handyman in his spare time and enjoys building bookcases for his ever-growing library.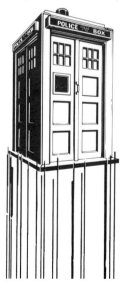

Before commencing work on his first *Doctor Who* story, Peter made a careful study of the performance of his predecessors and resolving how he would develop his own version of the Doctor. That he had to follow in the footsteps of four accomplished actors did not deter him at all.

'I don't consider it a disadvantage taking on a part that is well known,' he told the *Radio Times* in January 1982. 'It is not as if you have to continue the same characterisation. You have to start from scratch. I can learn things from my forerunners, of course. I don't overtly copy them, but I do bear in mind a particular aspect of each one.'

Peter was undoubtedly aided in getting away from the style of the other Doctors by the striking clothes that were designed for him by Colin

Lavers. 'It seemed to me that in some respects the Doctor is essentially English,' he said later. 'So what could be more English than a cricket sweater and a pair of striped trousers like those worn by Victorian cricketers?'

Such inside knowledge of the game is a clear indication that Peter is a fan of cricket. He supports Sussex and also plays regularly for the Showbiz XI in the summer.

The idea of the stick of celery on the lapel of the Doctor's regency-style coat was John Nathan-Turner's, says Peter, and both men resolutely refuses to disclose just *what* the significance of it might be. But one day, perhaps . . .?

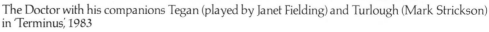
The Doctor with his companions Tegan (played by Janet Fielding) and Turlough (Mark Strickson) in 'Terminus', 1983

Naturally, Peter has ended up putting some of his own personality into the Doctor. 'Not an undue amount,' he stresses. 'A lot of the ideas for things I do are mine which come out at rehearsal, but there is really not much of my own character in him.'

He finds it interesting that some long-time viewers have drawn comparisions between *his* playing of the Doctor and that of Patrick Troughton. For, funnily enough, it was Troughton's Doctor that he watched most regularly when in his teens.

'Any similarities are not deliberate,' he says. 'I would say it has more to do with the fact that I am younger than any of the others. I felt, in a way, I had to be more fallible because I didn't want to play him as a hero as such. The implication always is that if you get someone younger to play a lead part like that you tend to try and make him dashing. I felt he should be a sort of anti-hero – not evil, of course, but someone who doesn't go about things in the way a normal hero would.'

To his millions of fans, Peter Davison *is* a hero, pure and simple. An occasionally fallible Doctor he may possibly be, but a continually exciting and engrossing one he certainly is. That he will eventually turn the role over to someone else is as inevitable as it was for each of his four predecessors.

Yet, for the moment at least, the affairs of the galaxy are undoubtedly safe in the hands of this the fifth and youngest regeneration of the Time Lord from Gallifrey . . .

I THOUGHT I WAS TOO YOUNG TO PLAY THE DOCTOR!

by Peter Davison

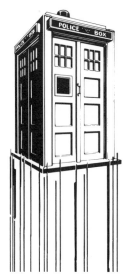

I was a fan of the *Doctor Who* programme eighteen years ago and it had a very big impact on me. Along with millions of other children I used to hide behind the sofa every Saturday evening. The stories used to terrify me and even now I can still vividly remember certain parts, in particular, the Hartnell–Troughton eras. For about five or six years I watched it absolutely avidly.

You can imagine, then, that when I was offered the part of the Doctor my reaction was one of disbelief! At first I didn't know what to think – the idea seemed crazy. But gradually it grew on me.

I think it was because I was the first *young* actor to be asked to play the part that I was so taken aback. It seemed to me I was too young for the role – that the character of the Doctor, as a kind of professor-type, was just not me. It also meant that I was much closer in age to the fans. So I knew there would be special problems I would have to face.

I had a starting point, of course. I could draw a little from each of my predecessors. So I watched old episodes of all the Doctors to see how they had played the part.

I also soon realised that as Tom Baker had played the Doctor for seven years there would be some young viewers who had never known anyone in the part but him. So I had to set out to create a character who was quite different – and this I hope I have achieved.

I see my Doctor as well-meaning – although he doesn't always act for the best. But his overriding consideration is still to sort out whatever problem he is faced with as best he can. He may even endanger his companions in doing this. And he always starts out being polite, but usually gets less and less so as disaster looms!

Funny things happen all the time when we are making *Doctor Who*. For instance, I remember an incident when we were filming 'Arc of Infinity' in Amsterdam. I was playing two parts, you may recall – the other being Omega who was trying to turn himself into the Doctor. Once he turned into me, he started to decay.

In one of the scenes I had to cross Dam Square, which is in the middle of Amsterdam, wearing horrific make-up – a mixture of rice crispies and glue and all sorts of things fixed down one side of my face.

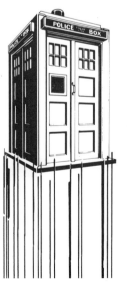

Anyhow, I had to run through the square – which is rather like our Trafalgar Square, full of people and pigeons. It must have been quite terrifying to those people – who, of course, had no idea we were making a film. They just couldn't believe their eyes as I ran by! It wasn't easy for me, either, having to dodge the trams and cars as well.

Getting that scene done was really hard work. We had to do it four times and after all that it was decided it was too horrific and cut from the story!

My total view of *Doctor Who* is that I am playing a part. However, I realise that there is a lot more to it than just acting on the screen. You somehow take on the mantle of the Doctor and a kind of instant charisma goes with the job. You have a responsibility – it is important to be always polite and cheery in public. Fortunately, I'm not a rebel rouser in my private life!

How long will I go on playing the Doctor? At the moment I don't honestly know. It will depend on a lot of things. In the past I have played a number of roles for about three years – so maybe *Doctor Who* will follow the same pattern?

It is really no surprise to me that the programme has been going for twenty years. It is unstoppable now, I think, and has a vast following that just goes on increasing all the time.

I just hope that we can keep on producing the goods and people carry on watching for another twenty years!

January 1983

A fascinating publicity shot for the twentieth anniversary special, 'The Five Doctors'

The sixth Doctor – Richard Hurndall

WHO'S THAT? A SIXTH DOCTOR!

The roll-call of Doctors is not *quite* complete with Peter Davison, however. For in *The Five Doctors*, the special 90-minute-long story to mark the twentieth anniversary of the series in November 1983, a further, *sixth* Doctor makes his appearance.* He is Richard Hurndall who appears in the role of the first Doctor, as played by the late William Hartnell.

Richard, in fact, bears a striking similarity to William Hartnell, and this was a major factor in his being selected for the role. 'Apparently,' he told me, 'John Nathan-Turner thought I would look right for the part. I admired William Hartnell very much and I have tried to play the part as he would have done.'

Curiously, there are interesting parallels in the careers of Hartnell and Hurndall, though Richard did not have to endure quite such a tough childhood. He was born two years after William Hartnell, on 3 November 1910, in Darlington, Co. Durham. After being educated at Scarborough College, he decided on a career in acting and trained at RADA.

Richard made his first stage appearance as a footman in *A Pantomine Rehearsal* in December 1930, and followed this with several years in rep. Like William Hartnell, an early landmark in his career was appearing in *Charley's Aunt* (in 1937) when he played Lord Fancourt Babberley. Similarly, he gained theatre experience in several Shakespearian roles including Bassanio in *The Merchant of Venice* and Laertes in *Hamlet*.

After war service, he continued his stage work and developed a considerable reputation playing legal roles – such as Sir Peter Crossman in *Hostile Witness* (1964). He extended his career by appearing in films – including *Zeppelin* and *Royal Flash* – as well as on radio and in television: most recently in *Enemy at the Door* and *Nanny*.

Richard's suitability for playing a Time Lord like the Doctor was underlined all the more for those who knew that his main hobby happened to be Genealogy!

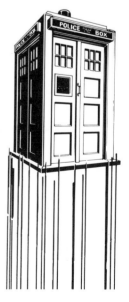

* An interesting feature about *The Five Doctors* was the appearance of Tom Baker. Unavailable for filming, his appearance actually consisted of sequences extracted from the story *Shada* made in 1979 but never shown because of a strike at the BBC. It was the first time any of this footage from Douglas Adam's story had been screened.

Peter Cushing – 'The Forgotten Doctor'

CHAPTER FOUR

THE FORGOTTEN DOCTOR

One of the most curious episodes in the history of *Doctor Who* concerns 'The Forgotten Doctor'. While there is no denying that only five actors have played the Time Lord's major regenerations on television (Richard Hurndall, notwithstanding) another person has also given a further dimension to the legend of the remarkable Doctor – yet today is scarcely remembered in this context. That actor was Peter Cushing and he portrayed the Doctor in two colour films made in 1965 and 1966 in the immediate aftermath of the successful TV launch.

There are those who will argue that, because *Doctor Who and the Daleks* (1965) and *The Daleks: Invasion Earth 2150 AD* (1966) were made specifically for the cinema and the Doctor was portrayed not as a Time Lord but as an eccentric earth-bound inventor, they have no place in our history. But this is not a view shared by many of the enthusiasts who have watched the television series since its inception and – like me – see the two films as very much part of the development of the *Doctor Who* success story. No commemorative volume such as this could or should ignore either the actor or the films.

The idea of transferring the burgeoning popularity of the Doctor – and in particular that of his most famous enemies, the Daleks – to the big screen was that of two well-known London businessmen, Walter Tuckwell, an entrepreneur in the toy field, and Milton Subotsky, a film-maker specialising in horror movies.

Tuckwell had first seen the potential of turning the Daleks into toys for children in the autumn of 1964 and, having agreed a licensing arrangement with creator Terry Nation, began the popularity boom which deluged the marketplace with products by the Christmas of that year. Next, enter Subotsky, who has subsequently earned a considerable reputation for making films based on successful television series. He instantly saw another avenue of exploitation to follow Tuckwell's success in the toy field – a film – perhaps more than one film, featuring the Daleks.

Subotsky therefore made a deal for the rights to make three films based on the series' characters, and then set about readying *Doctor Who and the Daleks* to burst on to the nation's cinema screens – larger in scope, more dramatic as it could now be freed from the confines of the television

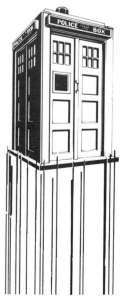

studios and, perhaps most importantly of all, in colour. (The *Doctor Who* television episodes were not made in colour until January 1970.)

Naturally enough, Subotsky chose to use Terry Nation's story 'The Daleks' as the basis for his first film, and signed up David Whitaker, the script editor on the TV series, to help him take care of the re-writing necessary for the transfer to the big screen. Apart from some changes in the characters and story line, the height of the specially made Daleks also had to be enlarged by over a foot and broadened for easier handling by the operators inside. A budget limit of £200,000 was put on the film (large then, but less than the cost of a four-part *Doctor Who* serial today!) and shooting took place in Studio H at Shepperton – at the time the largest film stage in Europe.

Although Milton Subotsky had his 'stars' in the shape of the Daleks, he needed a Doctor. William Hartnell who had, after all, created the part on television seemed the obvious choice. But Subotsky decided on the tried and tested cinema box office appeal of Peter Cushing.

Today, Peter Cushing regards the selection of himself in preference to William Hartnell with the gentleness and wry good humour that is so typical of him. He recalls how it came about:

'I had played Winston Smith in *1984* on television and it was probably the highlight of my television career,' he says. 'I'd like to have done the film version, but they gave it to Edmond O'Brien. I still don't know why.

'Then the next thing is, I'm playing Doctor Who while Bill Hartnell is doing it on TV! That's the way it goes. Down one minute and up the next. After a time you get used to it.'

Milton Subotsky also changed the Doctor's companions. He gave him *two* granddaughters, Barbara, played by the attractive Jennie Linden, and Susan, a vivacious schoolgirl played by Roberta Tovey. Ian Chesterton was lifted from the TV series but, instead of being a well-bred hero, was played by comedian Roy Castle as Barbara's boyfriend, a sincere but rather accident-prone buffoon.

In the light of the great interest which exists in the early appearances of the Daleks, the story line of this first film incarnation is, I think, well worth repeating here:

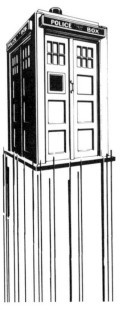

The TARDIS is the latest invention of the Doctor (Peter Cushing). A Time And Relative Dimension In Space machine, it can transport passengers to another world, at another time. With his granddaughters, Barbara (Jennie Linden) and Susan (Roberta Tovey), the Doctor demonstrates the machine to Barbara's boyfriend, Ian (Roy Castle). Ian trips and stumbles against the control panel and the four humans are instantly ejected away from Earth.

Landing in a vast petrified forest, they find a box of drugs mysteriously placed near their spaceship. Leaving these inside the TARDIS, they set out to explore a futuristic city, glistening beyond the forest on the horizon. This, they discover, is the all-metal city of the Daleks. A greedy war-mongering form of life, the Daleks are shielded by mobile metal cones and armed with flame guns which can temporarily cripple. The cones and city protect the Daleks from radiation, which has ravaged their planet since a massive neutron war.

The Doctor and his party are taken prisoner. And Susan, the youngest and least affected by the polluted atmosphere, is sent to collect the drugs – assumed to counteract radiation – from inside the TARDIS. The Daleks' aim is to copy the drugs, emerge from their protective city and ultimately to destroy the only other form of life on the planet – the Thals.

On her way Susan meets Alydon (Barrie Ingham). Gentle and friendly, he is leader of the Thals. It was he who had left the drugs for the visitors from Earth. He now gives Susan his white plastic cape and asks her to carry a message of friendship to the Daleks, together with a request for food for his starving people.

Back at the metal city, the Daleks trick Susan into inviting the Thals to collect food. But the Doctor deduces that the Daleks are generated by power from the metal floors. Covering their cell with Alydon's plastic cape, the humans capture their jailer. Cut off from the generating power, the gruesome creature dies . . .

Meanwhile, an array of Daleks lie in ambush for the approaching Thals. The escaped prisoners shout a warning just in time. And, as the Daleks open fire, most of the Thals escape from the city with the visitors from Earth. Discovering that they cannot be protected by the drug, the Daleks decide to explode a giant neutron bomb. This will increase radiation and exterminate the Thals.

Flashing mirrors to confuse the guards, the Doctor, Alydon and a party of Thals attack Dalek City. The trick fails. The Doctor is taken prisoner. But Alydon escapes to round up a relief army of Thals. Crossing massive chasms and monster-infested swamps, Ian, Barbara and two Thals enter the city through an unguarded front. In a corridor they are cornered by two Daleks who open fire. Alydon and his relief army arrive just in time. They up-end the Daleks, who are immediately destroyed by their own flames.

In the control room a countdown has already started on the neutron bomb. Daleks and Thals fight out a terrible battle. Ian helplessly tries to switch off the mechanism. The Daleks fire on him furiously. He ducks. And the whole panel goes up in flames.

With the countdown arrested and the power cut off, the Daleks are exterminated. The Thals are free to live in peace on their far-away planet. And the Doctor and his party can return to the TARDIS and – they hope – Earth . . .

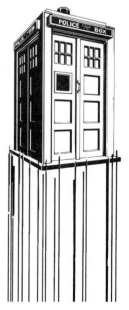

Once *Doctor Who and the Daleks* was completed, Subotsky and Regal Films instituted a vigorous publicity and promotion campaign which resulted in a summer of extremely successful box office business throughout the country. And this was despite an almost universally hostile reception from the film critics.

Leonard Mosley, one of the doyens of British film writers at the time, said the film 'hits you in the eye like a squirt of fly-spray' and declared of the Daleks, 'Their abrasive voices cut your ear-drums. Their spiny protuberances spit smoky venom. They pretended to be dead at the end of the film, but I don't believe it.'

Alexander Walker was even more depreciating: 'I am not at all surprised that the Daleks are so popular,' he wrote. 'I am only a bit depressed. For Terry Nation's armour-jointed serial on BBC TV, now mutated into a wide-screen Technicolor movie, embodies everything I shrink back from in daily life. Call me a prophet of doom for the under-twelves if you wish, but I find the whole set-up infinitely sinister.'

And he went on: 'Space ships in other science fiction fantasies have often been cosy old crates. But the Doctor's flying laboratory is camouflaged as one of those chilly mini-dungeons you find on street corners, namely a Metropolitan Police call box. No wonder it ushers us straight into a police state.

'The Daleks probably appeal most to people who live out of tins. They strike me as the final glorification of the juke box which has had servile TV panels pronouncing judgement on its "Hit or Miss" utterances and now rounds angrily on the humans belching fire and steam.

'Daleks talk in a hyphenated infant's primer way, which betrays a low level of literacy for all their technological know-how.'

Conversely, despite their lack of enthusiasm for the film, all the critics were quite prepared to admit that it *would* prove popular and that the Daleks would be back again on the screen before long. In this respect, if in no other, they were quite right.

Peter Cushing here takes up the story again. 'It was no surprise to me to learn that the first Doctor Who film came into the Top Twenty box office hits in 1965, despite the panning the critics gave us. That's why they made the sequel, *Daleks: Invasion Earth 2150 AD*. And why they spent almost twice as much money on it.'

The new picture was to be much more lavish than its predecessor, with extra money for location work and special models. Perhaps the most stunning creation on Studio H at Shepperton was a 120-foot flying saucer built by Ted Samuels which straddled the ruins of a London street.

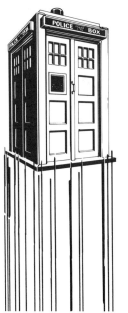

Peter Cushing and Roberta Tovey were again cast in the leading roles, although this time Barbara was replaced by Jill Curzon as Louise, a neice of the Doctor. Ian Chesterton disappeared altogether, with another comedian Bernard Cribbins moving in to play a central part as a rather ineffectual policeman, Tom Campbell, who mistakes the TARDIS for a real police box and is transported to the year 2150 along with the Doctor and his companions. Here the time travellers discover the Daleks busy 'robotising' the population.

One immediately noticeable fact about the film was that the Daleks were much more murderous in their intentions. This, apparently, had been brought about as a direct result of Milton Subotsky receiving many letters of complaint – mostly from younger viewers – who felt that the Daleks had not killed enough people in the first film: only one, in fact! So the new movie was liberally sprinkled with explosions, massacres and cries of 'Ex-ter-min-ate!'

Once again I think the story line of the film – another joint effort by Milton Subotsky and David Whitaker based on Terry Nation's serial 'The Dalek Invasion of Earth' – is worth including here.

Earth is an eerie and sinister place in 2150 AD. Subjected to a ferocious Dalek invasion, it has been bombarded with meteorites and cosmic rays. Its cities have been smashed. Whole continents wiped out. Human beings turned into living dead men – Robomen – able to act only on radioed instructions from their masters. Other humans have been commandeered to work as slaves in a massive mine in Bedfordshire. Only a small group of resistance fighters holds out in London . . .

A brilliant scientist, the Doctor (Peter Cushing) is transported into the future by a time and space machine. He arrives at the height of the crisis, bringing with him his niece, Louise (Jill Curzon), his granddaughter Susan (Roberta Tovey) and Tom (Bernard Cribbins), a passing policeman who stumbled into the machine when the controls were already set.

As the party from the present survey the desolate future, a Dalek saucer flies in to land in Chelsea. Two resistance fighters, David (Ray Brooks) and Wyler (Andrew Keir), escort the girls to safety in their hideaway. But the Doctor and Tom are taken as prisoners to the spaceship.

Despite widely broadcast threats of extermination, the morale of the resistance fighters remains high. They gallantly attack the spaceship with hand-made bombs. David helps the Doctor escape.

Daleks – Invasion Earth 2150 AD

Daleks – Invasion Earth 2150 AD

But Louise – separated from the resistance fighters – is left behind with Tom inside the spaceship. And the Daleks, immune to human bombs, emerge the victors.

Wyler returns to the resistance headquarters to take Susan and their crippled leader, Dortmun (Godfrey Quigley), to greater safety in the suburbs. As they leave they are menacingly surrounded by Daleks. Dortmun hurtles his wheelchair forward and is brutally exterminated. But Susan and Wyler accelerate through in a speeding van.

Forced to run for it when their van is ray-bombed by the spaceship, Susan and Wyler seek refuge in a cottage, where a family work at clothing the slaves. Desperate for food, the family betray them to the Daleks. And the fugitives are taken as prisoners to the Bedfordshire mine.

When the spaceship lands, Louise and Tom escape through a disposal chute. And in the mine they meet the Doctor and David who have discovered the cause of the invasion. The Daleks' aim is to blast out the planet's metallic core through a fracture in the Earth's crust and pilot it as a spaceship.

But the Doctor has also discovered the fatal weakness of the metal invaders. Any deviation in the aiming of their bomb would unleash a strong force of magnetic energy and destroy them . . .

Throwing himself at a master microphone, the Doctor commands: 'Robomen attack Daleks.' Under cover of battle, Tom boards up the main shaft of the mine and the bomb explodes in the wrong place, at the wrong time.

Sucked into the core of the Earth, the metal invaders are exterminated. And human beings are once again masters of their planet.

Strangely, though this film was to be generally praised by the critics, it did much less well at the box office than its predecessor. Cecil Wilson of the *Daily Mail* headlined his review, 'Oh, the joy of seeing the Daleks thumped again' and went on:

'There used to be a fairground sideshow called "Breaking up the Happy Home" in which for a small fee you could hurl wooden balls at a kitchen dresser just to see how much crockery you could smash. You did it with a free conscience because it was not a real kitchen anyway and I find much the same uninhibited destructive appeal about these Dalek films.

'From the moment Doctor Who is pitchforked by a time and space machine into a stark future and sees their flying saucer land in what he calls, "The vicinity of Sloane Square", I cannot wait for him to annihilate these metal monsters.'

And the previously scathing Alexander Walker conceded: 'Actually it's all much more inventive than the first Dalek film. The sets are quite an eyeful, so are the special effects, and director Gordon Flemyng can teach Disney a lot about packing in the action.'

Despite this praise, *Daleks: Invasion Earth 2150 AD* took much longer to recoup its cost at the box office and consequently Milton Subotsky has not

yet taken up his option to make a third Dalek film. But that is not to say, as he himself has declared more than once, that he will not bring back 'those motorised dustbins' (as one of the characters in the second film called them) at some future date.

In the meantime, the two films crop up from time to time at matinée shows and have also appeared on television. Recently, too, they became available as videos.

Peter Cushing, 'The Forgotten Doctor', remembers his part in the films with affection. 'They are among my favourite roles,' he told me recently. 'Especially because they brought me popularity with younger children.'

Prior to these parts, Peter was almost totally identified with horror films. 'I have to admit,' he says, 'that it got a bit tiresome when the neighbourhood kids all used to say, "My mum wouldn't like to meet you in a dark alley!" For, as you know, I'm really a very gentle person, happiest with my collection of model soldiers or reading.'

The two Doctor Who films, however, gave children in particular a new view of him.

'They just loved the Doctor,' he says. 'After all, it is one of the most heroic and successful parts an actor could play. That's no doubt one of the main reasons why the series has had such a long run on television.

'I shall always be grateful for having been a small part of such a success story.'

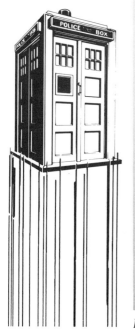

Doctor Who and the Daleks

CHAPTER FIVE

THE GOOD COMPANIONS

During his twenty years of time and space travel, the Doctor has been accompanied by a considerable number of companions of both sexes and varying capabilities. Here, in chronological order, are those 'good companions' with some notes on their characters, comments by the actors who played them and further details about where time has taken them since they left the series. We begin, naturally, with . . .

The William Hartnell Era

SUSAN FOREMAN, 1963–4

The very first of the Doctor's companions was his granddaughter Susan, a fifteen-year-old schoolgirl, who was played by Carole Ann Ford, then twenty-two years old. Carole was selected for the part by the original director Waris Hussein who first saw her, she says, screaming in a television play. 'I think they chose me because they wanted a good screamer. I certainly did an awful lot of that.' Susan Foreman appeared in 'An Unearthly Child' (November–December 1963) as a new pupil at Coal Hill Secondary School and, though she attracted the attention of two of her teachers, her origins were never made fully clear. 'It was never really explained how she came to be with the Doctor,' Carole says, 'but it was sort of accepted that they'd escaped together from another planet. Susan was originally going to be quite a tough little girl – a bit like *The Avengers* lady, using judo and karate – but having telepathic communication with the Doctor. Then they decided they wanted me to be a normal teenage girl so that other teenage girls could identify with me. But I was allowed to keep my scientific mind.' Susan ultimately parted company with the Doctor in the twenty-second century after 'The Dalek Invasion of Earth' (November–December 1964) when she decided to marry and help rebuild the devastated world. Carole Ann Ford herself got married – to a Czech businessman – and retired from acting in 1976 to have her second child. She has recently resumed her career, starting with a leading role in 'The Five Doctors', the twentieth anniversary special.

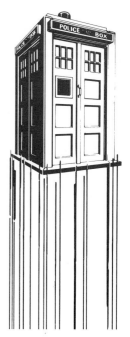

IAN CHESTERTON, 1963–5

'Mr Chesterton' was Susan's science master at Coal Hill Secondary School who have discovered the cause of the invasion. The Daleks' aim is fellow teacher Barbara Wright to investigate their mysterious pupil's supposed home in Totters Lane. He was played by William Russell, an actor already familiar to television viewers. 'I had also worked on the stage and made a number of films, including *The Great Escape* in 1962, when I was offered the part in the series,' William says. 'As the Doctor was something of an enigma, they wanted another man to play a kind of conventional hero-figure.' Ian Chesterton proved to be brave and resourceful, ever ready to fling himself into action, and he has the distinction of being not only the first of the Doctor's male companions but also the oldest! When he left the series in 1965 after 'The Chase' (May–June 1965) – along with Barbara Wright – both were to be replaced by much younger companions. William Russell, a former ex-president of RADA, is now at fifty-six a highly-regarded actor and at the time of writing was on a world tour with the Actors' Touring Company.

BARBARA WRIGHT, 1963–4

Barbara, the third of the original companions, was a history teacher at Coal Hill Secondary School, who stumbled into the Doctor's exploits along with her colleague, Ian. Played by Jacqueline Hill, Barbara was in her mid-thirties and proved to be the oldest female companion to date.

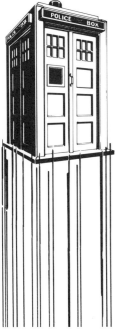

The Doctor with his first three companions, Ian (William Russell), his granddaughter Susan (Carole Ann Ford) and Barbara (Jacqueline Hill)

'As history was my subject it meant that I had a knowledge of the various people and customs that we encountered in the adventures,' says Jacqueline. 'Although I suppose my temperament meant that I often came into conflict with the Doctor who gave the impression he knew *everything*!' Barbara is also remembered for her ability to function without panic in even the most tricky situations, a quality missing in some of her female successors. Jacqueline Hill worked hard for her success on television, having first to seek employment as a wages clerk before her part-time studying won her an acting scholarship to RADA. She made her début in 1953 and, although she later became best known for her work on British television, she had periods on American TV and as a top fashion model in Paris. Jacqueline retired from acting in the late sixties to marry and have two children. However, in 1978 she returned to the stage, and has also appeared on television in *Romeo and Juliet* (directed by her husband, Alan Rakoff, in 1979) and in the ITV series *Tales of the Unexpected*. She came back to *Doctor Who* briefly in 1980 as Lexa in 'Meglos.'

Vicki (Maureen O'Brien)

VICKI, 1965

Vicki was a castaway on the planet Dido whom the Doctor saved in 'The Rescue' (January 1965) and thereafter replaced Susan. Although she was seen to be much the same age as her predecessor, Vicki was far more child-like and naive. She was played by 21-year-old Maureen O'Brien who recalls, 'I was cast as an orphan in the series and that fact along with my innocence and general clumsiness seemed to endear me to the Doctor – as well as the viewers.' Vicki left the series at the end of 'The Myth Makers' (October–November 1965) when she decided to change her name to Cressida and stay with the Trojan youth named Troilus – thereby creating the paradox of living and eventually dying before she was born! Actually born in Liverpool, Maureen worked as floor-manager at the Liverpool Everyman Theatre before successfully auditioning for the part of Vicki and beginning what has since proved a notable career on television and stage. Her major roles in the theatre have included *The Merchant of Venice* and *The Seagull* and her television dramas include *The Whiteoaks of Jalna*, *The Lost Boys* and recently as Morgan Le Fay in *The Legend of King Arthur*.

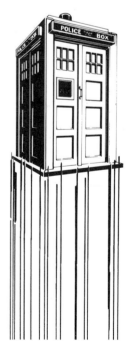

STEVEN TAYLOR, 1965–6

Steven Taylor was another human being found in dire straits in 'The Chase' and rescued by the Doctor to accompany him on his travels. He was an astronaut whose space craft had crashed on the planet Mechanus where he was held prisoner by the robot Mechonoids. Like his predecessor, the school teacher Ian, Steven proved something of a hero and was always ready to give the Doctor as good as he got in any argument. Peter Purves, who brought Steven to the screen when he was twenty-six and later became famous as a presenter on the *Blue Peter* television programme, recalls his introduction to the series vividly: 'The first *Doctor Who* audition I went to was for the part of a monster. They were looking for giant butterflies and moths who could "move well". As I'd just done a season dancing in the chorus at the London Palladium I thought I'd give it a try. But the director said, "Not really for you, I think, but I'll bear you in mind when I need a human."' The man, Richard Martin, was as good as his word, as Peter explains further: 'Sure enough, I was cast soon afterwards as a hillbilly American who was on top of the Empire State Building when the TARDIS landed there. Having done that, I was offered the part of Steven . . . he was argumentative and capable of making decisions for himself, if not always the right ones. Quite a together, headstrong young man.' Peter left the series after 'The Savages' (May–June 1966) when Steven remained behind as the leader of the primitive tribesmen. Thereafter he was out of work for over a year before working on Z-*Cars* and then landing the job as presenter on *Blue Peter* which occupied him for 900 appearances. He is married to Kathy Evans and appears now as a host on BBC's *Stopwatch* and as commentator on professional darts.

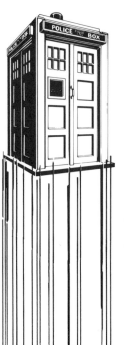

A problem for the Doctor and companions Steven (Peter Purves) and Katarina (Adrienne Hill). Bret Vyon (Nicholas Courtney, left) ponders the future—where he would return as the Brigadier

KATARINA, 1965

Katarina was the pretty and defenceless handmaiden rescued from the ruins of Troy by Steven during the historical story of 'The Myth Makers'. She was a servant to the prophetess Cassandra who found herself embroiled in the battle for Troy when the Greeks use a huge wooden horse (an idea thought up by the Doctor!) to gain entry to the city. During this attack Steven is wounded and Katarina comes to his aid. When she decides to leave the carnage of Troy and travel with Steven and the Doctor she finds herself transported to worlds beyond her imagination. 'She was really a very simple girl, lost once she was taken out of her ancient world into the high technology of the TARDIS,' said Adrienne Hill who played the role, 'but she returned the kindness of Steven and the Doctor by sacrificing her life for them.' Adrienne, an accomplished and forceful actress with a wide range of acting experience behind her, had to sublimate her natural instincts in order to play the timid slave girl. Katarina's tenure as replacement companion to the Doctor, after Vicki had decided to stay behind in Troy with Troilus, was, however, short-lived, for in the following twelve-episode story, 'The Dalek Masterplan' (November 1965 to January 1966), she was one of two companions (Sara Kingdom being the other) who lost their lives saving the Doctor from the infamous Daleks. Katarina's one object in life had been the hope that the Time Lord would transport her one day to the Palace of Perfection and, while death robbed her of this chance, Adrienne Hill's goal of going to America to continue her career was fulfilled shortly afterwards. She lives there still with her husband.

SARA KINGDOM, 1965–6

Although Sara Kingdom appeared as a companion of the Doctor in only one story, it was in the twelve-episode 'The Dalek Masterplan', the longest ever *Doctor Who* adventure. Sara was a ruthless and dedicated forty-first century secret agent of Mavic Chem, the Guardian of the Solar System, who had betrayed Earth by giving the marauding Daleks the necessary element to create the supreme weapon, a Time Destructor. Such was her dedication that Sara even killed her own brother, Bret Vyon (played by Nicholas Courtney, later to become famous in the series as Brigadier Lethbridge-Stewart). However, when she learned Mavic Chem's true intent and how misplaced her loyalty to him had been, Sara changed sides and joined up with the Doctor to defeat the Daleks. The cost of this triumph was, however, her own life when she was unable to pass through time with the Doctor and perished as she quickly aged hundreds of years. This central role was played by Jean Marsh, later to become enormously popular as the maid Rose in the long-running TV series, *Upstairs, Downstairs*, which she herself created with Eileen Atkins. 'I was a pretty cold-blooded person before I realised what was going on,' says Jean reminiscing about 'The Dalek Masterplan'. 'But once Sara saw the light most people took to her. It was a challenging role, about the only one where I have had to change my character so dramatically during the

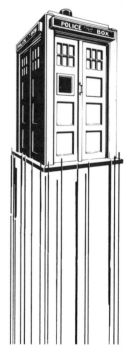

course of a story.' Jean, a naturally warm and sparkling person off screen, was later married to Jon Pertwee while he was playing the Doctor (although she never again appeared in the series) and now, aged forty-three, lives in America where she is very busy working in films, the theatre and on television, most recently in the series *9 to 5*. She also has plans to write a novel and create another TV series with Eileen Atkins.

The ill-fated Sara Kingdom (Jean Marsh)

DODO CHAPLET, 1966

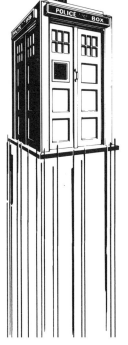

When Dodo, the mischievous cockney teenager, appeared in the series in 'The Massacre' (February 1966), by stepping into the TARDIS on her way home from school in the mistaken belief it was a real police box, it was almost as if time had gone backwards, for she bore a striking resemblance to the Doctor's granddaughter, Susan. Like her, she was dark-haired, elfin-featured and child-like, though somewhat different in her use of slang language which almost drove the Time Lord to the verge of distraction! There was another curious coincidence linking the two in that Jackie Lane, who played Dodo, had met Verity Lambert when the producer was casting the first companion. 'I very grandly said I didn't want to be in a programme for a whole year and promptly spent a year out of work!' she says. 'When I was asked three years later to join *Doctor Who* I was delighted to have a second chance, and particularly to be playing a character who I hoped would bring an element of comedy and fun.' Jackie had begun her acting career at the Library Theatre in Manchester, and then came to London where she made her TV début in *The Caucasian Chalk Circle*, followed by parts in the serials *Coronation Street* and *Compact*. Being only five feet tall and slight of build made her ideal for girl-woman roles, and she smiles impishly when reminded of her six

The elfin-featured Dodo (Jackie Lane)

Doctor Who stories. 'I found it very entertaining,' she says, 'and of course in those days a programme dealing with time travel was a novel idea. It was also enormously enjoyable. Although putting together any television programme is a serious business, there were lots of laughs and I worked with some fine directors and actors.' After bowing out in 'The War Machines', when she and the Doctor were forced to part company after she had nearly fallen victim to the renegade computer, WOTAN, Jackie Lane worked abroad for a time, ran an antiques business and then became an actors' agent. Among those she has since secured work for has been Tom Baker producing 'voice-overs' for TV commercials!

POLLY, 1966–7

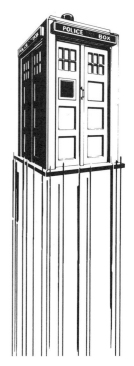

Polly was the 'dolly bird' who introduced the swinging sixties to a slightly bemused Doctor in 'The War Machines'. A vivacious, attractive blonde with blue eyes and a splendid figure, Polly worked as an assistant to the designer of the WOTAN computer, until she inadvertently walked into the Doctor's life when she also mistook the parked TARDIS for a real police box! With her at the time was a merchant seaman, Ben Jackson, and together they became the Doctor's new companions (continuing after William Hartnell's 'regeneration' into the Patrick Troughton era.) Polly was played by beautiful Anneke Wills, who had started acting at eleven, been 'chucked out of RADA' to use her own words, but still secured a lot of work in plays, TV and films before she joined *Doctor Who*. Anneke had her own very definite ideas about how she was going to portray this particular female companion. 'I wanted to play her like myself,' she says, 'scatter-brained, or "kooky" as the newspapers persisted in calling me. I thought it would be a very good idea to play a total coward. Television was full of brave ladies in those days. I wanted to be a sort of feminine anti-hero, a weedy, frightened lady who screamed and kicked and shouted, "Doctor!" at the least sign of danger. I think Polly got a bit braver towards the end.' Anneke says she enjoyed her role, particularly after Patrick Troughton joined the cast. 'The series was much more "me" when Patrick took over, because I always felt it should have been played more for comedy.' At the time of her appearances, Anneke was married to Michael Gough (who had himself appeared in the title role in the story of 'The Celestial Toymaker' in April 1966 and as Hedin in 'The Arc of Infinity' in January 1983), and she left in 1967, also at the same time as Ben Jackson, following a nasty brush with the Chameleons at Gatwick Airport in a story called 'The Faceless Ones' (April–May 1967). 'I suppose *Doctor Who* really brought me to the public eye,' she says, 'though when I left the series I couldn't get a job for months!' For a time Anneke ran an arts centre, but today lives in India.

The second Doctor, Patrick Troughton, with his first companions, Polly (Anneke Wills) and Ben (Michael Craze)

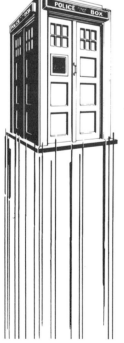

BEN JACKSON, 1966–7

Although only a cockney merchant seamen, Ben Jackson proved himself among the most resourceful and loyal of all the Doctor's assistants once he found himself caught up in the Time Lord's adventures. His practical experience of the sea made him well aware of the need of discipline on board ship – even a 'ship' like the TARDIS – and his technical knowledge more than once enabled him to help the Doctor outwit his enemies. The only difficulty in the relationship between the seaman and the time traveller was caused by the transmogrification of the serious-minded first

Doctor into the comic second one – this was a factor Ben found difficult to accept and several arguments developed between them. The seaman was played by Michael Craze, an actor who had first appeared on the stage as a boy soprano in *The King and I* and graduated to television when he was fifteen. *Doctor Who* was, though, his first series. He recalls: 'Ben wasn't as arrogant as I'd have like to have made him, but he was a tough bloke. Anneke and I spent much of the time being chased by Cybermen, who had just been introduced into the series. We also did quite a lot of time-travelling.' The stories proved very hard work as Michael still recalls. 'There are more problems working in *Doctor Who* than in most other TV series. It's tough making your mark when you're continually surrounded by a bunch of scene-stealing monsters! But it's no fun being inside those costumes, either.' Michael actually met his wife who was an assistant on the set of the series, and continued in acting until 1974. He has since been a publican in Egham, Surrey.

Michael and Polly also bridged the first regeneration of the Doctor which now leads us to . . .

The Patrick Troughton Era

JAMIE McCRIMMON, 1966–9

Introduced into the Doctor's company in 'The Highlanders' (December 1966–January 1967) when he escaped from the terrible slaughter of the English rout of Bonnie Prince Charlie and his Scottish troops at the Battle of Culloden in 1746, Jamie was to show the same kind of devotion to the Time Lord that he had previously shown to his prince. Not the cleverest of people, he was none the less intensely practical and several times saved the vague and absent-minded Doctor from disaster. This loyalty was rewarded by his becoming one of the Doctor's most durable companions, as Frazer Hines who portrayed him recalls: 'Apart from the Doctors, I suppose I was one of the longest-serving members of *Doctor Who*. For three years Patrick Troughton, Deborah Watling and later Wendy Padbury and I had an absolute ball together. I think there's always room for fun when you're working – except, maybe, if it's Chekov or Shakespeare – and I've always been a practical joker.' With a Scottish mother, and a love of costume parts, Frazer took to the role of Jamie with ease and became such a favourite that his original booking for only four episodes was extended. 'The response was so good that they asked me to stay,' he recalls. 'And Jamie was given plenty of action which, again, suited me, because I'm always ready to swash my buckle.' Having to wear a kilt also brought Frazer its own particular problems. 'It could be a bit chilly at times,' he says, 'but the big question people always wanted to know was: Did I or didn't I wear anything under it? Well, I'll tell you: I did – usually football shorts, so I could get a game of soccer as soon as I'd finished on the set. But I always tried to keep it a secret and had it written into my contract that they had to watch their camera angles!' In the end Jamie McCrimmon did not leave his mentor voluntarily, but at the conclusion of 'The War Games' (April–June 1969) when the Time Lords

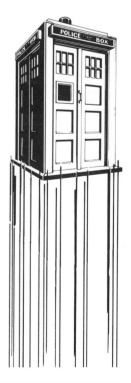

exiled the Doctor to Earth and changed his appearance (into that of Jon Pertwee), the young Scotsman was returned to his own time in the eighteenth century. Success has since followed success for Frazer Hines and his most recent television appearance has been as Joe Sugden in the popular series *Emmerdale Farm*, and he made a guest appearance in 'The Five Doctors'. He is married to the well-known television actress Gemma Craven.

A brisk walk for the Doctor, the redoubtable Jamie (Frazer Hines), and pretty Victoria (Deborah Watling)

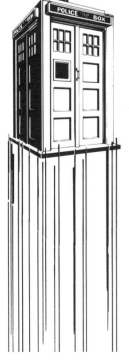

VICTORIA WATERFIELD, 1967–8

The demure and attractive Victoria, the daughter of a Victorian scientist, proved to have one particularly valuable asset during her exploits in the company of the Doctor and Jamie – a piercing shriek. Deborah Watling, who brought this young lady to the screen, confesses: 'I was first seen in *Doctor Who* screaming at the Daleks and I think I continued screaming for the next year. I screamed myself hoarse at every monster that came in sight, which was rather wearing but quite fun, because I'm not the timid type at all.' Victoria became a sort of adopted daughter to the Doctor after her father, Edward Waterfield, was killed saving him from a Dalek death ray in the story 'The Evil of the Daleks' (May–July 1967). The sheltered upbringing which Victoria had enjoyed until her confrontation with the Daleks was in stark contrast to that of Deborah Watling. Born into one of England's best-known acting families, her mother, father, elder sister and brother have all made careers in the profession, performing on the stage as well as in films and on television, Deborah was herself already appearing in public when a child. (The author of this book was himself fortunate enough to have appeared with young Deborah on a panel judging an Essex cinema's Saturday morning matinée contest for children back in the early 1960s.) In one of the Doctor's adventures, 'The Abominable Snowman' (September–November 1967) Deborah appeared with her father, Jack Watling, and remembers the time vividly. 'I'd never acted with him before and it proved hysterical,' she says. 'At one point Frazer and I were meant to be running down hill away from the Yeti when my dad, playing a professor, met us. Well, Frazer and I charged down the mountainside to be confronted by this incredible figure with a grey beard and white hair. I couldn't believe it was Dad and just stood there until the three of us collapsed in giggles.' Victoria left the series as she had come in – screaming. Her screams helped put an end to the Weed Creatures in 'Fury From the Deep' (March–April 1968) whereupon she decided to give up her life of time-travelling and settle with the Harris family. Deborah herself has remained anything but stationary in her professional career, featuring with Cliff Richard in the film *Take Me High*, and in several television productions including a recent appearance as 'naughty' Norma in *Danger UXB*.

The delightful Zoe (Wendy Padbury)

ZOE HERRIET, 1968–9

'The Doctor is almost as clever as I am,' Zoe once declared and, as a former computer scientist and astronomer from a Space Wheel who joined the time traveller from a future Earth age, there was a certain justification in her claim. Undoubtedly she was quite capable of coping with dire emergencies (she destroyed a Cyberman invasion fleet), had a very high intelligence (outwitting a computer), yet could still be puzzled by the commonplace (Jamie had on one occasion to explain to her what a candle was!) The uniqueness of this particular companion was heightened all the more by her very youthful looks, a feature that caused actress Wendy Padbury to be often cast in roles much younger than her true age. Wendy, who joined the Doctor on 'The Wheel in Space' (April–June 1968) to thwart another Cybermen invasion of Earth, recalls that she was twenty-five at the time. 'I'd always been cast as schoolgirls,' she said, 'because I was small and looked young. But Zoe was supposed to be ageless even if she did look young. She was originally intended to be a computerised type of lady without many human emotions. At the start she was different from the other girls the Doctor had been involved with – a bit more in control, I suppose. But it didn't take long for her to become a gibbering wreck, screaming in the corner like everybody else. She did maintain her super intelligence, though.' Wendy had worked in television, on the stage and appeared in the film *Charlie Bubbles* (1967) before joining *Doctor Who* and playing opposite a childhood favourite. 'It was super to work with Pat Troughton and Frazer Hines all that time,' she says. 'Patrick had been my favourite actor since I was a child. My mother and I were absolutely potty about him. He's got such a fantastic face. The three of us all left together (after *The War Games*). What a sad day.' Wendy married another well-known television actor, Melvyn Hayes of *It Ain't Half Hot, Mum*, and has continued to work in television recently making a children's series, *Over To You*. She made a guest appearance in 'The Five Doctors', and also achieved the unique distinction of playing another companion of the Doctor when she took the part of Jenny to Trevor Martin's Doctor in the stage production, *Doctor Who and the Daleks in Seven Keys to Doomsday*, at the Adelphi Theatre in London in 1974.

With Jamie and Zoe returned to their respective times, the 'cosmic magician' regenerated again into a very different Doctor and we enter . . .

The Jon Pertwee Era

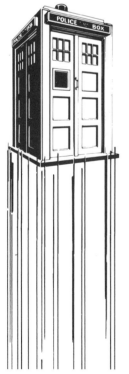

LIZ SHAW, 1970

Although Liz was a Cambridge University scientist with degrees in physics and medicine, she was also a very pretty lady who most attractively decorated the series as the third Doctor's first companion. Despite her high IQ, Liz was never quite able to comprehend some of the Doctor's more advanced reasoning, yet still provided him with a useful and adept assistant. The part provided a particularly exciting challenge for actress Caroline John who wanted the opportunity to prove that 'I wasn't just a long-skirted wench.' She explains, 'Until then I'd done nearly all classical theatre – with the National Theatre Company and reps around the country. So, in an effort to change my image, I had a picture taken in a bikini (rather pin-uppy, really, and not me at all) and then I got the part in *Doctor Who* . . . Liz Shaw was a mini-skirted lady, at least. With a first-class brain, mind you. I bought an encyclopedia especially to look up half the things she was talking about. I joined at the same time as Jon Pertwee ('Spearhead From Space', January 1970) which was lovely because the programme was getting a new sense of purpose and being taken rather more seriously.' Caroline remembers driving the Doctor's car, Bessie, as one of her fondest memories of the series. 'The only trouble was I hadn't passed my driving test,' she says. 'When I drove we had to use a disused airfield and the director, cameraman and lighting man all piled in the back. I think they were very relieved when I stopped!' Liz Shaw also provided the link between the Doctor and the British Division of UNIT – the United Nations Intelligence Force based in Geneva and set up to fight extra-terrestrial threats. Ultimately she resigned from UNIT to return to Cambridge after defeating the threat of Professor Stahlman's terrible gas in 'Inferno' (May–June 1970). Caroline herself retired from acting after her marriage to actor Geoffrey Beevers, to have a family, but has now returned to work on television, most recently appearing with Tom Baker in *The Hound of the Baskervilles* and in a cameo role in 'The Five Doctors'.

The third Doctor, Jon Pertwee, and his companions from UNIT, Brigadier Lethbridge-Stewart (Nicholas Courtney) and Liz Shaw (Caroline John)

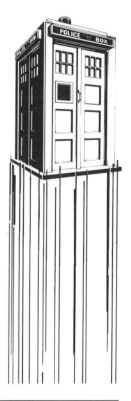

ALASTAIR LETHBRIDGE-STEWART, 1968–

Lethbridge-Stewart, 'the Brigadier' as he is known, became regularly associated with the Doctor during the period of the Time Lord's exile on Earth. A career soldier, he first met the Doctor during the events of 'The Web of Fear' (February–March 1968), and they were reunited in 'The Invasion' (November–December 1968) when UNIT was formerly established. The Doctor later became scientific adviser to UNIT in 'Spearhead From Space' (January 1970) when Lethbridge-Stewart presented him with the yellow roadster, Bessie.

Born into the distinguished Scottish clan Stewart, the Brigadier had been destined to a military career from his childhood, and quickly showed all the characteristics of a fine officer – the ability to command, act swiftly and precisely, take no nonsense and display great courage when needed. Actor Nicholas Courtney who made such a convincing personality of him was never in any doubt as to the kind of man the soldier was. 'I wanted the Brig to be a human being, not a cypher,' he said in 1973. 'I tried to make him endearing and get some fun into the action, the sort of unintentional humour that arises out of character and situations. I sometimes had my tongue in my cheek with the Brig, I admit, but I was not doing a Monty Python and trying to send him up. I didn't want him to look a twit. I think he has always appeared genuine. At least a brasshat from the War Office once told a producer, "He's exactly like our lot!"' Nicholas also has the unique distinction of being the *only* actor to have appeared with all five Doctors: he played the ill-fated Bret Vyon with William Hartnell in 'The Dalek Masterplan'; introduced Colonel Lethbridge-Stewart in 'The Web of Fear', in which the idea of UNIT was born; was promoted to Brigadier and then worked extensively with Jon Pertwee; sought the aid of Tom Baker to fight 'The Terror of the Zygons'; and most recently came out of 'semi-retirement' as a teacher to help Peter Davison in 'Mawdryn Undead'.

It is interesting to find, in the light of his subsequent career, that Nicholas had a grandfather who was a drama critic and wrote plays and a father who was an Army Officer before entering the Diplomatic Service. He himself was born in Egypt and spent much of his early life moving about the world with his parents from one diplomatic posting to another. He got a taste for acting while at school and when he settled in London, in 1948, he trained at the Webber-Douglas Drama School after completing his National Service. 'I never did any acting in the Army, except in keeping out of trouble,' he says. 'It's an interesting observation that people make when they suggest the Brigadier came from my years in the Army, because in actual fact I never rose beyond the rank of a trooper, which is the equivalent of a private in the Armoured Corps! So I never had any ambitions to be a real officer which I suppose is strange, because, despite all my years in the acting profession, the Brigadier is the role by which I am best known.' Of this role which made him famous, he adds: 'The Brigadier was based on General Mitchell, "Mad Mitch", who was around at the time, in so far as, like all good officers, he would lead his men from the front and never ask them to do anything he couldn't do.' Not surprisingly, Nicholas is highly regarded because of his unique contribution to *Doctor Who*, has a very large fan following, and is frequently asked to conventions both in Britain and overseas. Speaking of his association with the five Doctors, he gave this view of each of them recently: 'Hartnell I think you would describe as tetchy. Pat Troughton was whimsical. Jon Pertwee possessed great panache. Tom Baker I did not get to know well enough, and Peter Davison is very talented and will I am sure be a very successful Doctor.'

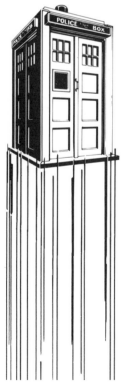

SERGEANT JOHN BENTON, 1968–75

Benton was a regular soldier brought into UNIT when the fighting force was introduced to viewers in 'The Invasion'. He became one of the few full-time members of Brigadier Lethbridge-Stewart's force and proved himself both a skilful soldier as well as a devoted subordinate to the Doctor. His knowledge of weapons, his training in military techniques and his sound sense of discipline not only saw him safely through UNIT's first terrifying encounter with the Cyberman in 'The Invasion', but through numerous later battles and ultimately earned him promotion to Warrant Officer. John Levene who played Benton says the role brought him similar success in his acting career. 'It was a really lucky break,' he recalls, 'I'd had no formal acting training, and before Benton I'd only had work as an extra.' In 1968 he came into contact with the series when he operated one of the Yetis in 'Web of Fear'. This was followed by the offer of playing a UNIT soldier. 'Originally, Benton was going to be just one of several soldiers,' he says, 'but he became so popular that the part was built up. The only thing was that whenever the story ran a bit long it was always my lines that were cut!' John's natural sense of humour and good looks made him a favourite with many viewers and he well remembers the day when the entire female staff of a Lancashire factory wrote a fan letter saying how much they liked him! RSM Benton was an ever-present character in the series until the last UNIT story, 'The Android Invasion' (November–December 1975), while John Levene continued in other television productions such as *Tightrope* and *The Adventurer*. He now runs a video advertising agency.

Off-duty – three of the men from UNIT (l. to r.) Sergeant Benton (John Levene), 'the Brig' and Captain Yates (Richard Franklin)

CAPTAIN MIKE YATES, 1971–4

Captain Yates, the archetypal, dashing young Army officer, was transferred into UNIT during the 'Terror of the Autons' (January 1971) and found himself immediately in conflict with that other infamous Time Lord, the Master, who was also making his first appearance in the series. Yates's skill as a leader of men was proved in 'The Mind of Evil' (January–March 1971) when he led the attack on Stangmoor Prison and again in 'The Daemons' (May–June 1971) when he once again helped thwart the Master in his demonic plans against the inhabitants of Devil's

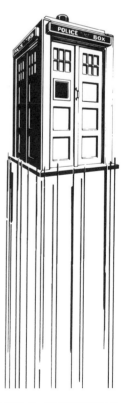

End. Richard Franklin, who played the Captain, took the part of an Army officer in his stride because he had actually been one! 'I served for a while in the Rifle Brigade before I took up acting,' Richard explains. 'So I had an immediate feel for the part. In fact there was a lot of me in Captain Yates, particularly the restless nature.' This restless nature had caused Richard to quit the Army and go into RADA where he trained in the classical roles. He performed a wide variety of parts for the Century Theatre Company before breaking into television. 'I found *Doctor Who* a very interesting series, but very different from playing Shakespeare!' he says. Mike's career with UNIT was not without its dangers and he was invalided out of the force after the terrible events of 'The Green Death' (May–June 1973). He did, though, make a valiant return from retirement in 'Planet of the Spiders' (May–June 1974) to warn the Doctor about the impending invasion of the insects from Metebelis 3. Since his role in the programme, Richard has continued in mainly theatrical roles with one appearance in that other space drama, *Blake's Seven*; he was also a guest artist in 'The Five Doctors'.

JO GRANT, 1971–3

The zany Jo, pretty, scatter-brained and accident prone, had to overcome an initial resentment on the part of the Doctor when she was foisted on him by Brigadier Lethbridge-Stewart. The Brigadier had himself taken her rather reluctantly into UNIT when a relative in the United Nations had pulled some strings to gain her entrance to the special group. Although

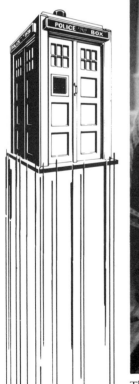

The Doctor with the delectable but scatterbrained Jo (Katy Manning)

trained in espionage techniques, Jo invariably found it difficult to put her training into practice and this led to the despairing Brigadier turning her over to the Doctor. The Time Lord never quite managed to make her the scientist he thought she could be, but still formed a warm, personal relationship with her and they shared many hair-raising exploits. Introduced in 'Terror of the Autons', Katy Manning, the daughter of one of Fleet Street's most famous sports journalists, J. L. Manning, explains how she managed to make the part of Jo so appealing to audiences: 'You can't really separate me from Jo Grant,' she says. 'As I grew up, so did Jo. When I started I was a right little teeny-bopper, even if I was twenty-one. Five feet tall with a mini-skirt tiny enough to match my height and rings on every finger . . . I suppose Jo ended up pretty much as she started – short-sighted and screaming. Still a freak, only a more sophisticated freak.' To the Doctor's evident sadness Jo eventually departed from the series in 'The Green Death' to marry the scientist Professor Jones. Katy herself was sad to leave the programme. 'I shall never forget *Doctor Who*,' she says. 'I only left because I thought I ought to branch out a bit to see if I could really act. But it was a wrench. I'm a bit like him in a way – an adventurer. Nothing ever freaked me out – mainly because I'm so short-sighted I couldn't see what was happening!' Since her departure, 32-year-old Katy has made headlines by posing in the nude with a Dalek for a girlie magazine, marrying and separating in just two months and most recently starring as a junkie in the series *Target*. She is now married to actor Dean Harris and they have four-year-old twins. They live in Australia.

SARAH JANE SMITH, 1973–6

Sarah Jane was the first of the Doctor's liberated female companions – unlike most of her predecessors she was more inclined to take action when in a difficult spot than resorting to screaming for help. She was a freelance journalist by profession and fiercely independent by nature, a trait she had developed from being orphaned when young and brought up by an aunt, Miss Lavinia Smith, who also happened to be a distinguished scientist. It was indirectly through this aunt that Sarah Jane joined up with the Doctor, having assumed the indentity of Professor Smith to gain entry to a top secret research centre to investigate the mysterious disappearance of some scientists and their equipment in the story of 'The Time Warrior' (December 1973–January 1974). It was here she encountered the Doctor who was on the same mission at the instigation of UNIT. Although her belief in women's liberation made her rebel at the churlish way the Doctor first treated her, Sarah Jane soon grew to like him as his attitude softened and together they tackled a host of strange monsters and devious enemies. Elisabeth Sladen, the Liverpool-born actress who played Sarah Jane, says that for all her self-assurance the young journalist did have her weaknesses. 'She did need a bit of protection. She thought she could stand on her own feet and would always have a bash at things believing she was right. But somebody normally ended up telling her she was wrong – and that was

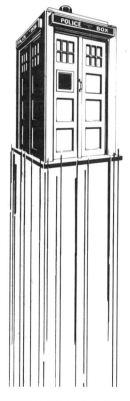

The fourth Doctor, Tom Baker, with the resourceful Sarah Jane (Elizabeth Sladen)

usually the Doctor.' Elisabeth, who had gone to drama school in Liverpool and then appeared in stage productions of plays like *The Crucible* and *Othello* in the north before coming to London and finding work in television, (*Coronation Street* and *Z-Cars*) took to *Doctor Who* because she loved science fiction. 'I'm easily spooked,' she says, 'I don't mind monsters like the Daleks, but it's the smaller ones, the little moving things, that frighten me. I hate creepies.' The lengthy partnership was broken when the Doctor was unceremoniously summoned to Gallifrey in 'The Hand of Fear' (October 1976) and knew it would be impossible to take Sarah Jane with him. Elisabeth has continued to be busy in television – most recently in the BBC classic serial *Gulliver in Lilliput* and she made a guest appearance in 'The Five Doctors'. She is married to actor Brian Miller. (For further details, see 'The Story of K9' p. 109.)

Before the parting of the ways with the Doctor, Sarah Jane was a witness to his fourth incarnation into . . .

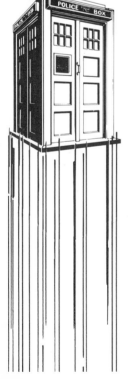

The Tom Baker Era

HARRY SULLIVAN, 1974–5

Dark-haired, handsome Harry Sullivan was a member of the UNIT team who was directed to assist the Doctor immediately after his fourth regeneration in 'Robot' (December 1974–January 1975), although unfortunately his ability to innocently cause near-catastrophes made the Time Lord explode on one occasion, 'Harry Sullivan is an imbecile!' None the less this former Royal Navy officer and qualified surgeon proved a loyal assistant and ever-ready protector of Sarah Jane. Like several other actors who have appeared in *Doctor Who*, Ian Marter, who played Harry Sullivan, had made an earlier bow in the series as a young Merchant Navy

The naval man turned companion, Lieutenant Harry Sullivan (Ian Marter)

officer named Andrews in 'Carnival of Monsters' (January–February 1973). 'Barry Letts, who was the Director of "Carnival", remembered me when he became producer of the series and that's how I was offered the role of Harry Sullivan,' says Ian. 'Harry really had a knack at getting others into trouble!' The role may have somewhat belied Ian's talent as a serious actor – prior to the series he had been a member of the Bristol Old Vic and since it he has appeared on the stage in *Conduct Unbecoming* among other notable parts – but his good looks made him a firm favourite with many viewers. Harry Sullivan eventually parted company from the Doctor in 'The Android Invasion' (November–December 1975), having been safely returned to his own time; and Ian is still busy in the theatre, as well as retaining his link with the series by writing novelisations of some of the stories for Target Books! His one regret is that the screenplay he wrote for a full-length feature film of *Doctor Who* with Tom Baker back in 1976 has never come to fruition.

LEELA, 1977–8

Leela could hardly have been a more striking contrast to Sarah Jane when she appeared as the Doctor's new female companion in 'The Face of Evil' (January 1977) – although she was just as independently minded and very willing to stand up for her own rights. Brought up as a fighting warrior in the fierce tribe of the Sevateem who had degenerated over the years from advanced star travellers to a near stone-age culture, Leela both looked and behaved like a glamorous female Tarzan. As strong and deadly as any man when it came to fighting, she was initially baffled by the Doctor's humanitarian ideals, but her savage skills were gradually harnessed under his influence for more worthwhile purposes. Louise Jameson came to her part of the female warrior after training at RADA and a string of

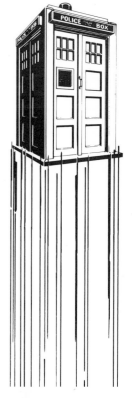

distinguished roles with the Royal Shakespeare Company as well as appearances in the West End and on the New York stage. 'It was quite a change of roles for me,' Louise admits. 'For Leela, the only good enemy was a dead one, and she was an expert at bringing about this state of affairs as quickly as possible. Even when the Doctor ended the war her tribe had been fighting all their lives, she still decided that a life of peace and industry was not for her. So she more or less forced her way into the TARDIS knowing that if she stayed close to the Doctor she would still get all the action and adventure her violent heart desired!' During their partnership, Leela's habit of killing first and asking questions afterwards often annoyed the Doctor and led to quarrels, but he was the first to recognise her skill when she more than once saved him from potentially fatal encounters. Leela finally chose to stay on Gallifrey to marry the handsome Captain Andred after the defeat of the Sontarans in *The Invasion of Time* (February–March 1978). After her time in the series, Louise changed her image yet again to play a resilient cockney, Blanche, in the television drama series *Tenko* about women prisoners of war in the hands of the Japanese during the Second World War.

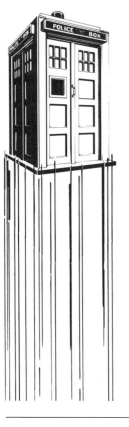

The all-action woman, Leela (Louise Jameson)

The first Romana (Mary Tamm)

ROMANA (First Incarnation), 1978–9

Leela's successor as companion was another striking change, for Romana – or Lady Romanadvoratrelunder to give her her full name – a tall, rather haughty girl, was actually a Time Lord herself and had been seconded to the Doctor's mission to find the all-powerful Key to Time in 'The Ribos Operation' (September 1978). The Doctor had been despatched on this voyage through the cosmos by the White Guardian, who decided that his occasionally erratic subject would benefit from having a companion of his own kind – and a strong-minded, intelligent and determined woman into the bargain. A simmering resentment between the two was natural enough and Romana did not initially help their partnership by declaring herself to be academically far superior to the Doctor. Actress Mary Tamm who played Romana has explained how peace between the two was ultimately achieved. 'Although Romana was very bright and could do everything the Doctor could, what she lacked was his *experience*,' Mary says. 'Once she realised that for all her superior book-learning there was just no substitute for the practical knowledge that her fellow Time Lord could bring to bear in any tricky situation, they got on famously. I loved the part, especially working with Tom who is such a character.' Before joining *Doctor Who*, Mary had been a pupil at RADA in London (a contemporary of Louise Jameson who had preceded her in the role of the Doctor's companion) and the series proved her big break into television. She has since appeared in the BBC drama production *The Assassination Run* and in the film *The Odessa File*. She is married to a stockbroker and they have a small daughter.

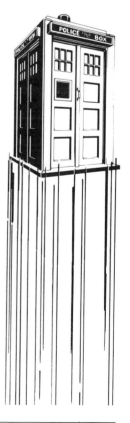

Once the Doctor and Romana had reached a better understanding of each other – and completed their mission in search of the Key to Time – Romana decided at the start of 'The Armageddon Factor' (January–February 1979) to regenerate her body into a more gentle, less bossy companion and became . . .

The second Romana (Lalla Ward),
who became Mrs Tom Baker

ROMANA (Second Incarnation), 1979–81

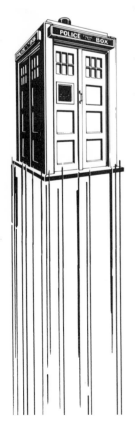

The second Romana, a small, laughing, effervescent figure, was much closer to the traditional type of female companion, although she was still the same highly skilled and occasionally temperamental girl she had been before. This Romana had taken on the face and features of Princess Astra of Atrios whom the Doctor had discovered in 'The Armageddon Factor' to be the final segment of the Key to Time. Regenerated in this shape in 'Destiny of the Daleks' (September 1979), Romana immediately found herself plunged into a dramatic confrontation with her fellow Time Lord's oldest adversaries. The part of this former Princess turned Time Lord was taken by Lalla Ward, herself more correctly known as the Honourable Sarah Ward, daughter of the Viscount and Viscountess Bangor. 'My Romana was a contrast to the first one because it was felt the Doctor got on better with somebody who didn't seem stuck up,' says Lalla, 'but although I was more bubbly, I still didn't allow myself to be pushed into the background or bossed about as some of the earlier girls had.' Lalla's happy on-screen relationship also developed off-screen and in 1981 she and Tom Baker got married. Sadly, though, they parted after sixteen months, with Lalla declaring, 'We were committed every bit as much to our careers as we were to one another. It's that which has driven us apart.' The second Romana departed from the adventures of the Time Lord in 'Warriors' Gate' (January 1981) when she decided to stay in E-space, taking K9, as a gift from the Doctor, with her. Lalla has continued to work on the stage (in the play *The Jeweller's Shop* written by the Pope) and on television (recently in the BBC's *School Girl Chums*).

ADRIC, 1980–2

The appearance of Adric was another new departure in the series, for he was the first young boy to become one of the Doctor's companions – albeit that he achieved this status by initially stowing away on the TARDIS. Adric was one of a group of lads known as the Outlers whom the Doctor and Romana encountered on the planet Alzarius in the story 'Full Circle' (October–November 1980). He helped the two Time Lords to escape a nasty fate at the hands of the marshmen and then stowed away to join in their adventures. Adric was played by eighteen-year-old Matthew Waterhouse, who had been plucked from the BBC's news information department to appear in the series *To Serve Them All My Days* and then moved on to *Doctor Who*. 'It was a great challenge,' says Matthew, 'because I love science fiction and horror and I knew all about the appeal of the series before I joined.' Matthew was ever-present through the following two years, bridging the Doctor's next regeneration in 'Logopolis', but suffering a fate only inflicted on two earlier companions – a heroic death. In yet another of the Doctor's many battles with the insidious Cybermen, 'Earthshock' (February–March 1982), Adric demonstrated his devotion to the Time Lord and his cause by getting blown up by one of their bombs while trying to save Earth. After the episode Matthew confessed that he was 'a bit disappointed and upset' about being killed off rather than written out of the series. He said, 'The Doctor's companions normally leave by falling in love or going off to help some underdeveloped planet – there's never been one of them killed before.' In fact, of course, Katarina took her own life to save the Doctor in 'The Dalek Masterplan', as did Sara Kingdom who could not travel in the TARDIS without instantly ageing hundreds of years.

Adric (Matthew Waterhouse) the young companion who met an unhappy end

NYSSA, 1981–3

With Nyssa, this survey moves into the latest group of companions continuing the saga of twenty years of travelling with the ever-unpredictable Doctor. She, however, was not introduced initially as a companion in 'The Keeper of the Traken' (January–February 1981), but as the beautiful daughter of the noble, peace-loving Consul Tremas. This plan was thwarted by an evil statue-creature name Melkur who corrupted the happy world and then revealed itself to be none other than the Master's TARDIS in disguise! When exposed, the Master, now at the end of his twelfth and final regeneration, took over the body of Tremas. Nyssa was later brought to the Tom Baker Doctor by the Watcher (a future projection of the Peter Davison Doctor). And, like Tegan, Nyssa is actually a link between the two eras – the Tom Baker Era and the Peter Davison Era. She joined the Doctor in the hope that on their travels she might meet up again with the evil Time Lord and be able somehow to help her father return to his former self.

Sarah Sutton, who plays Nyssa, came to the series as a nineteen-year-old with ten years of acting experience already behind her. She did not come from an acting family, however, for her father was an airline pilot. 'It all started because I went to ballet school for nine years,' she explains, 'and there was an agent for the whole school who happened to be there visiting one of the performances we did at our little theatre, and she suggested that I went for an audition. And thereafter audition just followed audition.' Her first professional engagement was aged nine years old at the Phoenix Theatre playing Baby Roo in a musical version of *Winnie the Pooh*, which she repeated for three Christmas seasons. She went on to be Alice in a major BBC production of *Alice Through the Looking Glass* and eventually came *Doctor Who*. She was auditioned, landed a part and then found her involvement in the series growing far beyond what she had expected. 'When I did "The Keeper of Traken" I didn't know that Nyssa was going to be carried on as a companion. She is a very intelligent girl, she's of noble birth and she's very technical, unlike Tegan, her companion, who has no particular skill. Different script-writers do see Nyssa in different lights and so in each story she does end up doing different things and appearing slightly differently.' One of the most striking differences in Nyssa has been her change of costume – from her original all-enveloping maroon outfit designed to reflect her gentle innocence – which she felt was 'rather like something out of *A Midsummer Night's Dream*' – to the revealing lace underwear which delighted all the older boys and men among viewers. This change, along with a similar restyling for Tegan, came about because of specific requests, says producer John Nathan-Turner. 'We granted viewers their wish,' he said in May 1982, 'and decided to show lots more leg!' Rather sadly, Nyssa parted company from the Doctor in February 1983 to minister to the sick Lazars on *Terminus*.

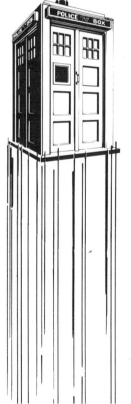

The fifth Doctor, Peter Davison, with his two beautiful companions, Nyssa (Sarah Sutton) and Tegan (Janet Fielding)

TEGAN JOVANKA, 1981–

The striking young air hostess Tegan who inadvertently walked into the
TARDIS while it was grounded in England having its chameleon circuit
repaired by the newly reincarnated Doctor in 'Logopolis' (February–
March 1981) proved an ideal foil to the other companion, Nyssa. For
while the one is quiet and intelligent, the other is easily distracted and
quick to anger. Apart from her more aggressive character, Tegan did of
course have reason to be upset when her aunt was murdered by the
Master, once again plaguing the life of the Doctor and all those close to
him. Janet Fielding, the Australian actress who plays Tegan, says that she
is a character 'you love to hate – rather like a Lucy figure from the Charlie
Brown strip'. Janet herself came to England in 1977, having gained a BA
honours degree in English and Drama at the University of Queensland
and then working in several theatre companies 'down under' for three
years before flying to Britain. More theatre work in England was followed
by her television début on ITV's *Hammer House of Horror* and then into
Doctor Who. 'They were looking for an Australian to play an Australian,'
Janet recalls, 'and although my application was a bit late I got the part . . .
I hope I'm not as aggressive as Tegan. I mean Tegan's reaction to

anything she can't cope with is to get angry – on the assumption if she gets angry then maybe she'll beat it into submission. That's her sort of outlook; take the offensive when you're on the defensive.' Janet also thinks that Tegan is much more meticulous than her. 'She's also totally anti-maths and anti-science whereas I wasn't . . . I once actually thought of going into computers or something like that!' The one thing she would not like to be, she says, is an air hostess. 'I'd loathe it! If I listed all the other occupations I'd rather do, that list would be infinite before it got anywhere near air stewardesses.' Although Janet sees all these differences between herself and Tegan, she believes the character she plays is gradually getting closer to her own. 'I think she is softening. Now that she's getting to know the people in the TARDIS better she is becoming more friendly with them. She is a warm person really. She's not cold by any means, just a little highly strung.' Like Nyssa, Tegan's original stewardess's outfit has been changed to a shoulder-revealing 'boob tube' and shorts, much to the delight of the male fans.

The Peter Davison Era

TURLOUGH, 1983–

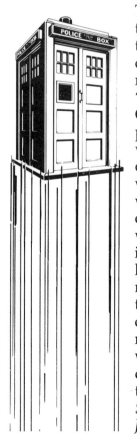

The red-headed, mercurial public schoolboy Turlough is the very latest of the Doctor's companions and, amazingly, he is only the sixth male to be taken on board the TARDIS in the show's twenty-year run (excluding, of course, the Master and the three members of UNIT). Turlough's relationship with the Doctor grew out of most unlikely beginnings in 'Mawdryn Undead', when he fell under the power of the evil Black Guardian and was commanded to destroy the Time Lord. His intriguing personality and unpredictable nature, plus the excitement of the 'will he, won't he succeed?' factor in his mission, gave actor Mark Strickson the opportunity to make an immediate impact on the series – which he took with both hands. Having previously worked mainly in the fringe theatre world with the occasional television series, Mark was delighted with the chance of appearing in the programme because, as he says, 'I remember watching *Doctor Who* as a kid and it's strange to find myself taking part in it . . . It's an amazingly different world, but it's great fun!' Born in the heart of Shakespeare country, Stratford-on-Avon in 1961, the son of a musician, it comes as no surprise to learn that acting and music were the two main interests of his young life. Mark trained at RADA and also took courses in classical music and is now an accomplished player of the recorder, guitar, piano and French horn. His first acting work was touring with the Mikron Theatre Company and during this time he also developed his skill as a musician as well as a composer and writer. Mark's television work to date includes two Granada productions, *Celebration* and *Strangers*, along with the BBC's very popular hospital series *Angels* and *Juliet Bravo*. As one of an increasing number of young actors who have

The unpredictable latest male companion, Turlough (Mark Strickson)

entered the series after being childhood fans, Mark certainly had one of the most imaginative introductions to the Doctor and their relationship is sure to continue along similarly unexpected lines. For as all those who travel with the Time Lord find, no one can be quite sure what the future (or the past, come to think of it!) will hold.

And neither, for that matter, can the Doctor himself!

CHAPTER SIX

THE STORY OF K9

The most unusual of the Doctor's companions – while also being numbered among the most popular – was K9, the Time Lord's electronic friend who combined the merits of a portable computer with the faithfulness of a dog. For three years (in two models) he dogged Tom Baker's footsteps, earning himself an enormous following among viewers and generating a howl of protest when he was put to kennels from the series.

K9 was introduced to viewers on 8 October 1977, in 'The Invisible Enemy'. He had been created by a research scientist, Professor Marius, as a companion in his space laboratory on the Bi-Al Foundation asteroid, where real pets were strictly forbidden. Able to help the Professor with his experiments, as well as keep him company, K9 proved an invaluable aid. His ability to converse with other computers, his sophisticated sensory devices, along with his means of self-protection and advanced weaponry, made him an ideal companion in a tight corner – as the Doctor was later to find out.

The computer dog became the companion of the Doctor and Leela after they had successfully defeated the Virus Nucleus. Realising that he would not be able to take his 'pet' back to Earth with him because of weight restrictions on the space shuttle, Professor Marius bequeathed him to the two time travellers. K9 remained an ever-present companion until after the Doctor's successful battle with the Sontarans in 'The Invasion of Time' (1978) when he decided to remain with Leela on Gallifrey where she was to marry Andred, the Commander of the Chancellery Guards. The smart mut also apparently had designs on increasing his own knowledge with the help of the Time Lords!

Despite the initial reservations that the Doctor had had about the robot hound, he had become more than a little attached to K9 (as had millions of viewers) and he promptly constructed a Mark II model which contained all the features of its predecessor and a number of improvements including more mobility, the power to stun rather than kill adversaries and the ability to respond to a sonic whistle. This new model fearlessly aided his master through various exciting and rigorous adventures, but in 'Warriors' Gate' (1981) was severely damaged and, in order to continue functioning, had to part company from the Doctor, remaining with Romana in E-Space. The loss of the lovable robot was as deeply felt by the Doctor as by many viewers and, as we shall see, led to an attempt to 'reactivate' him in his own series.

The background to the introduction of K9 into *Doctor Who* is an interesting story in itself. Part of his inspiration was the fabulously successful film, *Star Wars*, not long released, which had featured two delightful robot heroes, C-3PO (See-Threepio) and R2-D2 (Artoo-Detoo). The other was a script for a proposed adventure of the Doctor, 'The Invisible Enemy', in which the authors, Bob Baker and Dave Martin, had described a scene in which a character named Professor Marius 'bent down to a mobile computer that vaguely resembled a dog'.

The idea of this 'robot dog' caught the imagination of script editor Robert Holmes and producer Graham Williams and they decided on developing it further. They could call him something like 'Fido' and perhaps make him a new type of companion for the Doctor? The basic concept was handed over to special effects designer, Tony Harding, and within two weeks from his first sketch (reproduced here) K9 was born.

The original concept for K9 sketched by Tony Harding

The finished model did not make its début in the series without problems, however. When the first K9 was cued to enter a set, it suddenly raced off in the opposite direction! Investigation showed that its radio circuitry was being confused by the similar signals of the studio cameras and hence its unpredictable actions. There were occasions, too, when the robot dog careered into pieces of scenery and it proved to be extremely difficult to operate on location when the ground was uneven. It was also noisy and, although incidental music was used to disguise this, only when a rubber belt replaced the chain drive was this annoyance solved.

After two seasons, in which most of the problems had been successfully ironed out and the robot was a firm favourite with viewers, another
more serious one emerged. John Leeson, who had provided K9's
distinctive voice, decided to leave the programme. Knowing that fans
would instantly spot a change in tone in the dog, the Doctor was called
upon to tamper with his mechanism, and in so doing change the sound
he emitted. The result was that the new voice provided by David Brierley
was readily accepted. However, after a gap of one season, John Leeson
returned to *Doctor Who*, as the voice of K9.

The technical wizardry which was employed both on and off screen
undoubtedly went a long way to establish K9's popularity and so it was
perhaps not surprising that when John Nathan-Turner, the new producer
of the series, announced in the autumn of 1980 that the faithful dog was
leaving, a veritable flood of protest letters poured into the BBC. Although
there had been outcries in the past when a companion left *Doctor Who*, no

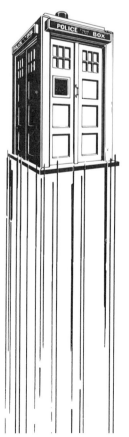

Sarah Jane, K9 and a genuine canine friend, Jasper, filming the special show *K9 and Company* for
Christmas 1981

one in the production office had *ever* seen such a mountain of mail as this
before!

The issue was taken up by the *Sun* newspaper which mounted a 'Save
K9 Campaign' and a nationwide petition was also organised by a book
publishing company. John Nathan-Turner defended his decision in the
press by saying that the dog was no different to any other companion
and, like them, could not be regarded as a permanent fixture.

John could, however, see that there was a quite unique attachment to
K9 and decided to see if the dog could support a programme of its own.

He also felt that such a series – if it came to be – might answer the constant requests he received from fans for the reappearance of earlier companions. First, though, a fifty-minute 'pilot' was required.

The result was *K9 and Company*, in which the dog was co-starred with another of the Doctor's most popular human companions, the journalist Sarah Jane Smith, played by Elisabeth Sladen. The programme was scripted by Terence Dudley, who had earned a considerable reputation as producer of the *Doomwatch* and *Survivors* series, and the director was John Black, who had been in charge of the memorable story 'The Keeper of Traken'.

In the adventure, Sarah Jane found herself the surprised recipient of a K9 Mark III (also voiced by John Leeson), sent by the Doctor, which she promptly used to help solve a mysterious case of witchcraft in the rural Cotswold area of England. Strong support from Bill Fraser as a no-nonsense old soldier and Linda Polar as a suspected devil worshipper made for an exciting programme which was screened on 28 December 1981.

Sadly – for K9's most fervent fans – the response to the programme was not strong enough to justify going ahead with a series, although public demand did lead to *K9 and Company* being re-screened again in 1982.* It does, though, still have the distinction of being the only *Doctor Who* spin-off that has actually been made. And when you consider that at one time or another there were quite advanced plans for separate programmes featuring the Daleks, the men of UNIT and those two extraordinary characters from 'The Talons of Weng Chiang' (1977), the explorer Charles Litefoot and the theatre-owner Henry Gordon Jago, this is no mean achievement!

Thus K9 remains an affectionate memory, though still an important element in the legend of *Doctor Who*. And if, as one fan remarked not so long ago, a dog is man's best friend, then certainly this computerised canine was a Gallifreyan's favourite pet, too!

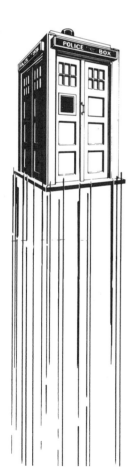

* Curiously, just as the screening of the first episode of *Doctor Who* was bedevilled by events beyond the producer's control – the news of the Kennedy assassination – so *K9 and Company* was hit by a transmitter failure in one of the BBC regions which almost certainly cut down the potential audience.

CHAPTER SEVEN

THE TARDIS – AND THE REALITY OF TIME TRAVEL

'The TARDIS is more than a machine. It's like a person. It needs coaxing, persuading, encouraging.'

The Five Doctors

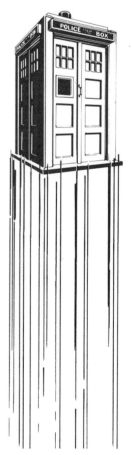

The Doctor's most valuable, not to say most remarkable, possession is surely the TARDIS. For to step into this machine is to be transported into another world – while it, in turn, can transport its occupants through time and space to other worlds with a facility still beyond the capabilities of mere Earthmen.

But is it just a piece of fantasy? A dream given substance and shape only in the adventures of the remarkable time traveller from Gallifrey? The answer is NO – for scientists have for years believed the construction of a time machine *is* theoretically possible: and later in this section I shall try and explain the theory.

First, though, let us take a look into the TARDIS – this magic carpet which can whisk the Doctor and his companions back into the distant past or forward into the far future. And unprepossessing as it looks to our eyes – brought up as we are to equate space travel with sleek rockets and craft shaped like slim projectiles – it is perfectly constructed for the missions it is called upon to perform.

The word TARDIS is an acronym for Time And Relative Dimensions In Space and the machine's primary purpose is as a research and study laboratory: at least that is what the Time Lords of Gallifrey originally built them all for, rather than gallivanting around the galaxies as the Doctor does!

In appearance the machine is like a square metal cabinet, entered by way of a single, sliding door on one face. But this appearance requires disguising for the varying and often dangerous missions upon which Time Lords engage and hence each possesses a chameleon circuit which enables it to take on any suitable appearance wherever it lands.

The Doctor's TARDIS has, of course, been constantly seen in the guise of a 1960s Metropolitan Police call box, a fact which derives from a malfunction in the circuit which occurred when the Doctor materialised it at that point in time in his adventure 'An Unearthly Child', and so far he has been unable to correct the fault. This is not the only trouble which the Time Lord has experienced with his TARDIS, an old Type 40 according to the best information, for it also suffers from erratic steering.

Because of the extremes of speed and the varying types of atmosphere and conditions to which the TARDIS is subjected on its travels – not to mention the fire-power of enemies – the craft is surrounded by its own enormously powerful force field which makes it virtually invulnerable to any attack. Should the enemy attack seem to have any likelihood of succeeding, the TARDIS can, of course, simply dematerialise. In basic terms, then, this remarkable craft is indestructible.

Stepping inside the TARDIS is a remarkable experience, for the senses are immediately overwhelmed in much the same way as entering a hall of mirrors distorts and changes our normal perceptions. For though it seems so small on the outside, inside, the craft is huge, a mass of rooms and passageways which seem almost infinite. In truth, we have stepped across a dimensional bridge.

We are now in a different, but relative, dimension, and perhaps for the first time can truly appreciate why the craft is referred to as Time And Relative Dimensions In Space. For, basically, its actual existence is *outside* time.

How is it possible to have such an extensive complex as we discover within the confines of a police box has long exercised the minds of the Doctor's companions as well as his viewers. He once tried to explain the puzzle to Leela. Taking two boxes, one large the other small, he placed the big one some feet away from his pretty assistant. The small one he then held up near her face and asked which appeared to be the bigger.

'This one,' Leela replied, indicating the little box in front of her eyes – though she knew full well it was in fact the smaller of the two.

'Exactly!' the Doctor grinned. 'Now if you could keep that larger box over there, and yet still have it here, then the larger one would fit inside the smaller one. Temporal Physics, a key Time Lord discovery!'

There is neither the time nor the space for us to see over all the TARDIS – indeed it is doubtful whether the Doctor himself has fully explored his remarkable craft! What little we are privileged to see along the maze of passages and corridors include a huge laboratory for research and study, a workroom for repairing or renovating items of TARDIS equipment, and the power room which houses the energies which drive the craft. There is a dormitory with couch-like beds which swing down from the walls, a bathroom the size of a small swimming pool, and a special alcove containing a food machine geared to satisfy any taste in the universe. Mention should also be made of the wardrobe room – which can supply outfits to suit just about any planetary climate – and a greenhouse in which flourish specimens from the ends of the universe. Perhaps most surprisingly, though, there are *two* control rooms. The second of these two rooms, with wood-panelled walls and an antique control system, gives every indication of now being out of date and only for use in emergencies.

The rarely seen secondary control room of the TARDIS with Tom Baker at the console in 'The Masque of Mandragora' (1976)

However, the main control room, with its brilliant illumination and familiar walls covered by sunken circular designs, has in its centre the most important piece of equipment in the TARDIS – the six-sided control console. This is the heart of the machine and on its smooth functioning depend the lives and well-being of the Doctor and his companions.

Each of the six sides of the console governs specific functions. The most important, naturally, controls the drive system of the TARDIS. On this section is mounted the master dematerialisation switch which, when operated, engages the machine's power sources and 'dissolves' or transports it from one point in time to another. A crucial part of this switch is the circuit which ensures that it does not materialise in a disastrous situation such as in the heart of a burning sun or inside solid rock!

Another of the six sections contains the guidance controls, while alongside this a third panel gives navigational read-outs. A fourth is linked to the machine's computers via the telepathic circuit link, while a further bank of switches and dials controls all the various recording and scanning equipment so necessary on the Doctor's missions. (Opposite this, on the wall, is a screen which enables those inside the TARDIS to see what is going on outside.) The last of the six sections supervises the protection of the machine.

In the middle of the console is the time rotor, a glass column which originally indicated by its movement what the TARDIS was doing. When the column was seen rising and falling the machine was in motion; when it became still the TARDIS had materialised. Then as the rotor swivelled around, the Doctor could collect precise information on the location in which he had landed before actually stepping outside and thereby avoid any unnecessary risks. It has since been simplified and its movement restricted, although still performing the same functions.

A close-up of the console: the very heart of the TARDIS which makes all the Doctor's travels possible

A second batch of very important pieces of equipment is contained in an alcove in the control room. There is the astral map which can project three-dimensional images of all the star systems, and the time path indicator which gives read-outs of relative positions when the TARDIS is in flight. These all help the Doctor to make his incredible journeys in the fourth and fifth dimensions.

Two other interesting features about the machine is that it has an emergency escape door (which exists through the back of the police box) and that it is quite impossible for anyone to fire weapons inside the TARDIS. According to the Doctor, anyone inside the machine is in a state of temporal grace, thereby prevented from conducting any harmful or violent act. However, at the present time, there is a fault . . .

Because of the almost omnipotent power of the TARDIS there are those who see it more as a thinking entity than a machine, somehow able to commune mystically with its master. Certainly, it was able to help in the regeneration of the Doctor into his second incarnation when he lay dying inside it, too weak to summon help. And, again, there are those who argue that some of the machine's more erratic manoeuvres are due to the equally eccentric behaviour of its master!

It is true, of course, that as the Doctor took the TARDIS from Gallifrey without permission – and had not been fully trained in its use – that he is learning things about the machine all the time. Hence his occasional recourse to the TARDIS manual. And it is because of his ignorance of certain things, plus his deliberate avoidance of some of the safety factors, that he gets himself into many of his adventures: in a perfectly functioning TARDIS nothing could go wrong – but what a boring existence *that* would be for our Time Lord!

Two other points of note are, firstly, that although the interior decor of the TARDIS has changed on a number of occasions during the Doctor's adventures, the actual design, and in particular that of the control console, has until recently, for 'The Five Doctors', scarcely been altered since it came from the drawing board of designer Peter Brachaki, twenty years ago. As to the TARDIS actually being seen in spinning flight – although this has naturally been suggested in most stories – it did not occur on our screens until 'Frontier in Space' in March 1973. Certainly there had been shots of the machine prior to this, but this was the first flight sequence.

Now that we have had a brief look at the complexities of the Doctor's time machine, what chance is there that scientists here on Earth might be able to duplicate it? The answer, according to one of the world's leading authorities on space/time travel, Dr Frank Tipler of Tulane University in America, is that it is *not* beyond the realms of possiblity. Dr Tipler is the first to concede that 'the materials needed would be unwieldy and the energy requirements enormous' but is fully convinced that 'the construction of a time machine is theoretically possible.'

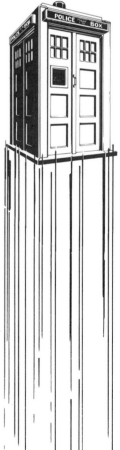

Dr Tipler prefaces his hypothesis by saying that we first have to rethink our traditional notions of space and time. These concepts, which were once considered distinct entities, were inextricably linked by Einstein's theory of relativity. In this statement, the famous mathematician showed how light from the stars does not travel in straight lines but in enormous curves in space. These curves were caused by stars enormously larger than ourselves and the planets in our own system and, because of their strength, could bend light in many ways, even back on itself, so that it is just possible one of the stars we see in the sky could be our own Sun millions of years ago.

Einstein also demonstrated how time moved at different speeds in different parts of the universe. He said that no matter how fast you might travel in a spaceship, light would always appear to you to be travelling at the same speed. However, if you had a clock on board this would be running slower and slower and equally your body would slow down. Hence, said Einstein, it would be feasible if you took a journey lasting hundreds of years in Earth time, you would arrive back at Earth to find people who had been younger than yourself when you left, now long since dead. So you had, in truth, travelled into the future of Earth.

Scientists now recognise time as the fourth dimension of our universe and also that we move through it as well as through space. To visualise space–time, a scientist named Paul Minkowski devised the diagram shown here:

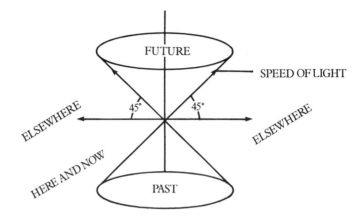

Minkowski said that the horizontal axis represents the three space coordinates while the vertical axis measures times. The diagonal lines – which represent the speed of light – are the outer boundaries of our travel through space–time. Since we cannot go faster than this speed, we can never reach the space–time outside the Minkowski light cone. Information comes to us from the past in the form of light through the lower half of the cone, while light from the present travels towards the future, or top half.

However, Dr Tipler says, the diagram has to be adjusted to account for the theory of relativity that light can be bent by gravity. Hence, if a massive object appears to one side of the light cone, the cone may lean toward the object and the light rays are thereby forever trapped within the attracting object.

Now, says Dr Tipler, if the object were rotating very quickly, its angular momentum would force the cone to tip over and start circling around the rotating body, as is shown in this second diagram:

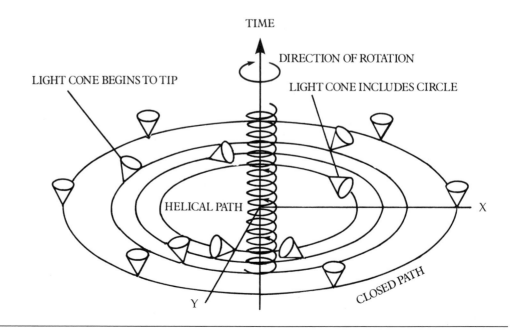

The amount of angular momentum then determines the degree of tipping, says Tipler. As the light cone tips, the coordinate that once measured space begins to measure time. Time, traditonally linear, would then twist around the rotating body in various paths.

Reaching the crux of this theory, Dr Tipler goes on: 'The critical angle for a time machine is forty-five degrees. Once the cone tips farther than that, one edge of the cone will fall below the space coordinates (shown on the diagram as X and Y) and into negative time. A space traveller equipped with a powerful rocketship could travel along any path contained within the light cone.

'If the traveller chooses to glide along the space axis, he will trace a closed path around the rotating body. Though he would be convinced that he was moving forward in time as well as travelling through space, a distant observer would say that his trip spanned only an instant, because he never moved up or down the time axis. Because his path is closed, he would eventually find himself at his original time and place of departure.'

But, says Tipler, if the traveller opted instead for a path *below* the space coordinates – but, of course, *above* the edge of the cone – he would trace a helical path down the axis of time and, therefore, travel backwards in time.

'Each descending revolution would take him that much farther into the past,' says Dr Tipler. 'At any point, he could enter a time earlier in history. And, with some fancy manoeuvring, he could hop back on to another helical path and return home. All along, he is travelling forward in time in the sense that he is travelling in the forward direction of the light cone.'

Tipler believes that the traveller's choice of destinations is only limited by the lifetime of the rotating mass. Before and after the object's existence, there is no angular momentum to tilt the cone and create the time machine. Without the object, the direction of time and light points back up, out of the plane of rotation, never to be reached from this area again.

Dr Tipler has naturally given much thought to the possible construction of his time machine. 'A rapidly rotating neutron star or man-made cylinder might suffice,' he says. 'But it seems more likely that a time machine would require the presence of a naked singularity – a star that has collapsed so completely that it has literally disappeared. A naked singularity differs from a black hole only in that the light that passes near it can, though distorted, escape its strong gravitational pull.'

Even in his enthusiasm for his theory, Dr Tipler is ever the realist, though never a defeatist. 'The stability of massive rotational bodies is questionable,' he emphasises. 'The energy associated with a strong angular momentum would have to be about equal to the rest-mass energy – energy so great that the accompanying centrifugal force may tear the rotating body apart.'

The reader should not for one moment imagine that this is an isolated viewpoint. Scientists in Britain, Europe and even behind the Iron Curtain share similar views to those of Dr Tipler. And his opinions were reinforced only a short time ago when the science correspondent of the British weekly newspaper the *News of the World*, Michael Cable, reported on the work of astrophysicist Dr Vincent Icke of Cambridge Institute of Astronomy, under the eye-catching heading, 'Doctor Who's Time Machine Is Not Just Kid's Stuff.'

Cable wrote, 'When Doctor Who steps into his time machine and travels thousands of years into the future, most TV viewers raise their eyebrows in disbelief. But it is just one more example of a science fiction dream which may become a reality.'

Dr Icke has been researching the possibility of sending a man deep into the Milky Way, says Cable. 'To the centre of our galaxy is a distance of more than 33,000 light years,' he writes. 'Even if an astronaut could travel at the speed of light – 186,000 miles a second – it would take nearly 70,000 years to go there and back.

'But the journey is not as impossible as it sounds, say some experts. Their theory is that if a rocket can maintain a constant acceleration, a speed will eventually be reached at which Earth time no longer applies to those on board.'

Dr Icke now takes up the story. 'This curious effect of time dilation means a spaceman could travel to the centre of the galaxy and back while only ageing forty years. Assuming you could find a volunteer to spend forty years of his life in space, there's still one nightmarish problem.

'For Earth time will have passed normally in his absence. And when the spaceman gets back he'll find himself 70,000 years in the future. By that time the planet may have become uninhabitable. Or worse, the people on it may have evolved into a different race.'

These considerations apart, Dr Icke feels that the greatest problem will be finding the immense power required for such a trip. He believes, though, that eventually 'some matter trawled from space' may provide the necessary fuel.

So, for the moment, the Doctor's TARDIS remains a little beyond our grasp, though not beyond our imagination or that of our scientists. That we *shall* ride to the stars like the Time Lord one day now really seems just a matter of time . . .

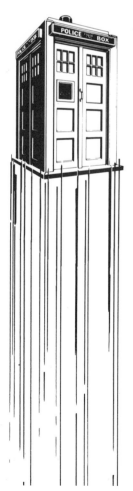

CHAPTER EIGHT

THE WORLD OF GALLIFREY

The Planet of the Time Lords

One of the most ancient dreams of mankind has been to achieve eternal life and be the possessors of all knowledge. Such, indeed, are the attributes of the Time Lords, of whom the Doctor is one, and from whose planet, Gallifrey, he fled one day to begin his wanderings across time and space. These remarkable people and their mysterious planet are, in truth, at the very core of the Doctor's adventures, and as such of primary importance in the study of his legend.

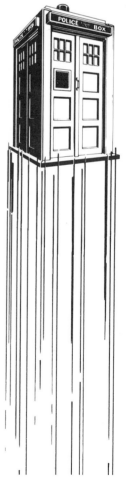

If we could step into a TARDIS of our own, what might we find on Gallifrey?

The planet lies far beyond our earthbound vision, far indeed beyond the range of even our most powerful telescopes, in the constellation of Kasterborus, on the very edge of time and space. It is a sun-lit planet seen from space to be covered by high mountain ranges and vast wastelands. Only occasionally is the wasteland relieved by huge domed constructions, in which are located the planet's highly sophisticated cities carefully protected from the harsh environment. Herein dwell the Time Lords and their society.

Gallifrey is, however, also inhabited beyond the cover of these domes. In the wilderness live the Shobogans, a group of Time Lords who have rejected the society of their fellows and withdrawn into solitude. Here, under the leadership of Nesbin, they watch out for their own interests as well as – when required – those of their planet. They are tough and resourceful beings, as indeed they need to be to survive in the hostile endless wastes of desertland.

The domed cities are in marked contrast to the terrain outside. Hushed like great cathedrals or the hallowed halls of some ancient university (which to a degree they are), they provide an equitable climate in which the Time Lords can perform their eternal tasks. The most important of these domes is Capitol City, a title which speaks for itself, which is located deep in the wastelands of Outer Gallifrey.

To a first-time visitor one strange fact becomes immediately apparent on approaching the dome of Capitol City – it has no aerial entrance. There are a few massive metal doors around the perimeter, but these show no evident signs of having been opened for generations. In fact there is no normal method of entry as we understand it into this temple of profound and timeless knowledge.

Because the Time Lords are of such age and have assembled the wealth of the universe's knowledge, they have long since ceased to need anything as basic as a passageway to leave or enter the city. The manipulation of time which is theirs to command has seen to that.

No traveller could, though, approach the city without his presence being registered and entry is only possible through the transduction barrier. Once the guardians of the capital have established the purpose of the incoming visitor, a split-second gap is created in the barrier to allow entry. Returning Time Lords will generally leave their TARDIS for servicing on arrival: and with their chameleon circuits switched off they make a strangely unimpressive sight, revealed then as little more than plain metal cabinets with a single sliding door on the front. (It should also be noted that while most life forms in the universe require transport craft of one form or another, the senior Time Lords can even do without their TARDIS by using time rings – metal bangles worn on the wrist – which allow them to move freely in the fourth and fifth dimensions.)

On arrival in Capitol City, the visitor is immediately struck by the silence – and the sense of *timelessness* about everything. There is no sense of urgency, no undue bustle here, none of the signs of activity one would expect in a sophisticated modern city. The simply dressed, gowned figures to be seen in the corridors and walkways go about their business as if time had no meaning.

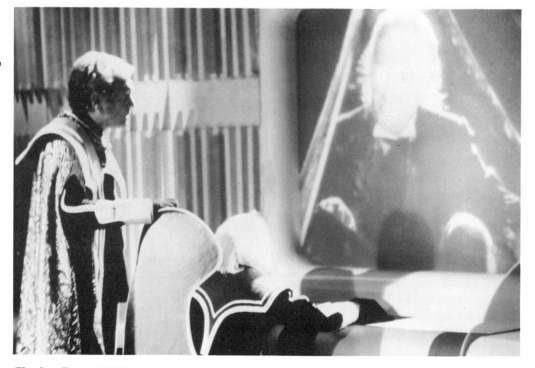

The first Doctor (William Hartnell) communicates with his fellow Time Lords on Gallifrey in 'The Three Doctors' (1973)

To save Gallifrey in 'The Deadly Assassin' (1976) Tom Baker seeks information in the records room from Castellan Spandrell (George Pravda) and Coordinator Engin (Eric Chitty)

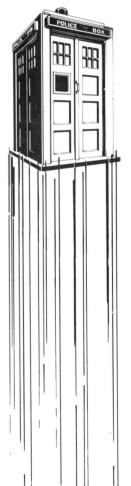

It would be wrong to think time has no importance to the people of Gallifrey – it does, but in rather a different way to that which it does for mere mortal beings like ourselves. When eternity stretches before you, there is no cause to hurry, no cause to make needless haste. In Capitol City time almost literally stands still.

One also becomes aware of a sense of order about everything. Indeed, the whole of life on Gallifrey is governed by order, from the inhabitants themselves to the way they proceed over every one of their tasks. To some observers this sense of order has become stultifying, giving an air of staleness, of lack of drive about the place. But such observation seems not to concern the Time Lords at all as they go their measured way.

It is easy at first glance to think that the people of this planet are much like us on Earth. In appearance they are humanoid, tall and imposing, with solemn, learned faces. Their clothes, too, are not far removed from the flowing white robes we associate with men of great wisdom and learning. But, of course, as we know from the Doctor, Time Lords possess two hearts, a bypass respiratory system, and a body temperature of sixty degrees Fahrenheit. They also have the unique ability to regenerate their bodies, an ability they can perform twelve times. They are spoken of as the people who can live forever – barring accidents! (But such facts apart, little else is really known about the Time Lords, who prefer to shroud themselves and their origins in mystery. Our own Doctor has, of course, spoken of himself as being over 750 years old, but has declined to reveal anything of his family and his youth preferring, as he says, to let such memories 'sleep in his mind'.)

There can be no denying from the first encounter that these are a people with an immense power at their finger-tips, an enormous knowledge at their control. As one might expect of such intelligence, their society is carefully ordered.

Although it is only inhabitants of Gallifrey who become Time Lords, they themselves can only aspire to such an honour as a result of heritage, breeding, intelligence and the most demanding study. There are in fact ancient hierarchies into which the Time Lords are divided: including the three most important, the Pyrdonians, the Arcalians and the Patraxes. Each wears distinguishing robes – the Pyrdonians, as the most famous, are in red and gold, the Arcalians in green and the Patraxes in heliotrope. Each wear their robes when at study or on ceremonial occasions.

Training at the academy is long and arduous for the acolyte Time Lords and may be followed by a period of apprenticeship during which they work as servants, guards, technicians and minor administrators. Only after satisfying their elders can such men (and occasionally women, for both sexes are found on Gallifrey) be allowed to follow the Time Lord's traditional role of monitoring the happenings in space and time. Although they are constantly aware of what is going on in the galaxies, the Time Lords rarely interfere in the matters of others, leaving such tasks to their secret branch, the Celestial Intervention Agency, who will only intervene in the most extreme cases. The Doctor has, though, become their more commonplace representative now!

The teachers at the academy are called Lord Cardinals, Time Lords of great age and experience, who instruct their students in the laws laid down by Rassilon, the first of the Time Lords, whose great prowess aeons ago created both the power sources and protective field upon which life on Gallifrey depends. The essence of the accumulated wisdom of the planet is said to be contained in the mysterious book, *The Ancient Law of Gallifrey*.

At the very centre of Capitol City stands the enormous circular building known as the Panopticon where all matters of state, law, government and administration are settled by the Gallifreyan Parliament. This body consists of the Cardinals who, apart from teaching, govern the planet and maintain its law, and the High Council who are concerned with all aspects of time. At the head of this august body is the Time Lord President, the elected leader of the community, who also lives in the building.

Directly beneath the Panopticon lies the source of the Time Lords'

Peter Davison's Doctor in confrontation with another Time Lord (Michael Gough) in 'Arc of Infinity' (1983)

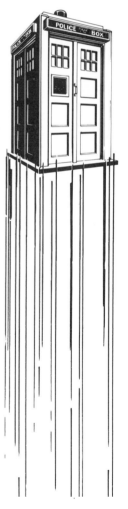

power, the Eye of Harmony, a huge ebonite monolith in which reside incalculable forces upon which the Time Lords can draw to make time travel a reality.

Close by the Panopticon stand the Archive Towers which house the mind-boggling storehouse of knowledge known as the Matrix. This most advanced and perfected kind of computer is the repository of all the knowledge of time and space which the Time Lords have assembled over countless generations. The information has been collected from the past, the present and the future, and such is the Matrix's complexity that it can drain from the mind of a dying Time Lord all his collected wisdom so that nothing be lost. Not surprisingly, it is considered the ultimate source of reference by even the President and such is the Matrix's capabilities that nothing has ever been known to go wrong with it.

These, then, are the important edifices of Capitol City – all geared to serving the ageless purpose of the Time Lords. Yet, according to legend, even they are not the most powerful race in the universe. For the Doctor himself was once sent on a mission by an even higher life form, the Guardians, almost godlike in status, who hold the balance of universal good and evil. Together, though, with the Time Lords as the law enforcers and the Guardians as the keepers of the forces of nature, there are mighty forces at hand to combat those who would attempt to disrupt the peace of the cosmos.

Yet, as we have seen in many of the Doctor's adventures, there are just such elements abroad in the vast reaches of space. Primary among these, of course, are the Renegade Time Lords. These are men who left Gallifrey to pursue ambitions of their own. Although the Doctor himself might be counted among this number, the term is generally used to refer to those with evil intentions as their main motivation – men such as the interfering Monk who first appeared in the story 'The Time Meddler', the War Chief featured in 'The War Games', the pioneer time engineer Omega, who was involved with 'The Three Doctors', the 'Arc of Infinity' and the terrible Morbius in 'The Brain of Morbius'. And, of course, the Master.

The Master is undoubtedly one of the most evil men in all of time and space. Dedicated to corrupting the pure of heart, terrorising the peaceful and destroying the beautiful, he is also an implacable enemy of the Doctor. A master of hypnotism, a cold-blooded killer with his compressor gun, he will also ally himself with any other evil force to suit his own ends – ultimately as callously betraying such 'friends' as he would his enemies.

The Doctor's foiling of the Master's various mad schemes has made their confrontations almost as important in the success of the *Doctor Who* legend as the Daleks themselves – certainly in its continuation. One without the other would somehow be unthinkable now, and the two remarkable actors who have given the Master such a grip on our imagination are featured in the next section.

Yet, while such feverish action continues in the galaxy, life goes on as ever on Gallifrey, steadily, methodically, inexorably. While there may be constant changes in other worlds, here nothing changes. On the planet which is at the core of our legend, time is truly timeless.

Patrick Troughton as the Doctor, on Gallifrey with Zoe and Jamie, during his trial in 'The War Games' (1969)

CHAPTER NINE

THE TWO REGENERATIONS OF THE MASTER

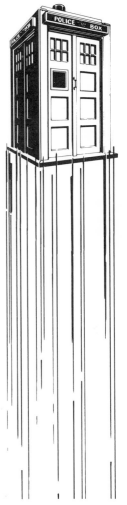

'Every good hero needs a good villain and the Doctor has the Master. Where the Doctor strives to make the realms of Time and Space better places for the indigenous populations to live, the Master delights only in their corruption and ultimate destruction. Unlike the Doctor, who holds compassion, mercy and high values of justice, the Master knows only the temptations of his own black hearts. He is evil but on a grand scale. He would burn a planet to light a match, destroy a world to test a theory; a personification of apocalypse, thinly disguised by a veil of elegant nobility. The Master ranks along with the Daleks as one of the intrinsic reasons for *Doctor Who*'s success. He is the epitome of all the Doctor fights to combat, and, played by the right actor, his role in the series can equal, and perhaps even overtake at times, the popularity enjoyed by the title character.'

Doctor Who Summer Special, 1982

The Doctor and his sworn enemy the Master are the Sherlock Holmes and Moriarty of our times. Like Sir Arthur Conan Doyle's famous detective almost a century ago, the Doctor now finds himself from time to time locked in battle with his cunning adversary, a man of similar background, equal intelligence and ingenuity, but as dedicated to the perpetration of evil as the Doctor is to sustaining peace and harmony throughout the galaxy. Like Moriarty, though, the Master has one fatal flaw . . .

Both men are, of course, Time Lords, originating from the planet Gallifrey and, as both are roughly the same age, their paths first crossed when they were studying at the academy. Strangely, both became disillusioned with the life-style of their people – yet when the Doctor fled from the planet in a stolen TARDIS to pursue his desire for knowledge among the worlds of space, the Master also departed, but craving for power and conquest. Whenever the two have come face to face, their intellects have been immediately joined in battle to see who could think and act the quickest: a battle between a renegade bent on chaos and destruction and a man of goodwill personifying the finer qualities of ageless wisdom. The sparring of their minds has made for some of the most compulsively watchable and popular stories among all the Doctor's adventures.

The Master's particular attributes are his ability to impersonate others and his finely developed powers of hypnotism. These, together with his Satanic will-power, calculating and ruthless mind and total lack of scruples, have made it easy for him to subvert the minds of weaker species – Earth people in particular – and to overthrow civilisations he wishes to conquer. Another particularly unpleasant trait he has demonstrated from time to time is his cold-blooded use of a tissue-compression eliminator which reduces human bodies to corpses the size of toys!

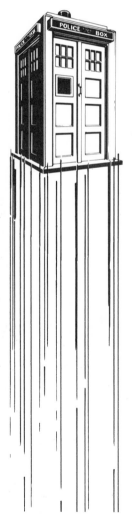

Yet, like all arch-villains – and the infamous Moriarty was no different – the Master has his Achilles' heel: his vanity. Although as cunning and clever as any Time Lord, the Master has this slight flaw in his character. He cannot resist boasting about his plans as they near what he imagines will be a triumphant conclusion. So whenever he finds it impossible not to gloat to the Doctor over his own cleverness, he leaves himself wide open to his adversary discovering an error in his planning and putting him to flight.

Despite their rivalry, however, the Doctor finds it impossible to totally dislike the Master. Maybe it is a combination of their common ancestry, or the dark good looks and air of superficial charm which give the Master an almost irresistible machiavellian appearance. Whatever the case, the Doctor has on a number of occasions quite evidently allowed his enemy to escape final capture and at one time even confessed to a companion that he would be 'really quite sorry' if something untoward happened to the Master! This grudging respect is one that Sherlock Holmes himself also shared towards *his* arch-enemy!

During the course of their encounters, the Master led several groups of aliens against the Earth, including the terrible Daleks, but only once was he imprisoned for any time (in 'The Sea Devils'), but again escaped with the help of some man-like lizards. Like all Time Lords, he is only permitted twelve regenerations and, when he neared the end of his 'life', he instigated a horrendous plan involving the destruction of Gallifrey to steal enough energy to start a new life-cycle. Fortunately, the Doctor managed to save his home planet, but his rival escaped and finally achieved his aim by taking over the body of Tremas, a consul of the planet Traken and the father of Nyssa, who became one of the Doctor's companions. Armed with this new body, he began the continuing story of the Master's second incarnation – a story already firmly bound up with the future of the Doctor. (The Doctor himself, of course, sacrificed his own fourth body to defeat the Master's evil machinations in 'Logopolis', 1981).

Much of the undoubted popularity of the Master is due to the two actors who have brought him to the screen. First, the late, devilishly versatile, Roger Delgado, and, secondly, the satanically accomplished

'I'm a citizen of the Universe, and a gentleman to boot!'
The Daleks' Master Plan

'I am not a student of human nature. I am a professor of a
far wider academy, of which human nature is only a part'.
Evil of the Daleks

'I remember saving to old Napoleon, 'Boney' I said . . .'

'I'm a Time Lord... I walk in Eternity.'
Pyramids of Mars

'A broken clock keeps better time than you!'
The Visitation

THE TWO FACES OF THE MASTER

The Doctor's most redoubtable adversary has, of course, been his fellow Time Lord, the Master, who is now in his second regeneration. Played first by Roger Delgado (above), his suave and charming manner concealed a most evil and cunning nature. In his present regeneration (left) played by Anthony Ainley, the Master is perhaps even more black-hearted and cruel. Tom Baker's Doctor once commented on him: 'A real black sheep. Wants to rule the world. Funny about that – so many others I meet have the same ambition!' Together the Doctor and the Master have become the Sherlock Holmes and Moriarty of our age.

THE MONSTERS WHO LOVES
TO HATE

In a survey taken recently among fans,
the five most popular monsters that
have appeared in the programme during
its twenty years are as follows:
1, The Daleks; 2, The Cybermen;
3, Ice Warriors; 4, Sontarans; 5, The Yeti.
On these last two pages of the Doctor's
colourful portrait gallery are some
suitably chilling reminders of these
monsters you love to hate.

1 Two Daleks about their evil work
2 A pair of well-armed Cybermen
3 An Ice Warrior (right) and friend
4 A Sontaran and his space ship
5 A Yeti more abominable than furry

1

2

performances of his successor, Anthony Ainley. Together, these two men have fleshed out and perfected the character and motivations of arguably the best-known super-villain on television today.

The character of the Master was devised in mid-1970 by the then producer of the series, Barry Letts, and his script editor, Terrance Dicks. These two had for some time been trying to find another villain of the piece who might capture the public imagination in the way the Daleks had done. They wanted a rather more human villain, however, and from their deliberations came the idea of a renegade Time Lord who would be the black figure to the Doctor's white. To introduce him to the series, Letts and Dicks chose one of their most imaginative script-writers, Robert

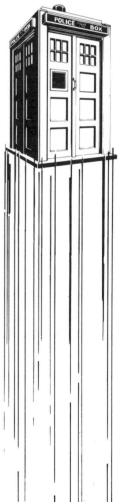

Evil personified – the first Master played by the late lamented Roger Delgado, here in 'The Sea Devils' (1972)

Holmes, who did not disappoint them or viewers with his *Terror of the Autons* which was screened in January 1971. The Master made a splendid entrance in the midst of a circus, stepping from a TARDIS shaped like a horse-box – and within weeks his villainy was earning him a following not equalled since the advent of the Daleks.

The impact of the character was also due to the inspired casting of Roger Delgado in the role. The actor's saturnine good looks, inherited from a French mother and Spanish father – although he was born in London in March 1918 within the sound of Bow Bells and was therefore a true cockney! – gave him exactly the right appearance for a man of such undisguised evil intent. His 'devil's beard' further enhanced the suggestion of a sinister intellect hell-bent on conquest and destruction.

Despite his screen *persona*, Roger Caesar Marius Bernard de Delgado Torres Castillo Roberto – to give him his full name – was a charming and kindly man remembered with great affection by fans as well as members of his profession. He was educated at the Cardinal Vaughan School and the London School of Economics, but turned his back on a business career to take up acting in 1938. He worked in repertory in Leicester until 1940 and then, following war service, continued in rep at York until 1950 when he joined the BBC Drama Repertory Company, playing a variety of parts.

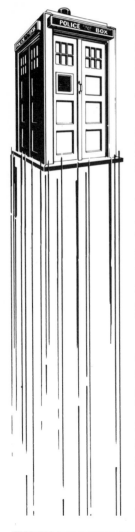

Although Roger clearly possessed considerable range as an actor, it was as a villain that he naturally excelled. But being type-cast was not something that unduly upset him, however, as he confessed in an interview in 1971.

'I love playing villains,' he said. 'I am chosen by directors to play wicked men because I have a beard, a menacing chin and piercing eyes.

'I have often been asked if I wouldn't prefer to play a hero. And though it isn't the sort of thing I like talking about, I did once star in a Brian Rix farce called *Diplomatic Baggage*. The audience cheered me nightly, and do you know I felt ashamed!'

In 1953, Roger appeared in his first film, *The Captain's Paradise,* and this was followed by roles of increasing importance in *The Battle of the River Plate* (1956); *First Man into Space* (1959) – rather appropriate considering what was to follow – and a number of spectaculars such as *Khartoum* (1966) and Charlton Heston's *Antony and Cleopatra* (1973). He also worked in radio and television, his beautiful speaking voice making his readings in the 'Morning Story' series memorable, while at the same time developing his 'villainy' to a fine pitch in TV serials such as *The Troubleshooters* and *Maigret.*

He later recalled that the series about the French detective had helped create his enduring image. 'I was responsible for killing Maigret's assistant Torrance (played by Euan Lloyd) by chloroforming him and sticking a large hatpin into his heart. I felt rotten about that. Think of poor Torrance's feelings. He had a regular part in the series and they brought me in for just one episode to bump him off and put him out of work! Still, afterwards Euan told me there were no hard feelings and we became great friends,' he said.

It was just such appearances which brought Roger to the attention of Barry Letts and Terrance Dicks when they were looking for a villain the viewers would love to hate.

The horribly disfigured Master in 'The Deadly Assassin' (1976) played by Peter Pratt

'I was thrilled to be offered the part of the Master,' Roger declared later. 'I had tried three times to break into Doctor Who, but the scope offered by this part was way and above any other I had considered.'

Roger saw the role as 'more than a Moriarty', though he accepted the relationship between himself and the Doctor was not disimilar to that of Holmes and his criminal adversary. Yet with skill and dedication he built up the part of the renegade Time Lord by such a clever mixture of evil and villainy, charm and humour, that he rapidly became second in popularity only to the Doctor himself!

Among his keenest fans were young viewers, who bombarded him with fan mail. 'I could tell from these letters that I was the man they loved to hate,' he recalled. 'There were even one or two kids who complained on occasions that I was not wicked enough!'

A famous incident involving children occurred when he was on location filming 'The Daemons' (1971). A group of youngsters watching the actors at work were asked to join in and hiss and boo when the Master was captured by the Doctor and some UNIT soldiers. Oh no, the youngsters declared emphatically, they liked the Master too much and wanted to cheer him instead!

Such incidents explain why Roger's tragic death on 18 June 1973 hit his fans so hard. He was killed when his chauffeur-driven car ran into a ravine while he was being driven to a film location in Nevsehir, Turkey, to play a part in a Turkish–French television production called *Bell of Tibet*. In paying tribute to his work, the august *Times* said:

'A dark, strikingly handsome man, he played with great panache the sinister scientist, versed in all the black arts, who repeatedly plots to do down Doctor Who (Jon Pertwee). Though entirely convincing in his sudden Mephisphelean appearances and disappearances and his blood-curdling threats of disaster for "the Doctor", he was a villain whom it was hard to hate.'

The passing of Roger Delgado made many people believe that it would also mean the end of the Master – *The Times*, for one, considered the actor to be 'irreplaceable'. He had, after all, made the part very much his own – creating it from scratch and playing it with unique style. Saddened fans were even more disappointed to learn that a final showdown had been planned between Delgado's Master and Pertwee's Doctor in which the true relationship between the two men would be revealed. Speculation was rife as to just *what* that relationship might be – could they have been related, some wondered, or maybe even *brothers*? – but with the tragic accident, the character disappeared from the series.

But not forever. For true to the nature of a Time Lord, time was surely only there to be conquered, and four years later the evil renegade returned once more.

It was Philip Hinchcliffe, the producer who succeeded Barry Letts, who had the idea of bringing back the Master – and he turned to the ever-reliable Robert Holmes who had scripted the Time Lord's first appearance to bring about his second incarnation. Once again, Holmes came up trumps with the story of 'The Deadly Assassin' (1976) in which the hideously decaying figure of the Master in his twelfth and final regeneration (played by Peter Pratt) attempted to outwit the Doctor on

Gallifrey and seize the energy needed to restore his life-cycle. Although he was thwarted in his main aim, the means of his escape was left ambiguous enough to suggest he might well be back . . .

And he was. In 1980, the latest producer of the series, John Nathan-Turner resolved on a full-scale return of the Master, complete with a new body and perhaps even more sinister appearance. He recruited one of his new team of writers, Johnny Byrne, to create this situation in 'The Keeper of Traken' which was screened in late January and February 1981. The Master (initially played by Geoffrey Beevers) was still swathed in shards of rotting skin and, if anything, more evil and diabolical than before, until a dramatic last-minute twist when he effected a transfer of his soul into the body of Consul Tremas (Anthony Ainley). From that moment, fans everywhere knew that the Master was back – new body, new face, but still the same sinister, hell-bent personality.

It was a notable demonstration of his skills as an actor that Anthony Ainley was able in the stories which followed not only to re-establish the Master in the series, but once again make him a household word.

Inspired casting was again at work in the choice of Anthony – and although his family have a number of connections with *Doctor Who* he is very emphatic that this had nothing whatsoever to do with his being chosen for the part! His father, Henry Ainley was Jon Pertwee's godfather: his brother Richard Ainley was Tom Baker's drama teacher; while he himself was first coached in an amateur production of *Rookery Nook* by no less than William Hartnell, the very first Doctor! With such strange coincidences at work, he could surely *only* have come into the series as a new Doctor – or a mighty adversary!

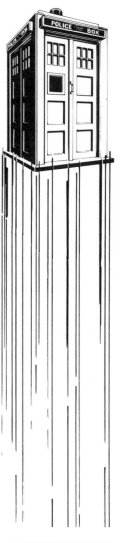

Anthony like his predecessor, is a Londoner. (Like Delgado, too, he is a friendly and aimiable man when off the set.) His first taste of acting came at the age of eleven when he sang in a school production of Gilbert and Sullivan's HMS *Pinafore* and, although acting was clearly in his blood, he began his working life as an insurance clerk. Dissatisfied with this, he enrolled at RADA and the correctness of his decision was underlined when he won the Fabia Drake Prize for Comedy. His initial stage work was in repertory, doing a season at the Liverpool Playhouse and he made his television début in the series, *It's Dark Outside*.

The West End called next and Anthony appeared in *The Right Honourable Gentleman* at Her Majesty's, in *Justice* at St Martin's Theatre and the lead part in a fringe theatre production of *Macbeth*. To this he added work in films, on radio and television.

A tall, dark-haired man with steely grey eyes, his ability to easily assume an appearance of villainy made him ideal for casting in such roles as Prussian officers or tough military men. Among his film roles to date have been parts in *Oh, What A Lovely War, The Devil's Touch, Assault* as well as a memorable appearance in *The Land That Time Forgot* as a brutal submarine officer. On television he chalked up roles in *Elizabeth R, The Avengers, Warship* and *The Pallisers* – the last of which led directly to his joining *Doctor Who*.

Anthony explains how this one serial led to the other. 'I was lucky enough to be in *The Pallisers* which was a big BBC production. I played a priest called Emelius who was a rather smarmy and devious character.

The regenerated Master (Anthony Ainley) surpasses his predecessor in cunning and deadliness in 'The King's Demons' (1983)

John Nathan-Turner was working on it and he remembered me when he took over *Doctor Who*. Later he asked me if I'd like to join him to play the part of the Master.'

Anthony sees a certain similarity between Emelius and the Master. Both wore a superficial air of charm and dignity which concealed a wicked and sly nature beneath. Indeed, some might even say the priest could have been a distant cousin of the Time Lord!

In any event, Anthony was able to transform himself into the Master with little make-up and revealed an astonishing resemblance to his predecessor which many fans of the programme have commented most favourably upon. But right from the start Anthony had no intention of just copying Roger Delgado's version of the role.

'There are obvious hazards in doing parts somebody else has already done,' he said when joining the programme, 'the most obvious of which is being compared, perhaps unfavourably, with the actor before. Nevertheless, I don't think I was ever in any real doubt about taking on the role because the Master is such a good part and such a joy to do. Certainly, at the back of my mind there is always the thought that everyone enjoyed Roger Delgado's portrayal, but that just means I've got to try and be pretty good in return.'

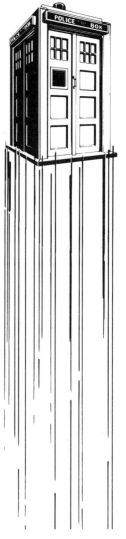

Anthony has succeeded so splendidly not only because of his own talent, but through subtle changes to the character of the Master. The Time Lord is, if anything, now a little more sadistic than his predecessor, and there is less humour though more wit in him. His entry into any new story almost invariably sends a shiver up the viewer's spine – a fact that can only delight such a dedicated actor as Anthony, although he is not one for being drawn into long discussions about his art.

'I don't really like to talk about acting,' he says, 'but I do feel that if it comes from one's centre, then it will be real, it will be exciting and it will be believable. You have to yield to your instinct in tackling any dramatic role.'

That Anthony's instincts have served him well is now in no doubt. He has given the Master a new lease of life with exactly the same degree of success as those actors who have taken over the part of the Doctor. It was undoubtedly a big gamble in bringing back the Master after such a long absence – but in what is now proving a time-honoured tradition of the whole series, the regeneration of a major character has proved to be an important ingredient in its twenty-year success story.

So let us hope for many more 'lives' for the Master!

The versatile Barry Letts who has been writer, director, producer and executive producer on
Doctor Who

CHAPTER TEN

BACK WITH WHO

by Barry Letts

I've always said that I'd never go back to *Doctor Who*. Five years as producer and about two in other capacities (as director, for instance, and writing one of the books), constitutes a large chunk of my working life. I'm not sure that I want to go back even in memory. Not that the memories are bad; quite the contrary. But the past is the past. I have other concerns.

I'd been an appreciative albeit intermittent viewer, along with millions of others, ever since that day in November 1963 when the good Doctor in his first appearance found himself competing for attention with the horrendous news of President Kennedy's assassination. In those far-off days I was an actor and a writer, though I neither appeared nor wrote for the series. I did try in early 1966 to flog some stories to Gerry Davis, then script editor. My favourite concerned a race of beings whose humanoid appearance was as different from their fully developed form as a caterpillar's from a butterfly's. Gerry rejected it (very amiably) along with the others as being too sophisticated. It is perhaps a measure of the extent to which the programme developed during the next few years that a very similar idea appeared in a story that was one of the great successes of our third season. This was 'The Mutant', written by Bob Baker and Dave Martin.

By the end of 1966 I was training to be a director and in less than a year I was asked by Innes Lloyd and Peter Bryant (who was taking over as producer) to direct 'The Enemy of the World'.

It was enormous fun to do but utterly exhausting. At that time the season lasted for forty weeks. To turn out so many episodes so quickly imposed a punishing schedule on everybody, but most of all on the Doctor himself. For example, in common with my fellow directors, I had to do my allocated week of exterior filming (complicated stuff with helicopter and a hovercraft) using doubles for the Doctor and his companions in long shot. After recording the current show Patrick Troughton, Frazer Hines and Debbie Watling were rushed to the location, spent their 'free' Sunday shooting the dialogue scenes in closer shots and were back in the dusty church hall which served as a rehearsal room the very next day.

Although of course this didn't happen every week, a studio recording

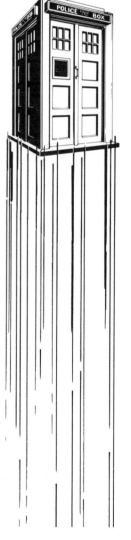

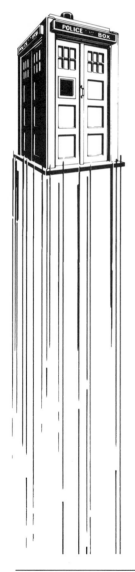

did, at least during the run of a particular story. One day off, five days' rehearsal and a very intense camera rehearsal culminated in the recording of a complete show in an hour and a quarter in the evening of the seventh day.

Now, I'd known Patrick for many years. Indeed, my very first television appearance was in the live production of a play entitled *Gunpowder Guy* in which Patrick played Guy Fawkes and I was one of the other conspirators. This was on 5 November 1950, when the famous BBC Television Centre was only a gleam in its architect's eye.

On the last studio day of 'The Enemy of the World', I was chatting to Patrick in his dressing room during the break before the recording and he asked me, as an old friend and colleague, for my advice. He was trying to weigh up the pros and cons of signing up for another year. Amongst other factors, the gruelling turn-round was a very large consideration.

'Why don't you suggest to Peter,' I said, 'that the Beeb should just present a six-month season: twenty-six episodes instead of forty. Then, if you still took nine or ten months to make them, you could have a gap between each story; time for everybody to catch their breath and do the outside filming properly.'

'Great! Great!' said Patrick, as he always does when he likes an idea. Unfortunately, the mills of the BBC grind almost as slowly as those of God. Although the idea was taken up, it was too late to apply it to the following season.

Quite unwittingly, however, I'd done myself an enormous favour. For in October 1969 I took over from Peter as producer at the start of the first season to see the new plan in operation, too late to benefit Patrick, but proving an enormous help in our efforts to regenerate the show along with the Doctor. For the powers that be were quite convinced that the show had come to the end of its natural life and had only very reluctantly agreed to the new season – thinking of it as a stop gap until a replacement could be found.

Auntie doesn't teach you how to be a drama producer. She just picks you up by the scruff of the neck and drops you in it, if you take my meaning. You'll have been a director, an actor, a writer or a script editor perhaps and so you'll have learnt a bit of doggy-paddle. If you swim hard enough you stand a chance of surfacing after a while. You might even be smelling of roses; although, until you learn to say 'No' to the wilder excesses of (rightly) ambitious directors and designers, the stink raised by the massive over-spending of your budget is likely to obscure the sweetest scent.

Such sci-fi blockbusters as *Star Wars* and *Superman* were, of course, a long way in the future. By 1970, though, the viewing public were becoming much more sophisticated. We were not exactly competing with movies like the James Bond epics but we were certainly in danger of being compared with them. Even to attempt to bear the comparison with the scale of budget and schedule which so constrained my predecessors would have been impossible. I'm proud to say that by dint of steady pressure over the next five years (and a certain amount of slightly machiavellian disingenuousness) I managed to change *Doctor Who* from a very cheap show to a definitely expensive one!

By the end of our first season we had changed our recording pattern from one a week to two a fortnight, i.e. ten days' rehearsal, followed by two camera days in the studio. Believe me, the difference is enormous: time to learn lines; time to make sets and costumes; time to work out camera shots; time to buy props; time to experiment with special effects, etc. Also, we soon nearly doubled our recording time – though we still managed to stretch the system to its limits and occasionally the plugs would be pulled on us before we'd finished and we'd have to pick up the remainder a fortnight later.

Still, all the time, money and resources in the world would have been quite useless without two prime factors: stories to intrigue and capture the viewer – and a successful Doctor.

Jon Pertwee was quite different from the two earlier Doctors. Both Bill Hartnell and Patrick were straight players; character actors of that great British strain which is the envy of the world. Although Jon's career had started in rep in the traditional way and he'd done his fair share of plays and films, he was best known as a comedian, especially on radio and in cabaret. His appeal, as Doctor Who, was the appeal of The Personality, larger than life and somehow different from the rest of us, even off the screen.

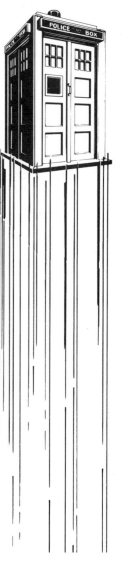

Peter Bryant and Derrick Sherwin had cast Jon. Derrick produced his first story. So when he was dumped in the lap of a strange Big Daddy whom he had never met and (I suspect) had never heard of, he undoubtedly felt very unsafe. He still hadn't quite found his feet in his new persona and wasn't absolutely sure in which direction to point them even when he had found them. If you were to see a playback of the first of Jon's shows ('Spearhead from Space') and then the last ('Planet of the Spiders') you would see quite a difference. There is, for instance, a far broader vein of comedy running through his performance in the earlier story.

We soon established a very good relationship. When Jon found that I'd been an actor for over twenty years (including some twelve in television), he felt he'd found a safe guide through the quicksands. I on my part felt that here was an ideal Doctor.

A showman, confident to the point of arrogance; a private man, as easily hurt as anyone; a middle-aged teenager whose musical taste ran to hard rock; an urbane man of the world priding himself on his knowledge of fine wines; a thoroughly likeable and amusing companion; a charming egocentric who would (unconsciously?) gather a retinue of willing servants from among his colleagues; a responsible leader of the company, keeping it in good heart and always concerned for the least of its members; Jon Pertwee was all of these.

One story sticks in my mind. In the second or third year Jon took on a great deal of outside work. Most of it was to appear as the Doctor, sometimes professionally, sometimes for charity. He was also appearing more and more in cabaret.

The result of this was that he had no time to learn his lines and would expect to be able to pick them up during rehearsal. He relied on the AFM (assistant floor manager), who acted as prompter, to feed him the words and would keep going back to make sure he'd got them right. All this took up a deal of time which should have been devoted to working on the scenes. It infuriated the other actors.

So during the summer break, at a private playback I'd arranged for him, I discreetly brought the subject up. 'Oh, come on, Barry!' he said, 'You've been through it yourself. You know how difficult it is to get lines into your head all by yourself at home, staring at a script.'

'Yes', I said, 'but I also know that if you don't at least try, it takes three times as long in rehearsal and wastes everybody's time.'

A month or so later, at the first relevant rehearsal, Jon put down his script and sailed through a complicated scene without a single prompt.

'Why, Jon!' said Sue Hedden, the outspoken AFM, 'you know your lines!'

'Yes,' replied our Star, before the entire assembled company, 'Barry took me into a corner and gave me a rocket!'

You have to love a man like that.

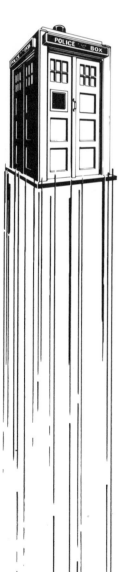

Jon was a great snapper-up of unconsidered trifles. He liked to have a souvenir of each show, if at all possible. If some unusual prop was going to be thrown away, Jon would always make sure it was steered in his direction. For example, the 'stone' carving of the grotesque Bok, from 'The Daemons', graced the Pertwee lawn in Barnes as an odd piece of garden statuary for quite a while until wind and weather ate away its polystyrene integrity.

One souvenir most appropriately can be said to have been 'steered in his direction'. In 'Carnival of Monsters' the Doctor and Jo Grant find themselves on a small ship steaming through the Indian Ocean in the mid-1920s. Chris D'Oyly John, our production manager, performed the usual miracle and found us an out-of-date paid-off Royal Fleet Auxiliary ship. Although she had no engines, we were able to arrange to be on board when the tug towed her down the Medway *en route* to the breaker's yard. (Incidentally, if you should ever see a repeat of 'Carnival of Monsters' you'll notice that you can never see the horizon – the Indian Ocean is slightly less cluttered than the Medway skyline!)

When shooting was over and we were all disembarking into a launch to take us to shore, the representative of the yard came up to me in a fine old state.

'I can't let you go,' he said. 'Somebody's taken the compass! We'll have to search the launch!'

'I don't think that will be necessary,' I said.

Sure enough, Jon cheerfully admitted to having taken it. A long job it must have been too, with all those brass screws.

'Why ever not?' he said. 'It's only going to be thrown away. The whole ship is . . . Ah. I see. They break it up to sell the bits . . .'

'That's right,' I said.

Jon has a great sense of mischievous fun. A big moment in the genesis of a show, or perhaps I should say in its gestation, is the producer's run. Having rehearsed the entire episode until it's nearly ready to go before the cameras, the director and the actors run it through under the critical gaze of the producer, who until now has kept well away from the rehearsal room (which is no longer an old church hall, by the way, but a large room in a purpose-built block known familiarly as the Acton

Hilton).

Of course, the director is very keen that the producer should see the best possible performance and so he'll run it through just before his arrival and make appropriate comments.

Now, the director of 'The Curse of Peladon' was Lennie Mayne, an ebullient Aussie with, to say the least, a very colourful turn of phrase. (During one camera rehearsal I nearly reduced Lennie to impotent silence by taking a visitor into the control gallery – an elderly vicar, complete with dog-collar.) The rest of this anecdote, perforce, will be somewhat bowdlerised.

In 'The Curse of Peladon', the monster, Aggedor, was a hairy creature like a ten-foot bear, with bloodshot eyes, the tusks of a wild boar and the horns of a rhinoceros. In the climactic scene of the last episode, Aggedor appears in the doorway of the crowded royal courtroom. At his roar, the entire company turns to look at him.

'No, no, no!' cried Lennie. 'Do you want me to show Barry *that*? If a ten-foot hairy nasty turned up in the rehearsal room right now, you wouldn't just stand like a lot of stuffed poodles, now would you? You'd swing round, look at all those teeth and eyes and all and you'd say, "Holy flaming cow!"'

And on they went.

Behold now, the producer's run. It's gone well. The drama is at its height. The villain has been exposed; the Doctor and Jo, the King, his court, all the delegates from the Galactic Federation, and a number of guards, twenty-two people all told, are at his mercy. Suddenly, the mighty roar of Aggedor echoes through the courtroom. The assembled company swings round in terror and in perfect unison twenty-two voices cry out, 'Holy flaming cow!'

Jon has had a little word.

One of the main reasons why I enjoyed my five years on the show so much, actually looking forward to going in to work day after day, was that I found in Terrance Dicks an ideal professional colleague and friend. The producer and the script editor, especially of *Doctor Who*, must be a two-headed Beeblebrox (as I've no doubt Douglas Adams himself discovered during the time he edited the show). To change the metaphor, if only slightly, if one member of a pair of Siamese twins is determined to go south and the other north, they'll end up standing still. Terrance and I found ourselves pointing in the same direction 95 per cent of the time (towards the light of the noonday sun? Or is that stretching the image too far?).

To start with, we recognised that the story situation we had inherited from Peter and Derrick (which Terrance had had quite a hand in setting up), with the Doctor stranded on Earth, cooperating with UNIT, implied a change, not to say a development, in the type of show we were presenting. Conceived originally as a children's serial it had, from the advent of Terry Nation's Daleks in the second story, captured a large adult viewing public as well. Nevertheless, its origins betrayed themselves in the uneasy zig-zag between science fiction and science fantasy which characterised many of its stories. What is the difference between the two? In science fantasy, the writer can posit such a different world from our own or such a radically different view of it that he can largely write his own rules. As long as they are self-consistent, they can ignore the accepted laws of science and the experience of our everyday lives. The science fiction writer, on the other hand, having dreamed up a possible (though likely to be highly improbable) basic idea (e.g. the invasion of Earth by Martians; the breeding of a mobile and deadly plant; the invention of a time machine) will be expected, in all other respects, to stick to 'reality' (and let's not go into ontology, phenomenology, epistemology and the rest of the gallimaufry involved in trying to work out what *that* means!). Especially, he must never get his science wrong.

Doctor Who had now become, willy-nilly, far more science fiction than science fantasy. Terrance and I had to recognise that and consciously plan for it. There are those who would argue that in so doing we lost an ambiguity, a poetic mystery, which informed the earlier programmes. I wouldn't quarrel with that. It's a valid criticism. I would hope that we didn't lose it entirely; especially in stories such as 'The Daemons' and 'The Time Monster', where we cross-bred science and myth. Nevertheless, I am convinced that one of the reasons why the show has lasted so long is that it has every so often changed considerably in style and outlook, just as each Doctor has been utterly different. If the second Doctor had been a Bill Hartnell look-alike, we shouldn't now be celebrating the twentieth anniversary.

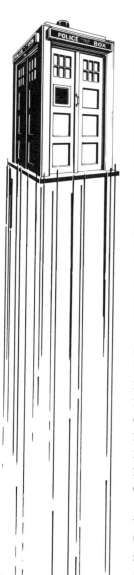

Terrance and I talked endlessly. (We still do, though nowadays the subject is more likely to be Dickens or Charlotte Brontë). We talked on several levels at once: we discussed, for example, the planning of the next season; the plotting of a particular story; the morality of showing violence and horror; and, in amongst the rest, we tried to work out a rationale of time–space travel, a model into which all the stories would fit.

It had always irritated me, for example, that when the Doctor travelled into our past, he would say, 'Now, we must be careful not to interfere with the course of history.' Whereas, when he travelled into our future he would happily interfere – to prevent the otherwise inevitable destruction of Earth, for instance. To a perpetual time traveller, there is no future and no past, except relatively. The history of 'the future' is as valid as the history of 'the past'.

To picture exactly what 'time' is, is like trying to get a firm grip on an eel. Time feels like a movement, doesn't it? This is so deep in us that it's taken for granted in our language. We speak of time 'passing' for instance, or 'going slowly'. But if its moving, how fast does it move; not in miles per hour, of course, but minutes per . . . what? Even to ask the question implies the existence of a sort of time beyond time: minutes per meta-minutes perhaps. But how fast does meta-time go? And how fast meta-meta-time? And so on, into what the philosophers call an infinite regress, before which our minds boggle as much as they do when we contemplate the infinity of space.

So really, what we were trying to do was impossible! But the attempt was worth it and threw up all the contradictions that we had to avoid. One of the outcomes, after our third season, which included two time stories, 'The Day of the Daleks' and 'The Time Monster', was a letter from a professor of philosophy asking if he could use our ideas in a paper he

Bok, Azal's terrifying Gargoyle, in Barry Letts' 'The Daemons' (1971)

was preparing on the subject of time for a seminar of a learned society!

The worst time-paradoxes we had to gloss over. For instance, in 'The Day of the Daleks' we ran slap bang into the old chestnut: what happens if you go back into the past and kill your maternal grandfather before he's even met your grandmother? Think about it. If your mother was never born, then neither were you. So how do you manage to be there to interfere? In the Dalek story, an underground resistance in a Dalek-conquered future sends back a guerilla with a bomb to a critical moment in history to try to change its outcome. He succeeds, thus preventing the Daleks' later victory. But if they didn't conquer Earth, the resistance movement wouldn't exist to send back a guerilla, so . . .?

We kept quiet about that one.

One device (useful to all storytellers) that we hatched up was to use a character to point out a difficulty before the viewer could. In the Dalek story I was just talking about, for instance, Jo Grant said to the Doctor, 'Well, if these guerillas can travel in time, when something goes wrong for them, all they have to do is to go back a day earlier, do it again and get it right . . .'

Now when you think of it, this is a point which makes nonsense of practically every *Doctor Who* story!

So the Doctor said, 'Oh no, they couldn't do that!'

'Why not?' said Jo.

'Because of the Blinovitch limitation effect.'

'What's that?'

'Well, you see . . .'

And at that moment, thank goodness, the guerillas came in and the Doctor didn't have time to explain.

This device proved very useful on the occasion when I had foolishly planned extensive filming on the exposed beaches of Dungeness during the first weeks of January. This was for 'The Claws of Axos' in which (surprise, surprise!) an alien spaceship lands and UNIT goes to investigate.

The weather that week was unbelievable. To start with, it was arctic cold. Katy Manning was wearing a purple mini-skirt and purple boots and you couldn't see where they stopped and her legs began. But worse than that, everything (except the cold) kept changing. There was snow, rain, fog – even a bright blue sky with full sun; and all this was supposed to happen on the same morning.

No problem. When, three weeks later, we shot the scene in the UNIT headquarters control room, the Brigadier was told, 'Reports are coming in of freak weather conditions in the area where the spaceship landed, sir!' The Brigadier wasn't surprised.

Another example: I've already mentioned our trip to the Indian Ocean. It was set 'after dinner' – say at 8 p.m. It wasn't until I got back with every scene shot in broad daylight that I realised that in the tropics the sun sets around six o'clock.

Luckily, in the story the ship was not in the Indian Ocean at all but in an artificial environment – a Galactic Peepshow. So guess what? One of the prime clues the Doctor had for realising that all was not as it seemed was this strange behaviour of the sun. Very clever of him to spot it.

Sometimes, of course, our mistakes were not as easily covered up. The late Malcolm Hulke was a very experienced writer, but no scientist. He relied on us to keep him on the path of scientific virtue. Unfortunately it was not until we received a fair number of letters, some infuriated, some gleeful, that we realised that his Silurians, those underground man-like reptiles the Pertwee Doctor met in his second adventure, were sadly misnamed. In the Silurian period, some 270 million years ago, there weren't even any plants on land, let alone animals. As for intelligent reptiles . . .!

So when we met the Silurians' cousins, the Sea Devils, a couple of years later, the Doctor said, 'Of course, the discoverer of the Silurians made a foolish mistake in calling them that. It would have been more accurate to call them Cretaceans.'

I wish he'd mentioned it earlier.

One of the best letters I had of this sort referred to the giant maggots which appeared in 'The Green Death'. When the Brigadier observed that, like so many of the monsters he encountered, the maggots were impervious to bullets, the Doctor told him that it was due to their thick chitinous skin. Jon, on my instructions, pronounced the first syllable of the word as 'chit'. Two days after transmission I received a very short letter:

Dear Barry Letts,
     The reason I'm writin'
     Is how to say kitin.
          Yours sincerely,

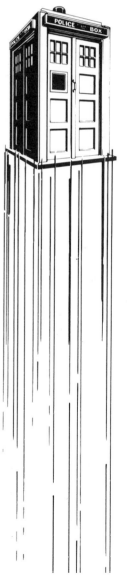

The time eventually arrived when I was to leave the show. To be honest, I had wanted to move on a year or so earlier (when the same problems started coming round for the thirteenth time) but I'd been persuaded not to by my bosses because the show was going so well. As Terrance said, 'This is the only prison where you get time *on* for good behaviour!'

When Jon decided that he'd had enough it seemed a good time to make the break. This left me with two highly important tasks: firstly, to make sure that Jon had a good send-off in his last story and, secondly, to find a new Doctor.

Now, Jon has had a life-long love affair with mechanical transport. As a very young man he had driven racing cars at Brooklands and he sometimes would arrive at rehearsal on an extremely large and powerful motorbike. In his first *Doctor Who* adventure, the Doctor 'borrowed' a beautiful old vintage car – and Jon was so delighted with it that he asked if it could become the Doctor's own. Unfortunately, the owner was unwilling to part with it. So Bessie, the little canary yellow 'old crock', was bought instead. Later Jon, at his own expense, had a beautiful silver saucer-shaped special designed and made, which he called the Whomobile. It made its first appearance on the screen beneath the legs of a giant dinosaur.

But this was not enough for Jon. Whenever he discovered some new method of mechanical travel he wanted to include it in the show. We had managed to indulge him at the beginning of his third year, by writing in a chase with the Doctor riding a fascinating little motor tricycle, with enormous balloon tyres. This was over ten years ago, when they were quite new and unobtainable in Britain. Since then they have become a world best seller.

During the five years Jon also spotted a sea-scooter, a one-man autogiro, a water-jet-propelled speed boat and a miniature inflatable hovercraft. Two sea-scooters were featured in 'The Sea Devils' in a wild and very wet sea-chase between the Doctor and the Master (my dear friend, Roger Delgado, so tragically killed in a car accident in Turkey a little over a year later).

I still hadn't managed to work in the last three machines. So it seemed only fair to make sure they appeared in Jon's last story. And so they did. In 'The Planet of the Spiders', starting with Bessie, in one spectacular chase we used them all – and even persuaded the Whomobile to fly, although the electronic trickery with which we lifted her turned her silver coat into a golden one. A fitting exit, perhaps.

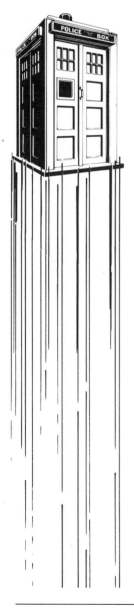

Still I hadn't found a new Doctor. I circulated the agents and spread the news on the grapevine. I wanted a good actor who, though quite different in type from Jon, was also a 'personality' in his own right – even an 'eccentric' perhaps. I wasn't necessarily looking for a star or a well-known name – but I didn't rule that out.

I evolved a method of inquiry. 'With no commitment on either side,' I would say to a possible contender, 'let's discuss how you would react if I were to ask you to be Doctor Who.'

In this manner I talked to a large number of very different possible Doctors, ranging from virtual unknowns to household names. It would be invidious to name those names, perhaps, as we never were able to come to a happy conclusion.

Having made a rule, I shall at once proceed to break it. I talked to the late Richard Hearne, for instance, loved by several generations for his famous character, Mr Pastry. He had, however, virtually retired, and seemed to think we were asking his *alter ego* to be the Doctor. 'I'm not sure that Pastry would be right for it,' he said. 'He doesn't do a lot these days – though he does appear for charity still.'

I was by now accepting and following up suggestions from all directions – and now one came from a most authoritative source. 'Did you see Tom Baker play the Egyptian Doctor when I directed *The Millionairess* for "Play of the Month"?' said Bill Slater, the newly appointed head of drama serials and hence my boss. 'No? Well, surely you must have seen his Rasputin . . .'

I arranged to meet Tom. Within less than two minutes I felt certain we had found our 'personality' at last. And surely he could act? Hadn't he played at the National?

'You can see me in Victoria this very afternoon,' he said. '*The Golden Voyage of Sinbad* is running there.'

So Terrance and I dropped everything and went to see Tom's remarkable performance as the evil magician, the villain of the film. When we came out I rang Tom at once and offered him the job. There was no question but that we had found the right man.

And as for being an 'eccentric' . . . Tom, at the time he was offered one of the most eagerly sought-after roles in British television, was working as a builder's labourer on a Wimpey site. Not because he couldn't get work as an actor. 'You see,' he told me, 'since Rasputin and Sinbad I've been offered nothing but staring blue-eyed psychopaths. I want a change. And I'd rather work than go on the dole.'

Another story: some time after Philip Hinchcliffe had taken over from me he asked me to direct one of Tom's stories, 'The Android Invasion'. We did our exterior filming in the heart of the English countryside in high summer. Whenever Tom wasn't actually needed, he roamed the fields and hedgerows, collecting the seeds of wild flowers until he had a large plastic bag nearly full.

'What are you going to do with those?' I asked him.

'Well, you see,' he said, 'I live in Notting Hill Gate and it's a bit drab. When I get back, a few of my friends and I will go round shoving these seeds into all the cracks and crannies we can find. Just imagine what it'll look like next spring!'

The deceptively beautiful Axons in 'The Claws of Axos' (1971)

I'm not sure whether or not London W11 was indeed a riot of colour in the spring of 1976, but one thing I do know: we could do with a few more eccentrics of the same kind as Tom Baker.

When I was asked to write 5,000 words about my time with *Doctor Who*, I was appalled. I'll never find so much to say, I thought.

But now I find it difficult to stop; I could write 50,000 words. It's like no other show, this one. It gets into the bones and blood of those who work on it. I said that I'd never go back to *Doctor Who* – but I find that I've never left it.

How very odd.

Barry Letts.

January 1983

Azal, the last of the Daemons who threatened to use his terrible powers on the village of Devil's End, from 'The Daemons' (1971)

CHAPTER ELEVEN

WHO AND I

by Terrance Dicks

It began with a telephone call.

'How would you like to be script editor of *Doctor Who*?' The caller was Derrick Sherwin, who had been script editor on *Who* for a fairly short time. Derrick had received the offer of a job he wanted much more – but he couldn't get away from *Doctor Who* until he had found someone to take his place in what had turned out to be a very hot seat.

In those days, back in 1968, I was just getting established as a script-writer, a late starter after Cambridge, National Service and far too many years an an advertising copywriter, a temporary stop-gap job that had lasted five years.

'Script editor of *Doctor Who*? How long for?' I asked cautiously.

'You start with an initial three-month contract. After that, well it all depends . . .'

Like most freelances I was on an economic tightrope. Three months' regular money! was the first thought that popped into my head.

'All right,' I said. 'I'll give it a try.'

It was a fairly casual decision that was to swallow up most of the next six years and have an influence that has lasted until this very moment! When I first joined *Who* the Doctor was Patrick Troughton, a quiet, intensely private man, who disappeared as if he'd dematerialised the second his work on the show was over. Current companions were Fraser Hines as the Scottish lad Jamie and Deborah Watling as Victoria.

The first playback I attended was the last episode of 'Web of Fear' which featured amiable droopy-drawered monsters called the Yeti, who looked like overweight teddy bears and made a noise *exactly* like a flushing lavatory when they roared.

It was their second appearance on *Who* and in an attempt to make them at least a little bit frightening, they had been given glowing eyes and fiercer teeth. But it was no use. The Yeti remained obstinately loveable.

In those days *Who* was recorded from the BBC's Lime Grove studios, smaller and more old-fashioned than those at the Wood Lane Television Centre. The show was on the screen for most of the year, the budget was minute and the schedule especially for the regulars was punishing.

If the Doctor was to get a holiday, he had to be written out! Towards the end of 'Wheel in Space' the Doctor was knocked on the head. He

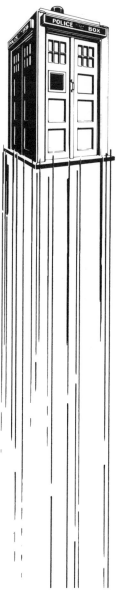

spent the whole of the next episode lying on a bunk with a blanket over him, check trousers and boots sticking out from underneath. Or rather, a double's feet stuck out, while Patrick Troughton was off having a well-deserved rest.

I think it would be fair to say that at that time *Who* hadn't really attained its present legendary, cult status. It was then just over five years old, an excellent run certainly, but a lot less than the up-coming twenty years. Much of the early impact of the Daleks had faded and there was a feeling at the BBC that when Patrick Troughton left, the show should be allowed to come to its natural end.

It was in these unpromising circumstances that I started as script editor on *Who*, with every indication that the show was about to disappear from under me.

Luckily for all of us, nobody came up with a replacement that sounded any better than the original and for this reason, as much as any other, it was decided to let *Who* carry on a little longer.

I spent much of the following year, the sixth season of the show and Patrick Troughton's last as the Doctor, in a state of total confusion, trying to find my feet in a world of continuous crisis.

Things were complicated by the fact that Derrick's new job had failed to materialise and he and Peter Bryant were trying to set up a new project that would get them off the *Who* treadmill.

Since the person I had been hired to replace hadn't actually gone I was left in an uncomfortably nebulous position, and for a time looked like becoming the longest-serving assistant script editor in television history. Derrick and I divided the editing work between us, fairly amicably, and Derrick took over some of the producer's functions while Peter was busy with the new show. There were times when *Who* seemed to be heading in three different directions at once. I stayed on, partly because I was too involved to think of leaving, partly because everyone assured me I was doing a grand job and things would be sorted out any day now.

It was about this time that not one but two script projects collapsed in ruins, leaving a ten-part gap in the schedules. I was given the task of writing a ten-part *Doctor Who* serial. I called in an experienced *Who* writer and an old friend, Malcolm Hulke, to help me, and we came up with 'The War Games'.

We wrote 'The War Games' at the rate of a script about every two days. Some of the time it showed. The opening and closing episodes are pretty good, but in between there is a great deal of chasing about through the time zones.

At long last 'The War Games' came to an end. The Patrick Troughton Doctor was captured by the Time Lords and sentenced to exile on Earth with a new face.

One of Peter Bryant's last jobs on *Who* was to find a replacement for Patrick Troughton. All kinds of names were considered and top of the final short list appeared a certain radio comedian, film character actor, light comedian and cabaret entertainer called Jon Pertwee. But would he want the job?

As it happened, Jon had liked the idea of the role as soon as word got round on the theatrical grapevine, but had felt diffident about applying for what was basically a straight acting role. His agent persuaded him to try – and Jon found he was already top of the short list.

Relieved to find an actor he wanted, who very much wanted to play the part, Peter Bryant cast Jon Pertwee as the new Doctor, and went off to his new show, accompanied by Derrick Sherwin.

Barry Letts, recently promoted from director to producer, took over his replacement and *Doctor Who*'s seventh season got under way with a new Doctor and a new producer and a new script editor. Seven turned out to be a lucky number for all of us, for the show took off with a new lease of life.

To begin with Jon Pertwee scored an immediate success as the Doctor bringing his own flamboyance, zest and enthusiasm to the part. Very much the born showman, Jon revelled in being the Doctor and joined in enthusiastically in publicity and personal appearances.

The important factor from my point of view was that Barry Letts and I hit it off immediately. We have remained friends, colleagues and collaborators ever since that first meeting. (At the moment we're working together again as producer and script editor on BBC 1's Sunday evening classic serial – but that's a whole series of other stories.)

In the days when I was still assistant script editor, part of my job was to read ideas and story lines submitted for the show. One story line called 'The Krotons' was sent in by a writer called Bob Holmes.

Although at the time no new scripts were actually needed, I managed to get permission to develop the idea into a four-part serial as a possible

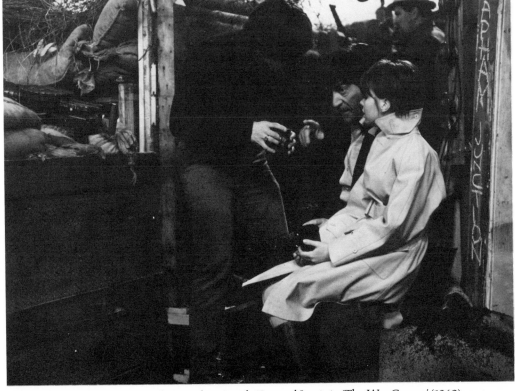

The beleaguered Doctor (Patrick Troughton) with Zoe and Jamie in 'The War Games' (1969)

'reserve'. When a particular set of *Who* scripts once again failed to work out, the reserve was hurriedly rushed into production. 'The Krotons' appeared at the end of 1968 starring possibly the most incompetent monster ever to appear on *Doctor Who*.

The Krotons were alien beings, giant crystalline creatures looking like many-faceted robots. Impressive enough in appearance, they were unable to move more than a few stumbling steps at a time, fell over rather frequently and had the greatest difficulty in holding their ray guns without dropping them.

They spent most of their time on the show simply standing there and looking sinister.

However, the script stood up even if the monsters couldn't and Bob became one of the regular writers on the show. He was asked to write 'Spearhead from Space', the first Jon Pertwee *Doctor Who* serial – the one in which the dummies smash out of the shop windows and mow down the passers-by with built-in wrist ray-guns. The show was a great success and so was Jon Pertwee.

Who was in the news again and the viewing figures went up and stayed up. In more senses than one, the Doctor had taken on new life. Next season we opened with another Auton story 'Terror of the Autons'.

Immediately we were in hot water. The show was criticised in the press for being too frightening and questions were asked in Parliament.

What really had everyone worried was the plastic Troll doll that came to life and killed its victims when activated by heat. All over England kids refused to take their teddy bears to bed – in case they grew fangs in the night and attacked their little owners.

However, as Sam Goldwyn once said, 'There is no bad publicity!' And once again the viewing figures rose dramatically.

Much of the next seven years passed in a kind of blur, with a general sensation much like that of running up a down escalator. You have to sprint like hell to make any real progress and if you relax for as much as a moment you find yourself back where you started.

There are several reasons why *Who* was, and probably always will be, a hellishly difficult show to work on. To begin with, it's science fiction and therefore expensive by definition. There is never really enough time, or enough money. We were trying to achieve then at least something of that 'sense of wonder' which *Star Wars* later produced with months of production time, millions of dollars and an immense special effects staff.

Secondly, the show is technically extremely complex. Douglas Camfield, one of our directors, used to say *Who* was the most technically complex show on British television – and therefore in the world!

From a writing point of view there was the fact that the show had to work on so many different levels. *Who* viewers ranged from the five-year-olds who watch from behind the sofa (so the monsters won't see them) through school children, university students (the viewing rooms in every university in the country are packed when *Who* is on) through all the ages of adults and up to and including the old. Grandparents to grandchildren, and everyone in between.

In addition, *Who* has the strange and unique property of being a series of serials. Four, five, perhaps even six different serials every season, each one by a different writer, each one directed by a different director bringing with him his retinue of assistants and the new cast for that particular story.

The continuing threads that run all through this circus are the producer and script editor, the Doctor, and his companions of that particular season. Sometimes the threads tend to get more than a little frayed.

Because of the mechanics of production, all five of these shows overlap to some extent.

Every year there is a lunatic period when all the shows are going on at once, in different stages of their production lives.

One show is just about to be commissioned, and you're involved in discussions with the writer about his story line.

The next is already being written, and scripts are coming in, needing discussions, re-writes, and final editing.

The third show is in rehearsal – calling for attendance at some of the rehearsals and the regular producers run. Perhaps the show is working out too long. You have to find cuts that don't harm the show and make the actors hate you. Worse still, perhaps it's too short, and you'll have to write a very quick scene using cast and sets available, something to lengthen the episode without looking like obvious padding. (I used to find quarrel scenes a great standby.)

I think it's true to say that scripts have always been a problem on *Who*, before, during and after my time.

Even a four-part serial has a total length of nearly two hours, as long as the average feature film, and a six-parter is a real epic, nearly three hours long. Multiply this by the four or five shows that make up each season, and you can see that there is a tremendous volume of sheer material to be got in each year. Original material too, specially commissioned, technically feasible on the show's resources and budget, and not too much like anything that has gone before, or is due to come after.

In addition the cycle is continous. All the scripts for next season have to be set up while the current season – and all the activity mentioned above – is going on full blast.

Over the years I evolved a few basic rules that made the job possible, if never easy. The key to everything is *time*. Get each show, each set of scripts, under way long, long before you actually need them. The script-writing process of initial discussion, story line, scene-by-scene-breakdown, first-draft, more discussion, second draft, final re-writes, editing, printing, distribution simply devours time. Multiply all this by five and you can have a director breathing down your neck and no scripts to give him.

Television is an intensely collaborative medium. *Who*, like every other show you see on your screen, is the combined work of producer, director, make-up and costume departments, special effects men, designers, carpenters, builders, scene shifters, electricians, cameramen, sound men, lighting technicians as well, of course, as the cast – the actors and actresses the public actually see.

None of these people can even start to do their vital jobs until the script

is written, finalised and distributed.

Recently at the BBC I attended a massive problem-solving meeting in which all the factors that bedevil shows and cause problems for those who make them were raised and discussed. After literally hours of debate, *one* factor emerged as all-important if a show was to run smoothly – *getting the scripts in on time.*

'Not just on time,' said a weary voice from the back. 'Are they any bloody good when you get them?'

As I've said, if a script is late, the huge gang of expert professionals who make television shows can't even start their work. If the script is weak, everything they do will be, to some extent, undermined from the very beginning.

Good scripts, in on time, is what script editing is all about. On *Who* particularly, it is easier said than done.

Something else that worked, at least for us was control and input from the top.

I soon discovered that it was no use sitting back and announcing that I was in the market for *Who* stories. Hundreds of ideas flooded in, most unusable, very often for reasons that the writers couldn't possibly know about. New writers in particular might not understand the limitations of the show and even experienced ones would come up with ideas that were against current policy, or too similar to others already in the works.

As long as possible before each new season, producer Barry Letts and I would have an unending series of discussions. How many shows? How many episodes each one? Same companions, or was it time for a change? What *kind* of shows? (Variety is the keynote of *Who* and every show must be different in look and tone from the one before and the one after.) Only when this was thrashed out, did we think of writers. Is A free? Do we want to use B again, or is it time to give C a chance? And what about that promising story line from D – unknown to us and new to television, but shouldn't we make room for new talent?

The whole question of new writers is a difficult one on TV in general and on *Who* in particular.

Given all the horrendous problems outlined above, producers and script editors are very prone to turn to writers they already know, not for any sinister reasons of closed shop exclusivity, but simply because when a writer has given you as set of well-written scripts delivered more or less on time, there seems at least a reasonable chance that he or she can do it again. (Though we writers are erratic creatures and even this is by no means a sure thing.)

Trying a new writer means a gamble of time and resources, and when you're running up that down escalator, your time for gambling is very limited. Yet at the same time there *is* a need for new talent and every producer and script editor accepts the responsibility for finding and encouraging it – when they can find the time!

A pair of newish – at the time – writers who did break in to *Who* and became regulars were Bob Baker and Dave Martin.

They made it by mistake, because of a totally misrouted script. They sent the BBC a comedy of Army life, which by some aberration of the internal post landed on my desk.

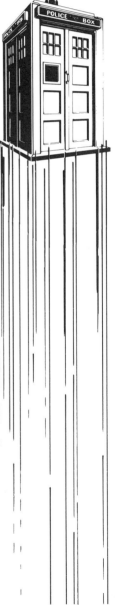

I read it with great enjoyment and some bafflement, since it didn't seem to have anything to do with *Doctor Who*. It was, however, very funny – fast moving, intelligent and witty. I got in touch with Bob and Dave – one tall, one smaller, known collectively as the Bristol Boys because that was where they lived – and after some discussion they wrote a story line.

In fact, over the next year, as I recall, they wrote about seventeen story lines and at least three draft scripts, all of which eventually culminated in the 'Claws of Axos'. Many other Baker and Martin shows were to follow.

Struggling all the time to get ahead of oneself – or at least, not too far behind, controlling and shaping the shows so that each script was a kind of collaboration between writer and production team we eventually evolved a routine that made the script side of things workable, though never simple. Nothing is ever simple on *Who*.

However, vital as the script is, it *is* only the beginning. Most problems are solvable on paper – it's when you take all these lunatic fantasies out into the real world that the trouble starts. I remember Katy Manning's first day of outside filming.

Katy had been cast as the Doctor's new assistant, Jo Grant. She was very small, very cute and, as it happened, very short-sighted, a fact she had naturally omitted to mention at her audition.

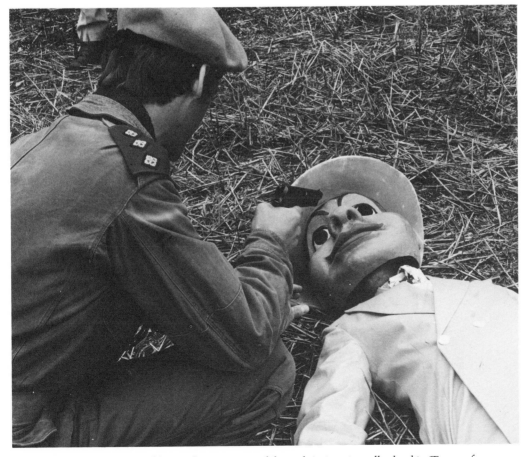

Captain Yates (Richard Franklin) makes sure one of the evil Autons is really dead in 'Terror of the Autons' (1970)

The show in question was 'Terror of the Autons' – the sequel to 'Spearhead from Space'. Katy and Jon had to run across country pursued by Autons. The scene was set up, the director called, 'Action!'

The Doctor shouted, 'Run!' and Katy ran – straight into a tree, knocking herself silly. In future chases, Jon took good care to take her by the hand and lead her in the right direction.

I remember back in the Troughton days, filming the Ice Warrior story 'Seeds of Death' on Hampstead Heath in the early hours of the morning. One lady motorist was so horrified at the sight of the scaly green giant lurching towards her that she drove straight into a tree, luckily with only minor damage as a result.

Even more suprised was the sleeping tramp who woke up one morning under one of the arches near the National Theatre to see a tall dragon-featured Draconian looming over him. He disappeared over the horizon, probably to sign the pledge.

I remember 'Inferno', an alternate world story. The Doctor and his companions are marched before the Brigadier's evil other self, a sinister autocrat with a black eye-patch.

When they arrived on the set, Jon, Katy Manning and every other actor in the scene were *all* wearing black eye-patches.

The joke however misfired since Nick Courtney, like the old pro he was, simply stared them coldly in the eyes – or rather eye – and went on with the scene. It was the practical jokers who collapsed, helpless with laughter.

I remember a story called 'The Dominators' in which a tubby balding actor had to play a tough no-nonsense rebel – and costume dressed him in something that looked like a ballet-dancer's tu-tu.

I remember some monsters called Gell-guards, in 'The Three Doctors' who looked like giant blancmanges and could do little more than stand there and wobble menacingly. (Shades of the Krotons!)

It was in 'The Three Doctors' incidentally that it became clear at the very last moment that William Hartnell, the first Doctor, was far too ill to play the extensive part that had been written for him. The scripts had to be hurriedly re-written so that he could appear from time to time on the screen of the TARDIS scanner and deliver a few words of advice to his usually squabbling other selves.

All of the first Doctor's scenes were filmed during one day at the BBC's Ealing studios. Without tiring the old man out too much, the director was able to get enough on film to enable the first Doctor to make a number of impressive appearances in all four episodes.

It was a busy and enjoyable five years, a period of continuous crises, each one dealt with just in time before the next came along. However, like all good things it had to come to an end. At the end of five years we were all very tired and badly in need of a change.

Jon Pertwee felt that five years as the Doctor was enough and was very anxious to leave at a peak of success. He was getting interesting offers from stage, television and films, most of which he had to turn down because he was committed to *Who* and as he said, 'If I keep on saying no, they may stop asking me!'

Barry Letts wanted a change and a return to the more satisfying work of directing.

Although my own plans were far from clear, I felt it was the natural end of an era and that I should go too. To give myself a boost into the cold hard world of the freelance I persuaded the powers that be that there was a tradition that retiring script editors wrote the first of the new shows. (There was no such tradition, but I was determined to start one.)

It was agreed that I should write the first show for the new Doctor – but what new Doctor?

Like Peter Bryant all those years ago, Barry Letts had the fearful responsibility of finding a new Doctor before he left.

To me the finding of each new Doctor is a recurrent miracle. It's always impossible and it always succeeds brilliantly. Somehow the miracle happened again and Tom Baker was cast as the Doctor.

Once everything was settled, I was able to get on with my script. Bob Holmes who was replacing me as script editor wanted a story about a robot and I eventually produced 'Robot', a kind of affectionate homage to King Kong, which successfully launched the new Tom Baker Doctor.

At this point, with a new Doctor, a new producer and a new script editor, it seemed my connection with *Who* was more or less over. In fact it was to continue for many years in a rather different way.

The *Doctor Who* books are novelisations of the television series. Their success has been as phenomenal as that of the show itself. Not that it looked that way in the beginning.

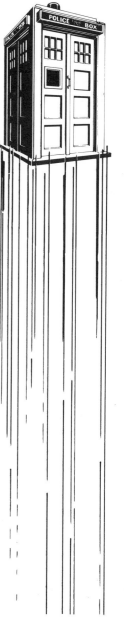

Back in the early sixties when the show first started and the Daleks scored their first big success, three of the television serials were novelised. *Doctor Who and the Daleks* and *Doctor Who and the Crusaders* both by David Whitaker and *Doctor Who and the Zarbi* by Bill Strutton. Published as children's hardbacks of the kind bought mostly by libraries, these three books had a modest success – and stayed forgotten for the next ten years.

In the early seventies a publisher called Tandem Books decided to start a new children's paperback list, Target Books. The editor, Richard Henwood, shopped around other publishers, looking for titles which could be paperbacked. Amongst his purchases were those three ten-year-old Doctor Who books . . .

The rest is publishing history. The three books reprinted in paperback with colourful striking colours were an instant sell-out. Target realised they had a hit on their hands – and they also realised they only had three very old titles.

They contacted the BBC, made a deal for the novelisation rights, and eventually Richard Henwood landed up in my office with the message, 'We need more Doctor Who books? Who will write for us?'

At the time, I don't think any of us realised what a phenomenon we were dealing with. The new wave *Doctor Who* books were simply a part of the Target publicity programme. Very soon they were to swallow it up completely.

My first novelisation was *Auton Invasion*, adapted from Bob Holmes's 'Spearhead from Space'. Barry Letts novelised *The Daemons*, Malcolm Hulke *The Space War*, adapted from his own 'Frontier in Space'. In those days, if the serial title wasn't thought exciting enough, it was simply changed – today book and serial title are always the same.

The books were shared around a small group of writers. The early days of the Target *Doctor Who* novelisation coincided with the time I finally left *Who* and went freelance again and gradually, over the years, most, though not all, of the other adaptors dropped away and I found myself writing the bulk of the Target output. That initial book has now turned into something like fifty. These in turn led to my writing a variety of other children's books and more or less by chance I turned into a writer of books rather than scripts.

In the years that followed, my connection with *Who* was continuous but, at the same time, detached. Other people racked their brains to get out the scripts, other people faced all the problems of production. When all the blood sweat and tears was over, I sat down with a set of scripts and a video recording and set about the enjoyable, though by no means easy, task of turning a television script into a book that would stand up on its own.

Occasionally in those peaceful years, I would be asked to write another *Who* TV serial – usually, I suspected, because of some sort of emergency.

American science fiction conventions were a kind of *Who* fringe benefit. American fans are organised, vociferous and very fond of holding massive conventions, or cons, where people connected with their favourite books and shows are invited to come as guests, speak, appear on panels and generally just be seen.

In recent years *Who* has become increasingly popular in America and over the past few years I have attended conventions in Los Angeles, Boston, Miami and, most recently, New Orleans.

It was in New Orleans one morning that the telephone rang waking me from a very short sleep – last night's party had ended at 4 a.m. As the fog receded I gradually realised that the voice on the other end was Eric Saward, current script editor of *Doctor Who*, and that I was being asked to write the Anniversary Special – a ninety-minute film with *all* the Doctors and a variety of companions and monsters. So many do's and don'ts were built into the brief that the whole thing was practically impossible from the start. It was a bit of an emergency. Certain earlier plans hadn't worked out and they were very short of time . . . It was an offer I couldn't possibly refuse.

Soon after my return to England, I was back on the *Who* merry-go-round. Script conferences, story lines, more script conferences, first draft, more script conferences and, just when the end was in sight, an unavoidable last-minute change in the brief that sent me back to the beginning again.

Nothing is ever simple – not on *Who* it isn't!

Now the script is finished, delivered, printed and distributed. And I'm at home, finishing this article – very much overdue, sorry, Peter. When this is finished, there's another pile of *Who* scripts waiting to be turned into a book and, unless I get a move on, *that*'ll be overdue as well . . .

Sometimes I refer to my time, the Pertwee days, as 'The Classic Years'.

It *is* only a joke. Time lends enchantment and today's shows are the classics of the future. But I like to think there's a gleam of truth in it.

Somehow, during those years, the show made the jump from a modestly successful five-year-old children's show that had nearly run its course, to a legend that looks like going on forever.

Now Peter Davison and the current producer John Nathan-Turner and his team are carrying the show into its twentieth incredible year and beyond.

I always used to say *Who* was like a relay race. You carry the baton for a while, drop back exhausted and hand the burden over to someone else. I shall always be glad that I helped to carry that baton for a while.

And I shall always remember something William Hartnell said in his years of retirement. 'Once you've been involved with the Doctor, some of the magic stays with you the rest of your life . . .'

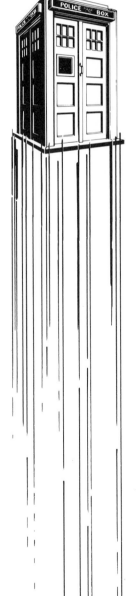

February 1983

Terrance Dicks signing copies of some of the many *Doctor Who* novelisations he has written

John Nathan-Turner with a few examples of the spin-offs *Doctor Who* has generated

CHAPTER TWELVE

THE CONTINUING STORY OF WHO

by John Nathan-Turner

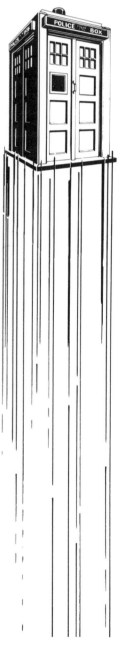

If someone today tried to sell the idea of *Doctor Who* to the controller of a television channel he would probably be committed to a lunatic asylum. I mean, just what kind of an idea is it that a man – the Doctor – travels around in space and time with a couple of sidekicks in a police box that is bigger on the inside than outside?

Yet it is a *brilliant* concept – and because we are dealing with space and time we have a completely empty canvas to paint on and consequently every story can be very, very different. Of course, there will be some people who say that a certain story is reminiscent of another. That's inevitable. After all, there are only supposed to be *seven* plots in drama terms – and we do seven stories a year!

Doctor Who is quite unlike any other television programme. It is outrageous and it is also very attractive. It allows you to explore new civilisations or old historical situations – what we call pseudo-historical sci-fi – whenever you want. I have been associated with the series, on and off, since 1969 and worked with all but one of the Doctors, so you can understand why it has such a great appeal for me. I started on 'The Space Pirates' in 1969 with Patrick Troughton and then did 'The Ambassadors of Death' (1970) and 'Colony in Space' (1971) with Jon Pertwee. I became production unit manager in 1977 and my first assignment was 'The Invisible Enemy', with Tom Baker as the Doctor. I've been travelling with the show ever since!

I became production unit manager in order, ultimately, to become a producer. It was a stepping-stone, but the job – which entails being a kind of general and financial adviser to the producer – gave me tremendous background knowledge about *Doctor Who*. When, in turn, I was made producer, it represented a fantastic challenge.

There were several factors that helped me in the job. First, I think my earlier background as an actor and in stage management was invaluable. Secondly, having been a great filmgoer when I was young – I used to write screeds to film companies in America – I had an appreciation of the fans' point of view. And that's very important with *Doctor Who*, I believe.

One of the first satisfactions I gained in the job was having the chance to drop the six-part stories. I thought that many of the six-parters in recent years had really been just two four-part stories condensed – with one villain being unmasked at the end of episode four and another introduced for the remaining two. There have been exceptions, of course, but a four-part story is after all one hundred minutes long – the equivalent of a full-length feature film. Now, there are not many films that can stand *six* times twenty-five minutes; two and a half hours. I just think that in six episodes you are pulling the story lines out too far, stretching them too much. Four is the ideal length for the programme in its current form.

The decision to move *Doctor Who* from its time spot of Saturday evening to two weekday spots was made by the Controller of BBC 1, though I was asked for my opinion. The twice-weekly slot *has* given the show a new lease of life – as I knew it would. I know there were a lot of protests from viewers and in the press that Saturday had always been regarded as the traditional day for the series, because children did not have homework and older people were not commuting. But times and viewing tastes have changed in recent years. BBC 1 no longer has the absolute hold it once had on Saturday evening audiences. In those days you started with *Grandstand* and went right through to *Parkinson* at the end of the day.

Nowadays, people do a lot more channel switching on Saturdays and I earnestly believe that if we'd stayed on Saturdays we would not have attracted the 10 million average viewing figures we are getting.

When I took over the programme, I had no idea that Tom Baker was going to leave. He had, in fact, just signed a contract for another year. But he did let me know what was in his mind and we decided to hold on to the information so as to be able to get the most publicity from it at the right moment. When, though, the news of his imminent departure did get out unexpectedly, it led to one of the most extraordinary rumours ever published about *Doctor Who* – that the next Doctor might be played by a woman! I'd like to explain how this came about and lay to rest once and for all any idea that such a thing might happen . . .

It all began on 24 October 1980 when Tom and I were attending a press photocall at Madame Tussaud's. Tom had become the first person to have two models of himself in the museum and the cameramen wanted pictures of him with his dummies.

After the photocall, Tom and I went for a quiet drink. No sooner had we ordered than I got a phone call from my secretary. Her voice sounded anxious. She said the *Daily Mirror* were chasing after me because they had got a tip that Tom was leaving the series.

I had to make a very quick decision. I have never believed in lying to the press, so I told Tom I was going to arrange a press conference in two hours' time to release the news. It was noon then and so Tom and I had to lie low in the meantime so that no journalist could steal a lead on another.

Well, as we drove in a taxi to the press conference two hours later, Tom suddenly said, 'Let's have a bit of fun. I'll feed you a line that the next Doctor might be a woman!' I looked at that marvellous, toothy grin of his, saw his eyes sparkling with mischief and burst out laughing. It was an irresistible idea – and I agreed.

When we walked into the press conference it was *packed*. I could hardly believe my eyes that so many reporters had been sent to cover the departure of an actor playing a television character. Naturally, the first thing they all wanted to know was why Tom was leaving.

'I've done seven years and been seen by 100 million viewers in 37 countries,' he replied, 'and I get recognised all over the world. I want to quit while I'm at the top. There's nothing more I can do but repetition.'

Tom added that he was finishing work on the programme in December and his last appearance on screen would be in March. Then that look came into his eyes which only I of all the people in the room appreciated.

'I would just like to add,' he went on, glancing around the reporters, 'that I wish the new Doctor, *whoever he or she is*, the very best of luck.'

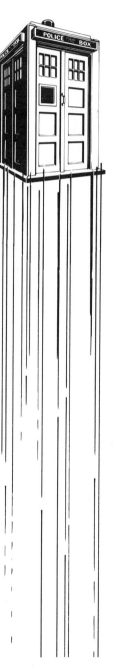

Well, of course, there was pandemonium. All the journalists pounced on his words and began to shout questions at once. A woman – playing the Doctor?

Tom kept up the pretence superbly and, when the clamour died down, he said simply, 'Oh, I've said far too much already. You must talk to John about the future.'

Then it was my turn. 'The part has not been offered to anyone yet,' I said, 'but we shall be considering either sex.'

There was no need to add any more. The following day the news made the front pages of most British newspapers: 'Tom Baker quits – the new Doctor may be a woman!

The idea had been a great success and certainly generated enormous interest in who Tom's successor might be. But let me say that there was never a chance *then* – nor do I think there ever will be – that the Doctor could be played by a woman. Absolutely not!

Tom's departure naturally opened up the possibility of more changes on the series – yet picking his actual successor was one of the easiest tasks I've had on *Doctor Who*.

My first decision was that whoever took over the part was going to be very different from Tom – and also much younger. Having settled this, I was sitting in my office shortly afterwards wondering who would fit these requirements. Idly my eyes roamed over one of the walls covered with photographs. My gaze fell on a picture of a young man in some cricketing gear taken at a charity match which we had both attended. The young man was Peter Davison and I had worked with him for three years when I was production associate on *All Creatures Great and Small*. During that time I had come to admire his performance as the vet, Tristan, tremendously. It was a very difficult and demanding role.

That's it, I thought – *he's* the one! And he really *was* my first choice for the new Doctor.

I know it sometimes sounds easy to say something like that in hindsight because you don't want to upset anyone else you might have had in mind beforehand. But I can honestly say there was no one else but Peter.

So I rang him at home and just said, 'How would you like to be the next Doctor Who?' He was absolutely astounded, I could tell.

'I can't answer that,' he replied after a long pause. 'Can I ring you back tomorrow?'

He did ring back the next day and said he hadn't been able to sleep because he'd been thinking about what I had proposed. But he had come to the conclusion he would like to try.

In casting Peter, I not only wanted somebody younger than his predecessors, but also more heroic, more vulnerable, with less reliance on the hardware – on the K9s and the sonic screwdrivers and that kind of thing. In a programme such as ours with its cliff-hangers, it's inevitably the Doctor who is in peril at the end of an episode. And no matter how much you try to steer writers away from it, they always put him in an impossible situation to get out of and then solve it by having him just take out his sonic screwdriver or whatever. That's a real let-down, I think, and you lose all the drama.

So we opted for a Doctor who was more inventive, more ingenious and would sometimes get out of a scrape using the kind of things most youngsters would have in their pockets – a safety pin, paperclips, bits of string, even a cricket ball!

To bring a freshness to the programme, I have also been trying new writers. *Doctor Who* is an incredibly hard series to write for, and it really doesn't matter how many scripts a writer has done before – it is still a very difficult format.

In creating a script, we have to have endless meetings and discussions and I feel that if you have to go through these with long-established writers just as much as with newcomers, why not give some new people a chance in the hope they come up with some fresh ideas? You are spending no more time in fact with a new writer – and it is nice to encourage some new talent.

I am a great believer in continuity – not just for the fans but also for the general viewer. If you decide to bring back a character who has been in the series before, there will be viewers who have seen him and will quickly spot if you have changed his mannerisms, for example. So I insist we take the trouble to look up the old episodes and scripts and make sure we get everything right.

I also like continuity in the people working behind the scenes on *Doctor Who*. It seems to me that the best programmes often have the nicest group of people working on them. I'm particularly proud of the kind of family atmosphere we have. It has taken time to build up and is really paying off.

For instance, I have a fine camera crew who have been with me for three years (and with the show even longer). Despite the fact that we only go into the studios once a fortnight for a couple of days, they have become so close with the actors and production team that they all send each other cards at Christmas! Then there are the designers. We never have masses of money – in fact I'm always complaining about a lack of it – but they nearly always come up with absolutely stunning designs in costume, make-up, visual effects and set designs. Somehow they take the pittance we give them and with a lot of skill and ingenuity create effects that are ten times better than shows with budgets many times bigger than ours. They are also very good at what I call jigsaw sets – detailed sets that appear to look quite different from opposite angles and look much bigger than they actually are.

The directors, too, play a major role in creating the finished product and each one seems to add some new dimension to the continuing saga. They, like everyone else, are part and parcel of a creative team making everything so exciting to watch. (It may surprise you to know that all

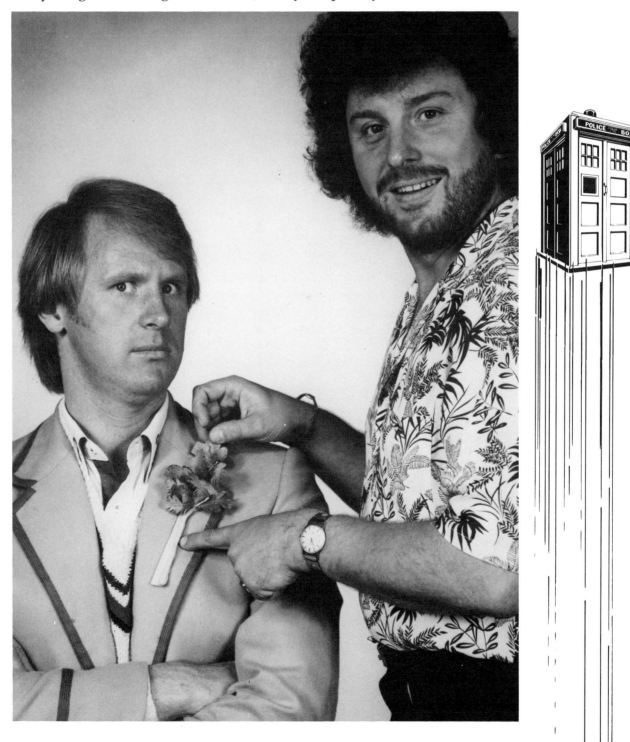

John Nathan-Turner with Peter Davison

these people only work on *Doctor Who* as part of their jobs at the BBC – the full-time members of the team are just script editor Eric Saward, production associate June Collins, my secretary Jane Judge, and myself!)

The impact of the various monsters and aliens on our audience is also very much down to the skill of this team. Although these creatures have been a very important ingredient in the success of the programme over the years, I don't believe they are essential in every story. Variety of theme is just as important as the monsters I would say.

Audiences tend to react best to monsters which are based on the human form. We have to be careful not to come up with something that is inadvertently funny, like a blob of man-eating jelly. The best frights can come from monsters you don't actually see. In recent years we've been going more for a Hitchcock treatment; a shadow flitting across the screen, a bulging eye, a foot behind a door.

With *Doctor Who* the intention is to scare, but not to horrify. To keep everyone on the edges of their seats, but without giving them lasting nightmares. Some of the monsters can be pretty scary for children. Most little ones tend to watch trembling from behind sofas or, on bad days, through the living-room keyhole – loving every spine-chilling minute of it, of course!

But we rarely show blood, or anyone killed with kitchen knives or catapaults. It can give children bad ideas. We also have to draw a fine line between scaring and actually terrifying. Not so long ago we had complaints because we used real bats in a vampire scene. The protests weren't because we were too scary, but because it was bad for the bats' image. The Bat Preservation Society was up in arms. There were even questions asked about it in Parliament!

Being the centre of controversy and attracting publicity is nothing new for *Doctor Who*, though. Stories about the show abound – as this book has already shown! – but as I'm always being asked to recall amusing incidents, I must surely find space for one more here.

A story that springs to mind concerns the filming of 'Arc of Infinity'. We were doing some sequences in Amsterdam and naturally had to take a lot of baggage with us – film equipment, costumes, certain props and suchlike. When we discovered the consignment was going to be more than our permitted allowance, we made a hurried check through the telex to confirm that all the baggage *was* being accommodated on our flight. It would cause all sorts of headaches if anything was left behind.

Sure enough, back came the reply confirming that arrangements had been made to accommodate the extra load. But there was one rather special exception.

'One Tardis,' the message read, 'making its own way.'

Somebody at Heathrow Airport obviously had a sense of humour!

So here we are with twenty years behind us. What of the future?

For myself, I plan to do one more season as producer and then – who knows? As far as the programme itself is concerned I am sure it will be endless.

For *Doctor Who* captured the public's imagination when it was born in 1963 and with the change of Doctors, producers, script-writers and others over the years has been kept fresh and full of ideas. No one has wanted to copy his or her predecessor – I did not want to duplicate what Verity Lambert had done in those far-off days and doubtless my successor will have different ideas from mine. *That's* what has kept it fresh – it has continued to update itself all the time and appeal to each new generation of youngsters.

It was a terribly bold thing to have decided back in 1966 when William Hartnell left, 'We love this show, let's not kill it.' And promptly have the Doctor regenerate in a complete new form. It *could* have been the end, the finish of *Doctor Who*. Instead it was just another beginning. And that brave decision has, I think, been most fittingly marked by the fact that the word 'regeneration' is now a very much more familiar part of the English language – and all due to *Doctor Who*!

February 1983

A twentieth-birthday cake for a very special programme

THE WHONIVERSE

THE TWENTY-YEAR TRAVEL LOG

The Doctors' Adventures and
Their Backgrounds

by Jeremy Bentham

An Unearthly Child/The Tribe of Gum (serial A) by Anthony Coburn (with additional material by C. E. Webber). Director: Waris Hussein
The Doctor's first trip through time as far as television audiences were concerned and, from a visual point of view, the best executed of the TARDIS's many time flights. To date this has been the only story ever to depict the ship tumbling backwards through time, an effect achieved by superimposing shots of the lead characters with the original *Doctor Who* title graphics. So startling was this trick that when first seen the reviewer for *Television Today* was inspired to comment, 'The Visual Effects Department have succeeded in transporting me through time and space more satisfactorily than I can ever recall having journeyed before – and that includes the cinema with all the trick effects at its disposal.'

The remaining three episodes of this serial concerned the efforts of the four hapless time travellers to stay alive in the savage environment of a tribe of sun worshippers desperately seeking the secret of fire as the Ice Age looms daily ever nearer. The climactic final battle between the two would-be tribe leaders – Kal and Za – made much use of burning torches thereby requiring this sequence to be done on film at the BBC's Ealing studios, rather than at the conventional recording studio at Lime Grove, for reasons of safety.

The Daleks (aka The Dead Planet) (serial B) by Terry Nation. Director: Christopher Barry and Richard Martin
The arrival of the Daleks and the serial which gave overnight fame and lasting fortune to *Doctor Who*. Although arguably not the best of the many Dalek serials this seven-parter overcame the limitations of its studio confines by stunning combinations of optical and sound effects. The first sight of the Dalek city on Skaro with the travellers in the foreground and the city seen in the distance set the mood of the story with its careful blending of live action recording, model shots and an eerie radiophonic soundtrack composed by Tristram Carey.

The Daleks caught the imagination of a generation of youngsters in a way seldom witnessed before or after. Their grating monotone voices, small squat shapes and lethal weaponry (the negative 'extermination' effect being achieved by the simple process of over-exposing the view seen through the TV camera) inspiring a fame and notoriety that has led the word Dalek to become part of the English language.

The Edge of Destruction (serial C) by David Whitaker. Directors: Richard Martin and Frank Cox
It is said that the cheapest and easiest play ever to do on television would be about a small cast trapped in a lift. To all intents and purposes this story was that play with the four regular members of the cast having to act alone for two episodes solely within the confines of the TARDIS which had inexplicably broken down.

It was 'force majeure' which led to this two-parter being done: the cancellation of a story entitled 'Beyond the Sun' meant that a story was needed that utilised the only stock set available – the TARDIS.

That said the somewhat speedily written script by story editor David Whitaker provided the *Doctor Who* production team with an excellent excuse to introduce viewers more clearly to the characters of Ian, Barbara, Susan and the enigmatic Doctor and to the abilities and facilities of the TARDIS, including its dormitories, food machine and navigation computers. In this story it was conclusively shown that the TARDIS is indeed far more than a mere machine and could take very drastic steps indeed to protect itself from anything that might lead, albeit inadvertently, to its own destruction . . .

Marco Polo (serial D) by John Lucarotti. Directors: Waris Hussein and John Crockett
The earliest of the Doctor's journeys into history and in many respects the best – a no-holds-barred costume drama of the kind at which the BBC is unexcelled and a good excuse to educate *Doctor Who*'s by-now huge legion of viewers in the travels of Marco Polo.

Right from the beginning it had been intended that *Doctor Who* would balance science fiction stories with historical epics that would hopefully fire the imaginations of school-age viewers. Of the many writers to have penned historical *Doctor Who* stories over the years John Lucarotti took his brief the most literally and included many let's-teach-history sections within his three scripts for the programme.

One of the ways this was achieved in 'Marco Polo' was through its unique 'Captain's Log' approach, the drama being broken up every now and then to show a map illustrating the journey from the plain of Pamir to Cathay with Mark Eden (as Polo) narrating the details and happenings *en route*.

The Keys of Marinus (serial E) by Terry Nation. Director: John Gorrie
The first of the quest-style serials to grace *Doctor Who* as the travellers are persuaded by Arbitan, Keeper of the Conscience Machine of Marinus, to hunt for the four missing operating keys to the device across the many continents of the planet Marinus using the convenient – and expense-saving – travel dials: wristwatch-like personal transportation systems. Exercising the capabilities of the BBC's design department to the fullest, the various episodes for this story took place in jungle surroundings, an icy tundra, a courtroom setting and a nightmare city

that one moment could look like an opulent palace and the next like a dilapidated ruin.

Oddly enough the billed villains of the piece, the Voord, only appeared in episodes one and six and only then for one half of the final episode. Despite this, however, they gained some fame and recognition through merchandising spin-offs, appearing in one story in the 1965 *Doctor Who* annual and by co-starring, with the Daleks, on the first ever set of *Doctor Who* sweet cigarette cards marketed by the Cadet company, also in 1965.

The Aztecs (serial F) by John Lucarotti. Director: John Crockett
The TARDIS arrives in Mexico at the time of the Aztec civilisation, pitting its four incumbents against the paradoxes of this strange civilisation. On the one hand, the Aztecs were cultured and artistic, on the other hand, they practised the barbaric custom of human sacrifice. In writing this four-part script John Lucarotti used the characters of his story line to mark out the differences in the Aztec people. Autloc, played by Keith Pyott, is a gentle and wise figure who believes absolutely in the dictates of the God Yetaxa – for whom Barbara is mistaken. By contrast John Ringham's superb Richard III performance as Tlotoxl is the advocate of sacrifice and it is Barbara's wish to end this practice that leads to Tlotoxl's conviction that she is not Yetaxa reincarnated after all. And eventually, of course, it is Tlotoxl who wins the day: an uncommon moral viewpoint incongruous to *Doctor Who* even then.

Commenting on this, his favourite *Doctor Who* script, John Lucarotti said, 'Their civilisation intrigued me. They were, at the same time, a cultured yet savage people who practised human sacrifice. Also, they didn't know about the wheel. So, as one became the key to the Doctor's escape, he took it with him so as not to interfere with history.'

The Sensorites (serial G) by Peter R. Newman. Directors: Mervyn Pinfield and Frank Cox
The least remembered of the first season's science fiction stories, *The Sensorites* perhaps failed to make an impact due to the goodly nature of its aliens. With their Mickey Mouse shaped feet, orange costumes, portly figures and bald heads, this curious race of aliens, with aversions to loud noise and darkness, did rather resemble a species of wise old men – which of course they were. Even the villain of the piece, played by Peter Glaze more notably of *Crackerjack* fame, was only allowed to be scheming rather than downright nasty.

One facet of this story was Barbara's absence for the whole of episodes four and five. With the season being recorded continually week in and week out, scripts were carefully written to allow the regular cast the odd week or two's holiday from time to time. Carole Ann Ford, as Susan, is seen only on pre-recorded film inserts for episodes two and three of 'The Aztecs'. Similarly William Russell, as Ian, appears only on telecine film for episodes two and three of 'The Reign of Terror'. Jacqueline Hill is absent totally in 'The Sensorites' and, in a move that would never happen now, William Hartnell, playing the title role of the Doctor, does not appear anywhere in episodes three and four of 'The Keys of Marinus'.

The Reign of Terror (serial H) by Dennis Spooner. Director: Henric Hirsch

Doctor Who meets *A Tale of Two Cities* as the intrepid travellers, still searching for a way back to England 1963, arrived in Paris during Robespierre's last weeks in power before the chain of events began which would eventually see Napoleon Bonaparte ensconced as Emperor of France – and a good many other places as well.

True to the flavour of the show at this time Dennis Spooner kept in the scene of the supposed first meeting between Paul Barrass and the young Corsican general, with Barbara and Ian keeping only a watchful eye on proceedings aided by the simple presence of a keyhole in the plot.

With *Doctor Who* almost a year old now and already well on its way to becoming one of the BBC's vanguard productions, this story saw the first use of any exterior location filming as the Doctor is seen trudging across fields and meadows on his way to Paris to save his friends from the guillotine. Another notable first for the serial it was the earliest *Doctor Who* story to be recorded in the newly completed Television Centre in Shepherd's Bush.

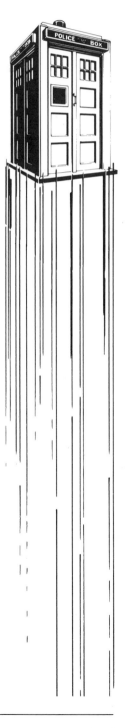

Planet of Giants (serial J) by Louis Marks. Directors: Mervyn Pinfield and Douglas Camfield

Doctor Who meets *Land of the Giants* might have been the press publicity had this serial been produced some eight years later. An accidental opening of the TARDIS doors mid-flight shrinks the ship and its four incumbents to Tom Thumb size, putting them in dire peril when they land in an English suburban garden.

Thanks to ingenious big-scale sets designed by Ray Cusick and the technical acumen of associate producer-turned-director for this serial, Mervyn Pinfield, neither giant animated flies, oversized telephones nor the dangers of finding oneself inside a sink sluice pipe as the plug is pulled were beyond this story. Racing against time to return Barbara back to the TARDIS before a lethal dose of insecticide poisoning kills her, Barbara, Ian and the Doctor also have to contend with thwarting the ambitions of a ruthless businessman who intends unleashing the insecticide DN6, knowing it will ultimately destroy all insect life on Earth.

Originally planned as a four-part story, 'Planet of Giants' ultimately had its last two episodes merged together on the instructions of Verity Lambert who felt they did not carry enough weight as they stood to sustain fifty minutes of television drama. The original title for episode four was 'An Urge to Live'.

The Dalek Invasion of Earth (serial K) by Terry Nation. Director: Richard Martin

'The Daleks are back', proclaimed banner headlines in most of the national dailies. Fuelled by an unprecedented wave of popular interest in the mechanical aliens by the youth of Britain, this serial attracted the highest consistent ratings for a Hartnell serial and cemented the festive period of 1964 as 'Dalek Christmas' in the eyes of toy manufacturers, all of whom had worked night and day the months before getting Dalek toys ready for the Christmas spending spree.

The story line was simple enough. The TARDIS at last returns Barbara and Ian to London, England, but to a point more than one hundred years ahead of their own time. The Daleks have invaded and conquered the world and now they intend replacing the Earth's core with a drive system that will enable them to pilot the world to a new point in space – effectively killing off the remains of humanity *en route*. Joining up with an underground resistance, the Doctor and company eventually use the invaders' own superbomb against them, thereby ending the threat.

This was the first *Doctor Who* serial to make use of major location filming although, as in the famous instance of the Dalek rising out of the Thames, some locations merely required the team to go out the back door of their own studios at Riverside, Hammersmith Bridge, for several key sequences.

The Rescue (serial L) by David Whitaker. Director: Christopher Barry
With Susan having stayed behind to help the remaining population of the shattered Earth rebuild their world, the saddened Doctor finds an able replacement for her vacant berth aboard the TARDIS in the form of orphan Vicki. She and the injured Bennett are the sole survivors of a passenger craft, the rest of whose crew were apparently massacred by the Didonians shortly after the ship crash-landed on this barren world. Now the pair are being menaced by a sinister witch-doctor-like figure, Koquillion, whose spined appearance terrifies Vicki. Koquillion, though, is Bennett in disguise, attempting to cover up the murders he first committed while the ship was in flight. Unmasked by the Doctor, Bennett is later killed by two Didonians whom the mad killer also thought he had slaughtered.

Originally planned as the first story of the second season this serial was put back into third place when the extra work required on 'Dalek Invasion of Earth' dictated that the first season should finish sooner than was originally scheduled. This was David Whitaker's last story as script editor, having fulfilled his contract to handle a year's worth of *Doctor Who* episodes.

The Romans (serial M) by Dennis Spooner. Director: Christopher Barry
The Doctor has taken Vicki to see the sights of ancient Rome but on the way gets mistaken for the famous lyre player Maximus Pettulian who is booked to entertain Nero's court. Meanwhile Barbara has been abducted by a band of slave traders and sold at auction to Tavius. But Tavius is master of Nero's household and so Barbara finds herself serving at Nero's palace totally unaware of the Doctor and Vicki's presence. At the same time Ian, also one-time prisoner of the slavers, has also arrived in the Roman capital searching for Barbara with the aid of a galley slave, Delos. The pair are captured and told they will die unless they agree to train as gladiators for the arena sports – with lions being their chosen opponents. Not only is Ian unaware of Barbara's fate at the palace – where she has been dodging the amorous advances of the Emperor himself – he likewise remains in total ignorance of the whereabouts of Vicki and the Doctor. Confused? You should be . . .

No strangers to comedy themselves, Derek Francis as Nero and

William Hartnell both gave virtuoso farce performances in this the first *Doctor Who* story to be played for laughs. Not so much *Carry On, Sergeant* as *Carry On, Cleo* with Dennis Spooner even hiring Gerton Klauber to recreate his galley master role.

The Web Planet (serial N) by Bill Strutton. Director: Richard Martin
An alien planet resembling the surface of the Moon, a race of hostile ant–beetles the size of a man, a malevolent parasite spider and a kindly race of giant flying moths. What more exciting plot devices for a *Doctor Who* story could anyone wish for? Or more expensive . . .

As the then script editor, Dennis Spooner, once pointed out everything on 'The Web Planet' was expensive. Every set, every costume, every prop had to be built from scratch. With the exception of the four travellers, none of the actors and actresses engaged for this production appeared in human shape – all had to be submerged beneath layers of make-up, costume and special props and then positioned on sets featuring craters, mica ridges, organic tentacles and acid pools. In some way the huge outlay paid off. Partly due to a *Radio Times* cover feature (the second that season), episode one gathered the highest ratings for a Hartnell serial with well in excess of ten million tuning in to watch the Doctor's efforts in aiding the beleaguered Menoptra recover their world from the eroding power of the Animus and its mentally enslaved Zarbi. In BBC terms the story was a success but its overheads had proved too high. To date there has not been another story like it.

The Crusade (serial P) by David Whitaker. Director: Douglas Camfield
Director Douglas Camfield pulled off a considerable coup with this story. Armed with what he considered, and still considers to this day, to be the finest script he has ever worked with, he managed to persuade big-name actor Julian Glover to play the part of King Richard I – Richard the Lionheart.

The main action of this story concerns the quest by Ian to rescue Barbara from her Saracen kidnappers and their sadistic leader, El Akir. However, easily the most watchable aspects of this show were the scenes at Richard's court where the Doctor and Vicki find themselves becoming ever more embroiled in Richard's plan to end the Holy War by marrying his sister, Joanna, to Saladin's brother. The grand confrontation between Glover, as Richard, and up-and-coming actress Jean Marsh as Joanna made for one of the finest moments of television drama ever witnessed in *Doctor Who*. From that serial onwards, the programme gained a kind of artistic respectability, drawing other big names, like Max Adrian and Michael Gough, into accepting roles in the series.

The Space Museum (serial Q) by Glyn Jones. Director: Mervyn Pinfield
With 'The Web Planet' having greatly overspent on the season's budget, this was the story which balanced the books through being made as cheaply as possible. Nevertheless what it lacked in production number sets and big name actors it more than made up with a superbly executed script submitted by Glyn Jones.

The basic story line – that of the travellers arriving on Xeros, finding the indigenous population suppressed by a gone-to-seed military government of Morok invaders and then pitching their lot in with the Xerons to end the tyranny – was simple enough. What gave this story such an ingenious twist was the notion of having the travellers land there before they had actually arrived. That is to say the TARDIS jumps a time track, depositing the Doctor, Ian, Barbara and Vicki on to Xeros as ghosts. Unaware of this at first, they discover, within the Morok space museum, the TARDIS, and themselves preserved forever in glass exhibition cases. As time catches up with them and they truly materialise, their impetus to help the young Xeron revolutionaries is galvanised by a need to avert the possible future they have seen.

With some highly technical on-air effects, needed to depict the travellers meeting themselves, direction for this show was handed to Mervyn Pinfield who had been hired as associate producer for *Doctor Who* to capitalise on his great technical knowledge of television and television recording techniques.

The Chase (serial R) by Terry Nation. Director: Richard Martin
The title sounds like a reworking of *The Perils of Pauline* and for six weeks this was exactly what *Doctor Who* viewers got. A madcap chase through space and time as a Dalek task force, complete with their own dimension-ally transcendental craft, hunts the TARDIS from the desert world of Aridius, to the top of the New York Empire State Building, to the *Marie Celeste* clipper (in time to see the crew frightened off ship by the arrival of the Daleks), to a haunted house exhibit at a World's Fair and lastly to the gleaming Mechonoid city atop the jungles of Mechanus.

The script was pure, fast-paced comic strip, with humour, action, drama and even tragedy interwoven as episode six sees the departure of the companions Ian and Barbara.

Director on this story was Richard Martin, known best for his film work. He used all the tricks of his trade – fast intercuts, overlays, even some animation effects – during the climactic final battle between the Mechonoids and the Daleks. Even now it still stands up as one of the finest battle scenes ever filmed for *Doctor Who*.

The Time Meddler (serial S) by Dennis Spooner. Director: Douglas Camfield
Having despatched Ian and Barbara back to twentieth-century England, the Doctor lands Vicki and the stowaway Steve Taylor nine centuries earlier in Northumbria on the eve of the invasion by King Hardrada's Vikings – subsequently defeated by King Harold's army before they lost the Battle of Hastings.

Despite the seriousness of its setting, 'The Time Meddler' relies much more on Dennis Spooner's propensity for comedy. Discovering where and when they are, the Doctor, Vicki and Steven are perplexed to find a modern-day wristwatch on a cliff top. This, it transpires, is the property of a local monk who is far from what he seems. Played with magnificent comic timing by Peter Butterworth, the monk is actually another renegade Time Lord like the Doctor; although at this point in *Doctor Who*'s history names like Time Lord and Gallifrey were not even figments of Terrance

Dicks's and Robert Holmes's imaginations.

The monk, a mischievous fellow also possessed of a TARDIS, has had the amusing notion of letting Harold win the Battle of Hastings, obviating his need to trudge up to Northumbria by destroying the Viking fleet for him using an atomic bazooka.

Naturally the Doctor deplores this monkey business and leaves his portly adversary stranded at the end of the serial by removing the dimensional control from his TARDIS.

Galaxy Four (serial T) by William Emms. Director: Derek Martinus
A much loved story at the time and sadly one that no longer exists in the BBC's film library, 'Galaxy Four' was the brain-child of school teacher William Emms who wrote the teleplay very much along the lines of the *Beauty and the Beast* parable.

In this case the beasts are the Rills – wart-encrusted sea-lion creatures who can only breath ammonia. Stranded on a barren planet only days away from global destruction, they are reliant upon their robot servants, the Chumbleys – named as such by Vicki after their curious wobbly locomotion. Likewise stranded are the Drahvins, the beauties of this story. Tall, leggy and blonde the Drahvins are a race of Amazon warriors who 'rescue' the time travellers after their first encounter with a Chumbley.

However, the moral of the story is never judge by appearances and it is quickly revealed that the Drahvins are the selfish aggressors, while the Rills, in fact, are a race who have achieved almost total perfection in mind and intellect. With the planet's sun due to go nova within a few dawns the Doctor agrees to help the Rills get their ship spaceworthy again despite the hostile opposition of the Drahvins.

Mission to the Unknown (serial T/A) by Terry Nation. Director: Derek Martinus
A curious story this for many reasons. First, it is the only one-part *Doctor Who* story ever done. Secondly, it was produced when the show's planners were abruptly granted an extra episode for the third season. Thirdly, it was used as a prelude to the mammoth twelve-part adventure 'The Daleks' Master Plan'. And fourthly, it is the only *Doctor Who* story in which neither the Doctor nor his companions appear.

The star of this prelude episode is space security agent Marc Cory, played by Edward de Souza, who has come to the jungle world of Kembel to investigate rumours of Dalek activity. He finds the Daleks there in force and planning a military operation of great magnitude against the Earth federation. As his crew are struck down one by one by the hostile life forms of Kembel, Cory battles against time and the Daleks to get a warning message recorded before he is discovered and killed by the patrols.

As with the rest of 'The Daleks' Master Plan', this episode was prompted on the direct instructions of the then BBC director-general Huw Wheldon, whose mother, so the papers reported, was a big fan of the Daleks.

The Myth Makers (serial U) by Donald Cotton. Director: Michael Leeston-Smith

Another excursion into comedy for the makers of *Doctor Who* as Hartnell, Max Adrian, Francis de Wolff and Barrie Ingham all compete for the funniest lines in these 'the most sophisticated scripts used in the series' (as it said in the BBC press handout).

Landing on the plains of Troy at the time of the siege by the Greeks, the Doctor is taken for Zeus by the less-than-overbrave Achilles when he suddenly appears, distracting Hector long enough for Achilles to slay him. Odysseus is more sceptical of the Doctor's divinity and insists he prove it by devising some means of ending the siege. Predictably the Doctor ends up designing the giant wooden horse (without shock absorbers . . .) thereby giving the Greeks ultimate victory. Vicki, with her new name of Cressida, leaves *Doctor Who* with this story, electing to flee with the Trojans and in particular with young Prince Troilus with whom she is in love.

Contrary to belief the BBC did not build a giant mock-up of the wooden horse for this story; the budget would not have stood it. It was all done by skilful combinations of model shots, shadows cast by studio spotlights and carefully angled camera shots.

The Daleks' Master Plan (serial V) by Dennis Spooner and Terry Nation. Director: Douglas Camfield

Quite simply the longest *Doctor Who* story ever recorded and also one of the best, although it is doubtful if director Douglas Camfield thought so at the time with the tremendous script and production problems doing a story of this length engendered.

Having agreed their plan to attack the Earth and her allies, the Daleks are enraged when the Doctor steals the prime component of their master plan – the Time Destructor. Firstly in spaceships and then in a time machine they remorselessly hunt down the Doctor and his friends with the treacherous help of Solar System Guardian Mavic Chen. Despite help from two Earth security agents and some hindrance from the Meddling Monk, the struggle proves a harrowing one for the Doctor as friends and companions alike perish in the struggle against the Daleks who are determined to recover their weapon. This they do but when the Doctor is forced to activate the Time Destructor it is they who are the victims – their personal time is rolled back to a point where the Daleks are nought but the husks of small embryos.

Due to its somewhat violent content at the time this story was not screened in countries with tighter censorship controls than England. Where it was sold abroad it was shown without the special Christmas panto episode, 'The Feast of Steven', which was the first *Doctor Who* episode ever to be destroyed by the BBC.

The Massacre (serial W) by John Lucarotti with Donald Tosh. Director: Paddy Russell

Almost two stories for the price of one with this tale. John Lucarotti contributed the three and a half episodes concerning the events leading up to the massacre of the Huguenots on St Batholomew's Eve, 1572, and did it in very grand opera style. Although with a much smaller budget the drama presentation of this story was every bit as good as the BBC's more celebrated period extravaganzas with, for once, the Doctor and Co. almost reduced to sitting on the sidelines as spectators throughout the story.

What 'Who' involvement there is concerns the conflict of identities surrounding the appearance in Paris of the Abbott of Amboise who is the exact double of the Doctor. Is it just coincidence, or has the Doctor adopted this guise for reasons of his own? The audience is left in suspense until episode four before the truth is divulged.

The final half of episode four is given over to script editor Donald Tosh who uses it, via one long scene set totally in the TARDIS, to re-establish the philosophy of *Doctor Who*. When Steven temporarily deserts him it does look as though the Doctor will be alone for the first time since the audience knew him. Then, through a stirring monologue, the Doctor reminds us, his unseen companions, of his reasons why he dare not change history, even though at times his decisions may seem harsh and callous to his human friends. It was a magical moment.

The Ark (serial X) by Paul Erickson and Lesley Scott. Director: Michael Imison
If 'The Massacre' had been almost two stories in one, 'The Ark' most definitely was. Episodes one and two comprised one story while three and four related another. The only uniting factors were the setting – a giant spaceship fleeing Earth with a population in cold storage, the travellers Dodo, Steven and the Doctor, and the new monsters – the Monoids.

The first half deals with the arrival of the TARDIS crew aboard this colossal ship and the horrendous discovery that the people of this century possess no immunity to the common cold brought by Dodo. Only the Doctor's medical skills avert disaster.

On their second visit, with the Ark approaching its new home on Refusis, the Doctor finds the Monoid servants have taken over and reduced the human guardians to obedient lap dogs. The Monoids intend to abandon the Ark, destroying it and its human incumbents with a bomb concealed within a huge statue. Again the Doctor finds himself the middle man, helping to overthrow the more militant of the Monoids and then negotiating with the Refusians to allow settlement on their world by humans and Monoids *if* the two races can learn to live together as equals.

The Celestial Toymaker (serial Y) by Brian Hayles. Director: Bill Sellars.
Few drama productions on television have ever achieved the unique atmosphere present in the four episodes of 'The Celestial Toymaker'.

The plot is quite simple. The TARDIS is drawn into the realm of a mandarin-like magician calling himself the Celestial Toymaker. If the three wish to escape the fate of being reduced to becoming his playthings they must win a series of games against the Toymaker's champions. Dodo and Steven play Blind Man's Buff, Musical Chairs and Ludo against Pierrot clowns, playing card kings and queens, toy soldiers and an obnoxious schoolboy hideously reminiscent of Billy Bunter. The Doctor's opponent is the Toymaker himself who sets the old man the task of playing The Trilogic Game – a sinister game with pyramids where one mistake can cost the game.

The success of this story lies in the way it visualises a child's nightmare – the secret world of toys from the nursery coming to life, harmless games that insidiously graduate into something far more sinister, smiling, happy faces concealing deadly menace. In short it was a perfect fairy-tale of the kind told by the brothers Grimm – a multi-level fantasy appealing to young and old alike, but strangely being more disturbing to adults than to children.

The Gunfighters (serial Z) by Donald Cotton. Director: Rex Tucker

If ever reviewers feel tempted to pour scorn on the attempts by America to emulate British costume drama, a good lesson in humility could be learned from studying this serial as a demonstration of how the British can not do westerns. It was billed as a show about the gunfight at the OK Corral, but it was more the massacre of the OK Corral.

So badly was this show received by the public that its audience viewing figures dipped below the horizontal axis line on the ratings graph in the *Doctor Who* producer's office for the only time in the programme's history!

What made this serial so poor is the cumulative effect of so many bad points which on their own would be forgiven in most other stories. The script was pure Talbot Rothwell, the acting was not even bad vaudeville and the direction was more West Ham than West Coast.

It was not good. It was bad and it was ugly. It was certainly the story that decided in the mind of new producer Innes Lloyd that the time had come to rethink the policy of using historical stories in *Doctor Who*'s framework.

The Savages (serial AA) by Ian Stuart Black. Director: Christopher Barry

From the ridiculous to the sublime. From the tombstone of the old west to a sand pit location in Esher for one of the archetypal *Doctor Who* story lines – the morality play.

The plot concerns two races living on a sandy, rough hilled world. One race calls itself the Elders and has apparently reached the peak of civilisation. They are all suntanned, beautiful people with great intellects and strong healthy bodies. In contrast to the fountains and colonnades of the Elders' city are the caves of the Savages. Yet despite their fierce name the Savages are a pale, depleted folk eking out a poor existence in fear of the Elders.

The reason for this fear is made clear in episode two. Such are the moral values of the Elders that they consider the Savages as we consider meat on a butcher's slab. They are food pure and simple. Periodically Savages are rounded up, herded into the laboratories and their life forces are drained off to be pumped into the bodies of the Elders to increase their own mental and physical energies. The resulting effect on the Savages is to reduce them to wrinkled husks who must then struggle to recover before the next round-up.

An unlikely-looking Doctor (William Hartnell) in 'The Gunfighters' (1966), which has been described as the poorest *Doctor Who* story

The only flaw visible in this story was its lack of a monster, otherwise it would deservedly be far better remembered than it is today.

The War Machines (serial BB) by Ian Stuart Black, based on material by Kit Pedler and Pat Dunlop. Director: Michael Ferguson
Though no one realised it at the time 'The War Machines' provided a template for the series' future; being the first story to bring the Doctor down to present-day Earth and combating a science fiction menace. The *Quatermass* principle, but with the far more limelighting presence of the Doctor.

The menace this time is a super-computer called WOTAN, housed within the new Post Office Tower, London, which suddenly gets the idea of swapping the servant/master roles between machines and men. Electronically hypnotising an army of technicians and engineers it goes about constructing mobile computerised war machines to dispose of London's population. When the Army fails to defeat them, a little rewiring by the Doctor provides a solution.

As well as setting a precedent for future stories 'The War Machines' is also the first story to pitch the show towards a teenage audience rather than at intelligent eleven-year-olds. It was a reflection of the BBC's market research at the time which showed that the series already had a markedly older audience. Hence the change of style as *Doctor Who* formally entered the swinging sixties.

The Smugglers (serial CC) by Brian Hayles. Director: Julia Smith
Not one of the most remembered of the Hartnell serials which is perhaps a shame as it was certainly one of the more ambitious.

The aim was to produce a rumbustious yarn of smugglers, pirates, hidden passageways, buried treasures and Cornish inns straight out of a Du Maurier novel.

The TARDIS lands in a cave some three hundred years before the mid-1960s. For his service in putting right the dislocated hand of a churchwarden, later murdered by one of the pirates, the Doctor is given a clue to the buried treasure of pirate Captain Avery. From then on it is trouble all the way for the Doctor, Ben and Polly as they discover the information is sought desperately by the local squire – head of the smugglers – and by Pike, one of Avery's former crewmen, now a pirate captain himself. In the final reckoning the three travellers are only saved by the timely arrival of revenue man Josiah Blake and a party of militiamen.

Director Julia Smith has a good knowledge of Cornwall and she used it in choosing the locations for this serial. The caves and the coastline were all real but to fake seventeenth-century inns and pirate ships her technical crew had to work very ingeniously, converting the side of an old barn and a contemporary trawler to accomplish the illusion.

The Tenth Planet (serial DD) by Kit Pedler and Gerry Davis with Pat Dunlop. Director: Derek Martinus
No one believed, when they saw the eight lumbering, cloth-faced giants with jug-handle ears and accordion-shaped computers positioned on their chests, that they were watching a new monster that would eventually come to rival the Daleks in popularity. But that is just what happened with this, the first of the Cybermen stories. Despite appearing in just two of the four episodes, the Cybermen immediately caught the popular imagination.

In concept the Cybermen were the brain-child of Kit Pedler, the show's uncredited technical adviser in those days. Fascinated by the notion of humankind's fate if it performs too many replacement surgery operations, the image in this story was truly that of Cyber-Men: survival specialists come to Earth to cream off the fittest of its human population and take them back to Mondas for body conversion into superior beings.

The Cybermen in 'The Tenth Planet' were overshadowed by one other momentous event. Everyone had been told about it but few believed it until the moment came when William Hartnell became Patrick Troughton.

The Power of the Daleks (serial EE) by David Whitaker with Dennis Spooner. Director: Christopher Barry
A new face, a new Doctor. The incredible had happened – the series was carrying on without the presence of its original title actor. It was a tense time for everyone concerned with the making of *Doctor Who*, seeing if the show could continue being as popular with Patrick Troughton at the helm.

To give him a good start, *Doctor Who*'s other big success agents, the

Daleks, were brought back in possibly their most intriguing story to date. At the outset of this six-parter the Daleks are the underdogs. Three of them are found inside a space capsule crashed a long time ago by human colonists on the planet Vulcan (no relation!). Well-meaning scientist Lesterson manages to revive them and few people heed the Doctor's frantic warnings when the Daleks proclaim their status as servants of humanity. Gradually the power of the Daleks builds as they manipulate the greed and self-assurance of the colonists' leaders to a point where they no longer need them. Then the exterminations begin . . .

The serial was a showpiece of BBC visual effects with easily the most memorable scene being the long sequence showing the conveyor-belt construction of hundreds of Daleks.

The Highlanders (serial FF) by Elwyn Jones and Gerry Davis. Director: Hugh David

'The Highlanders' was the last series of its kind in *Doctor Who*. Centred in and around Culloden Moor following the massacre of the Jacobite sympathisers in 1745, it was the last totally historical *Doctor Who* story, at least until 1982 when the policy of eliminating any science fiction references from a serial was tried again.

The story proved to be a fine testing vehicle for Troughton's Doctor, freed now from the overshadowing effects of the Daleks. Complete with stove-pipe hat, a tam o'shanter and a uniquely aggravating manner, the Doctor proceeded to have immense fun foiling the attempts of rascally lawyer Solicitor Grey to have the Scottish prisoners transported for profit to the West Indies.

It was during the making of this serial that producer Innes Lloyd spotted the potential as a regular for the series in Jamie McCrimmon, played by Frazer Hines. Two endings were filmed for this story, one with Jamie staying behind, one with Jamie coming aboard the TARDIS. Each was shown to the BBC heads of department responsible for *Doctor Who* and the rest was history, with Jamie staying on to become the longest-serving of the Doctor's travelling companions.

The Underwater Menace (serial GG) by Geoffrey Orme. Director: Julia Smith

So far *Doctor Who* has come up with no less than three versions for the reasons behind the destruction of Atlantis, but this was the earliest. 'The Underwater Menace' firmly establishes the lost continent to have sunk somewhere off the Azores, but when the four travellers finally reach the lost city they find another group of men there from the twentieth century, headed by Professor Zaroff. His claim to be able to lift Atlantis from the bottom of the Atlantic is disputed by the Doctor who realises that, if his experiments succeed, the bleeding of the sea into the molten core of the planet will cause the Earth's destruction.

Although *Doctor Who* is only partially done on film – relying mostly on videotape for its recording – this story made extensive use of the BBC's film studios at Ealing and especially the large water tank there. The climax to episode four called for the laboratory of Professor Zaroff to be flooded by the explosive inrush of the sea, thereby ending the threat to the world and drowning the mad scientist (played by Joseph Furst in very over-the-top manner reminiscent of Gene Wilder's more lunatic performances). For this scene hundreds of gallons of water had to be released into the tank on cue without harming any of the actors.

The Moonbase (serial HH) by Kit Pedler. Director: Morris Barry
As already mentioned, Dr Kit Pedler had a fascination with 'bionic' man and, unlike Terry Nation who had originally killed his Daleks off at the end of their first story, had planned for their return after 'The Tenth Planet'.

It was this serial that really cemented the fame of the Cybermen and established their trademarks: the electronic voice (again by Peter Hawkins of Dalek fame), the inexorable slow march, the Cybermen's great physical ·strength and their on-going costume updates.

Pedler's concept of the Cybermen, later altered by other writers, saw them as a race desperate to survive. Unable to reproduce themselves they saw in mankind a rich source of new Cybermen – hence their continuing attempts to force humanity into submission from which they could harvest their new recruits. This time an Earth weather-control base on the Moon is their objective and as the four episodes progress so the state of seige increases until, at the climax, the station is surrounded by a whole army of Cybermen.

Part of the success of this story was the nightmarish quality of those scenes set out on the Moon's surface. Slow motion was a key technique used to build up the nail-biting suspense as astronauts are chased along the surface by teams of pursuing Cybermen.

The Macra Terror (serial JJ) by Ian Stuart Black. Director: John Davies
With the historical stories now literally things of the past, Innes Lloyd was free to concentrate on what he believed to be the main factor to *Doctor Who's* popularity – the monsters. Monsters of all shapes and sizes was his directive to the writers and designers. Some in rubber suits, some in metallic casings and some, like the Macra, requiring the designers to stretch their imaginations to the utmost. The full-size Macra prop, and there was only one, had to be mounted on the back of a van to provide its movement. It stood nearly ten foot tall with a crab-like body far wider than the breadth of the van's rear platform. Operated by just one man, the moving claws, mandibles, steam breath and extruding slime presented an awesomely frightening image when the creature was first seen in close up at the end of episode one.

As the Doctor, Ben, Polly and Jamie fight to free a human colony from the brain-washing they have been subjected to by the parasitic Macra, their struggles take them deep into the gas mines whose products the Macra need to survive. Careful use of models made up the numbers for those scenes requiring more than one Macra in shot.

The Faceless Ones (serial KK) by David Ellis and Malcolm Hulke. Director: Gerry Mill
Where would any action/adventure series be without its obligatory story set in or around the glamorous surroundings of a contemporary airport?

'The Faceless Ones' had everything an airport drama demands save perhaps for the semi-obligatory crash alert: humour as an incoming jet reports the sudden appearance on a runway of a police box; glamour in the persons of Wanda Ventham and Pauline Collins; and some dramatic model effects as a VC10 folds its wings back into the silhouette of a rocket before blasting off into space and a rendezvous with a giant, orbiting alien space station.

The Chameleons, as the faceless ones are termed, have come to Earth to colonise it following a global disaster on their own planet which has left them with blank, featureless heads. They can, however, take on the shape of someone else, providing they can kidnap their models and hold them aboard their space platform from which blueprints of human bodies are taken and stored.

This is the last story to feature Ben and Polly, who leave after featuring only in episodes one, two and six.

The Evil of the Daleks (serial LL) by David Whitaker. Director: Derek Martinus

Every so often a *Doctor Who* story comes along which is universally recognised as a classic of its kind. 'Evil of the Daleks' is just such a show. Spanning seven weeks, it purports to show the final destruction of the Daleks by the Doctor after a long struggle in which he is blackmailed into helping the Daleks refine and synthesise the so-called 'human factor', that which has always caused the human spirit to triumph over the technical superiority of the Daleks. But, when the 'human factor' is put

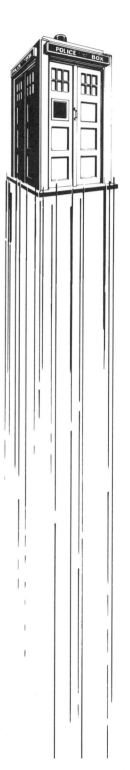

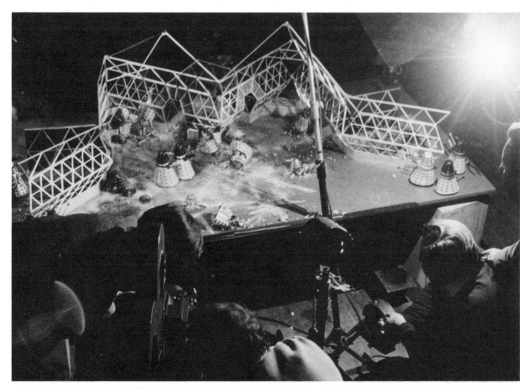

A rare shot of a special effects scene being staged with battling Daleks for 'The Evil of the Daleks' (1967)

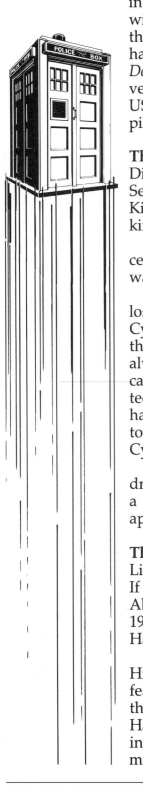

into three test Daleks the result is a Dalek which dares to question even the commands of its Emperor. As civil war erupts on Skaro (thanks to the Doctor 'humanising' hundreds more Daleks) the Doctor proclaims this fiery carnage as 'the final end'!

In truth this story was intended to be the end of the line for the Daleks in *Doctor Who*. By now Terry Nation had conquered the financial world with his robot-like creations and felt the time had come to try and launch the Daleks in their own show, financed and made in America. Owning half of the copyright on the Daleks he withdrew the rights to use them in *Doctor Who*. However, while the two Peter Cushing Dalek films had been very successful in this country, they had not gone down so well in the USA and, perhaps sadly, no backers were forthcoming for production of a pilot.

The Tomb of the Cybermen (serial MM) by Kit Pedler and Gerry Davis. Director: Morris Barry.

Set on the sandy world of Telos and looking remarkably like the Valley of Kings in Egypt, this story, like 'Evil of the Daleks', achieves the peak of its kind.

It is often said *Doctor Who* is at its best when its roots are showing and certainly the roots of this four-part Cybermen story can be traced all the way back to Universal's Mummy films.

A group of archaeologists arrives on Telos to seek out and explore the lost city of the Cybermen. They locate the hives containing the last of the Cybermen – supposedly frozen for eternity – but the ruthless ambitions of the expedition's backer leads the Cybermen to become re-activated. As always the Cybermen are interested in recruiting new bodies to their cause and it transpires this entire city was built as one great lure for the technologically competent, that is, bring the best to us rather than us having to find them. Fortunately the Doctor is on hand to reseal the tombs but not until the party has suffered a vicious attack from the Cybermen's servants, the Cybermats.

Looking rather like large, mechanical silverfish, the Cybermats were dreamed up by Gerry Davis in the hope they would catch on and provide a platform for merchandising based around the Cybermen. Only the apathy of the British toy companies prevented this from happening.

The Abominable Snowmen (serial NN) by Mervyn Haisman and Henry Lincoln. Director: Gerald Blake

If 'Tomb of the Cybermen' had been a remake of *The Mummy*, then 'The Abominable Snowmen' owed more than a passing debt to Nigel Kneale's 1950s' teleplay, *The Creature*, which, oddly enough, got translated by Hammer Films for the cinema and retitled *The Abominable Snowmen*.

Several themes recur: the lonely monastery on the slopes of the Himalayas, the western explorer, a group of monks some of whom hide fearful secrets and a group of apparently intelligent Yeti. With *Doctor Who* though there has to be sci-fi overtones and the excellent script penned by Haisman and Lincoln provides this in the form of a disembodied alien intelligence which has tapped a route into the physical world through the mind of the monastery's grand master, Padmasambhava. With robot Yeti to protect it the intelligence begins to manifest itself in a cave high up in the mountains. The Doctor soon realises that if it goes unchecked the glutinous mass may eventually encompass the world.

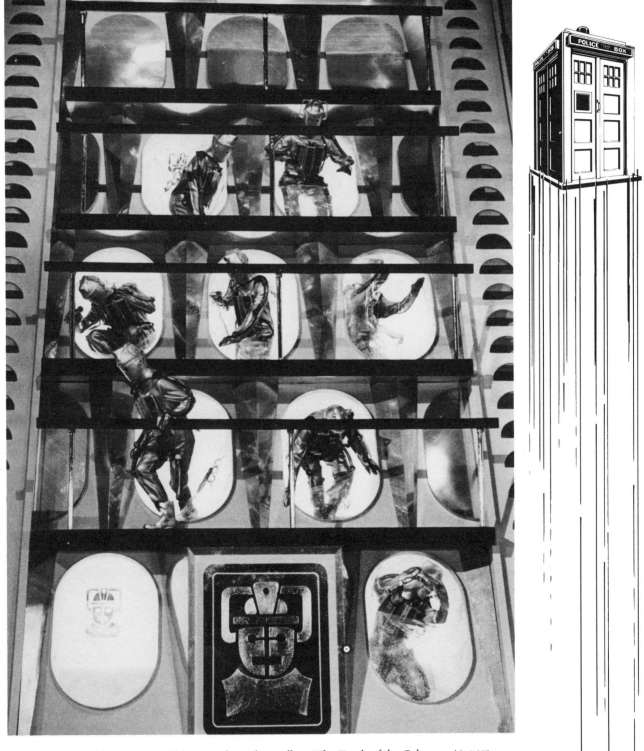

The emergence of the infamous Cybermen from their cells in 'The Tomb of the Cybermen' (1967)

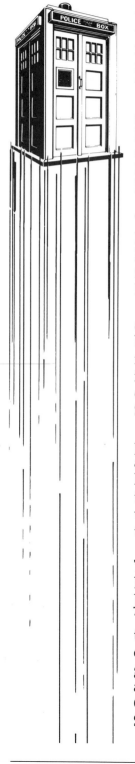

The Ice Warriors (serial OO) by Brian Hayles. Director: Derek Martinus
Another rewrite, this time borrowing from Howard Hawkes's 1950s' film *The Thing from Another World*. Director Derek Martinus even borrows one of the film's key moments as the block of ice containing the alien life form gradually melts releasing its still-very-much-alive inmate, Varga, the Ice Warrior from Mars.

A great strength of *Doctor Who* over the years has been its willingness to show the audience a whole race of monsters rather than just one or two. Sure enough, the episode ending to part two, with Victoria cowering in terror as Varga summons his four crew members to likewise awake from their icy slumbers, is an example of the programme at its most visually graphic.

The Ice Warriors were an immediate hit from this story, a fact attributable very much to the fine acting performance by Bernard Bresslaw, known mostly for his comedy roles, as Varga. In choosing his cast for this production Derek Martinus was very careful to emphasise the height of these Martians by hiring short actors to play the beseiged humans and artists in excess of six foot for the Warriors.

The Enemy of the World (serial PP) by David Whitaker. Director: Barry Letts
In a season known as the Monster Season, this story stands out in that it features no monsters or aliens and appears to be set only marginally in Earth's future.

Basically it is a political story, detailing the intrigues, machinations and power-forging of the ambitious would-be dictator Salamander who bears a startling facial similarity to the Doctor. Operating from his research station in Kenowa, Australia, Salamander secretly uses his invention, the Sun Store, to create global disasters which will reflect badly on the Controllers of the world's national zones. With these men deposed Salamander can replace them with his own puppet Controllers.

The highlight of this odd six-parter is the General Franco-like performance given by Patrick Troughton as Salamander, a portrayal he accomplishes both with his own talents as a character actor and with the help of facial make-up which appears to alter both his bone structure and to harden the lines of his face. In many respects this was the story in which the BBC made good its promise to Patrick Troughton to allow him to 'dress up a lot' in *Doctor Who*.

The Web of Fear (serial QQ) by Mervyn Haisman and Henry Lincoln. Director: Douglas Camfield
Just as 'An Unearthly Child' was the pilot for *Doctor Who* in the sixties, so 'The Web of Fear' was the pilot for the new directions the show would take in the seventies. Producer Peter Bryant, who later developed the changes to be made for the Jon Pertwee series, devised the setting of a group of scientists and soldiers fighting a menace from space against the all-too-familiar background of present-day England. Director Douglas Camfield supplied the fine details in the form of Colonel Lethbridge-Stewart, played so competently by Nicholas Courtney.

The story line is traditional *Doctor Who*: the goodies are heavily under seige and engaged in a deadly battle of wits against an encroaching alien menace – a battle they are losing until the arrival of the Doctor. This time around it is the Yeti again, given a slimmer, more frightening appearance after too many children found the original version cuddly and lovable. The intelligence has manifested itself again, this time as a suffocating cobweb which has filled the London Underground and cut off all roads within central London. Only with the Doctor's aid can the soldiers, under Lethbridge-Stewart, and the scientists, headed by Professor Travers, defeat the menace. It was the shape of things to come.

Fury from the Deep (serial RR) by Victor Pemberton. Director: Hugh David

The fifth consecutive story set on Earth takes a very topical theme for its subject matter – the drilling for gas in the North Sea. Penetrating a deep stratum, the technicians at a coastal refinery are horrified when they find they have opened a channel for a hostile weed parasite to attack both the refinery and the off-shore rigs. The weed absorbs humans into itself or else transmutes them gradually into creatures which are part man, part weed. In her last appearance in *Doctor Who*, it is Victoria who finally rids the world of the weed's menace via her electronically amplified screams which prove deadly to the invading organism.

Planning the special effects for this show the production team made ample use of a machine capable of generating vast quantities of soap foam which could fill a room in seconds. The speed at which even the largest room could become awash with this surging tide of weed infested foam helped to make this story one of the most visually frightening *Doctor Who* serials ever made. Like most of the well-remembered *Doctor Who* serials it flourished in the confines of a claustrophobic environment.

The Wheel in Space (serial SS) by David Whitaker, based on a story by Kit Pedler. Director: Tristan de Vere Cole

The Monster Season began with a Cybermen serial and it was perhaps fitting that it should end with a Cybermen serial. Getting away from Earth finally (for the time being), the TARDIS makes an emergency landing on an apparently abandoned rocket drifting within the orbit of a giant space station. The Wheel, as it is termed, governs one of the major space trade routes to Earth and it comes as little surprise to the Doctor when he finds Cybermats aboard. The Cybermen are once again planning an attack on Earth and for this to succeed they first need to take control of the Wheel. A high-powered, long-range laser beam eventually destroys the menace.

Although this was the last of the season of *Doctor Who*, it was not quite the final episode on television for a time. With Zoe Herriet pleading for a place aboard the TARDIS, the Doctor decides to show her some of the menaces she might encounter and does this by projecting a past adventure on to the TARDIS scanner. The adventure in question is 'Evil of the Daleks' which then leads into a re-run of that story over following Saturdays. Thus, in one season, viewers were treated to two Yeti stories, two Cybermen serials, the first Ice Warrior adventure and a re-run of a Dalek classic.

The Dominators (serial TT) by Norman Ashby (Mervyn Haisman and Henry Lincoln). Director: Morris Barry

From working with six-foot giants in 'Tomb of the Cybermen' the robot monsters in Morris Barry's latest *Doctor Who* required him, as director, to hire small schoolboys to fit inside and operate the three Quark costumes built for this story. So small were the Quarks that even the youngsters had problems operating them since they could only see out through the small apertures close to the arms on the main body. The movement of the heads were all done using a toggle control manipulated from inside the middle box section.

Far freer in movement were Kenneth Ives and *Crossroads'* Ronald Allen as the two Dominators named in the title. Breaking formation from the rest of the Dominator fleet, these two, Rago and Toga, bring their flying saucer to land on an island on the planet Dulkis. Their aim is to drill into the heart of the planet, drop an atomic seed device into the molten core and tap the resulting explosive radiation from the world's destruction as fuel for the main fleet. What neither of the Dominators reckons with is the cunning of the Doctor who figures out that the quickest way to dispose of an atomic bomb is to hide it aboard the ship from whence it came – and hope that the occupants decide to leave the planet before the big bang. And as ever when the chips are down, the Doctor was not proved wrong.

The Mind Robber (serial UU) by Peter Ling. Director: David Maloney

After having one of the big stars of *Crossroads* in 'The Dominators', it seemed almost too coincidental that the next story should be penned by the man who brought *Crossroads* into the world, Peter Ling. Yet such was the case and true to the traditions of ATV's series, 'The Mind Robber' was a serial steeped in total fantasy.

Dealing with the extraordinary idea of making fantasy into reality the show starts with the Doctor having to use the Emergency Unit aboard the TARDIS, a move which takes the ship out of the real universe and into the land of fiction. Here the Doctor, Jamie and Zoe must do battle against the Medusa, a charging unicorn, the Minotaur and a whole army of clockwork soldiers before they meet the ruler of the world, the Mind Master, and the computer which dominates him. With luck and some help from his companions, the Doctor defeats the power of this dimension and finds the Mind Master is really only a frail former writer for a boys' comic paper. They rescue him and return to reality – but one question is left unanswered. Who built the computer?

The Invasion (serial VV) by Derrick Sherwin, based on a story by Kit Pedler. Director: Douglas Camfield

If the birth of UNIT occurred in 'The Web of Fear', then its infancy was in 'The Invasion'. As the delighted reunion takes place in episode two between the Doctor and Lethbridge-Stewart, the former finds the latter has now been promoted to Brigadier and placed in charge of the United Nations Intelligence Taskforce's British division.

UNIT's baptism of fire comes as the Cybermen try once more to seize control of Earth's population – this time with the aid of a ruthless business tycoon Tobias Vaughan, whose corporation, International Electromatics, now has a virtual monopoly on the world's electronics industry. Every piece of IE merchandise now has a small micro-monolithic circuit built in which, at the correct moment, emits the Cyber-signal: a hypnotic sound that brings the world to a standstill and heralds the start of the invasion.

Like 'The Web of Fear' this epic-length serial – eight parts in all – is executed to perfection by director Douglas Camfield whose handling of the filmed sequences in and around central London gave *Doctor Who* one of its all-time classic scenes: the Cybermen walking down the steps of St Paul's Cathedral at the end of episode six.

The Krotons (serial WW) by Robert Holmes. Director: David Maloney
Repeated in 1981 as part of BBC 2's *Five Faces of Doctor Who* season, 'The Krotons' is the first story for the series to come from the pen of Robert Holmes, one of the most popular writers to script for the series in the seventies.

Originally 'The Krotons', submitted freelance to the BBC by Holmes, was not a *Doctor Who* story at all. In its original form it was conceived as a short story for the BBC 2 science fiction anthology series *Out of the Unknown*.

The premise concerns an isolated tribe of people, the Gonds, who are intelligent in some respects but dull in others. They worship and serve their unseen masters the Krotons, who live inside their gigantic crystalline machine – the Dynatrope. The Krotons educate the people and periodically select the brightest of their students to become their companions. But then it is found out that the Krotons are really bleeding the Gonds of their mental energy. Once the Gonds are intelligent enough to provide the Krotons with sufficient mental power, the crystalline monsters will use that power to get the Dynatrope spaceborn again, even though that will obliterate the Gond community in the process.

Thanks to the intervention of script editor Terrance Dicks the scripts were re-written to include the Doctor's party.

The Seeds of Death (serial XX) by Brian Hayles. Director: Michael Ferguson
It had not escaped the attention of producer Peter Bryant that the Ice Warriors had been tremendously successful in their first story. And so, since the costumes had been so expensive, the BBC decided to get its money's worth by commissioning Brian Hayles to write a sequel. This he did and, not only did it provide the visual effects technicians with an ideal opportunity to use their foam-making equipment again, it also gave costume supervisor Bobi Bartlett the chance to add another kind of Ice Warrior into the Martian ranks: the much slimmer Ice Lord, the villainous Slaar.

Once again the Earth is the target for invasion from space, this time well into the future where a matter transmitter device called T-MAT has replaced cars, planes, boats and rockets as the means of mass transport. The Ice Warriors seize control of the vital Moon station governing T-MAT and use it to send Martian seed pods to Earth. The pods, when burst, release deadly spores that in time will remove most of the oxygen from

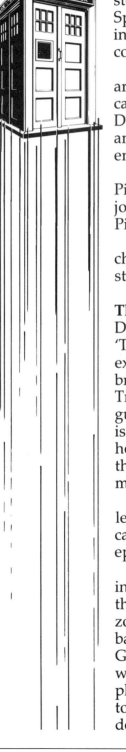

the planet's atmosphere and submerge much of the surface beneath a layer of thick, white fungus. Luckily for Earth, and especially for Britain, the Doctor saw to it that rain stopped play . . .

The Space Pirates (serial YY) by Robert Holmes. Director: Michael Hart
With man poised, in spring 1969, to take his first giant leap on to the Moon, the *Doctor Who* production crew opted to do a grand space opera story the models for which would be provided by the BBC's blossoming Space Unit – an adventurous title given to the visual effects men involved in turning out highly detailed and working models for the Apollo coverage.

There is certainly no denying that the model sequences for this story are of a very high calibre. The battered old ship LIZ 79, the aircraft-carrier-sized V-Ship, the Minnow fighters and especially the sleek Beta-Dart operated by the Pirates, are beautifully designed, constructed, lit and filmed. Even small details like working retro engines are included to enhance the realism of the scenes.

Unfortunately it is the quest for realism which slows 'The Space Pirates' almost to a snail's pace. Careful to stress the enormity of space journeys between planets, events such as the V-Ship's pursuit of the Pirates to the planet Ta take up most of this story's six episodes.

Luckily the live action is salvaged to some degree by the murderous character of Caven, leader of the Pirates, played in the coldly malicious style which was the trademark of actor Dudley Foster.

The War Games (serial ZZ) by Malcolm Hulke and Terrance Dicks. Director: David Maloney
'The time has come for you to change your appearance, and begin your exile.' With these words the Time Lords end the reign of a Doctor, and bring to a close an era for the five-and-a-half-year-old programme. Patrick Troughton's role as the second Doctor finishes as his peers try to find him guilty of breaking their most important laws. The era of the renegade exile is explained and closed off as it is revealed just who the Doctor is and why he has chosen such a nomadic lifestyle. And it was the end of the road for the black-and-white *Doctor Who* serials as the BBC prepared to launch its major channel into colour later in 1969.

All of this transpires in the final episode of 'The War Games', an epic-length serial spanning no less than ten episodes after the enforced cancellation of another story necessitated the padding out of four extra episodes by writers Hulke and Dicks.

They succeeded, just, by introducing as many colourful and interesting characters as their inventive minds could devise to flesh out the story of the Doctor's adventures on a world divided into several war zones by a race of belligerent aliens. Each zone was made to look like a battleground from one of Earth's major wars up to and including the Great War. Thousands upon thousands of kidnapped soldiers from Earth were brainwashed into thinking they were still fighting on their home planet although their officers were all aliens. The object of the games was to distil the finest fighting force in the universe which the aliens could deploy in their bid for galactic supremacy. Helping them was another renegade Time Lord and, in the titanic struggle needed to defeat him and his alien masters, the Doctor was compelled to call upon help from his own race from whom he had escaped so long ago.

It was the end of *Doctor Who* in the sixties.

Spearhead from Space (serial AAA) by Robert Holmes. Director: Derek Martinus
Another new face in the form of Jon Pertwee as the Doctor and also some familiar ones such as Brigadier Lethbridge-Stewart and the men of UNIT returned, this time as regulars in the new-look format for the programme.

With his TARDIS inoperative, for the time being, the Doctor's adventures would be set solidly on Earth in the present day, with more conventional modes of transport like vintage roadsters and helicopters replacing time machines.

Although UNIT was over its birth pangs, it still suffered some teething problems in this story as a strike by studio staff at the BBC forced the entire production to be done on location and on film – which resulted in a very glossy looking début story for Jon Pertwee but also a frighteningly expensive one as far as the BBC was concerned.

The basis for these new serials by producers Peter Bryant, Derrick Sherwin and Barry Letts, was the famous *Quatermass* trilogy of stories from the 1950s, e.g. the forces of science and stability versus the alien unknown come to Earth. In homage to this Robert Holmes and Derek Martinus almost repeat the opening of *Quatermass II* shot for shot as a radar station detects the coming of a shower of meteorites bearing the substance of an alien conciousness in the first scenes of 'Spearhead from Space'.

Doctor Who and the Silurians (serial BBB) by Malcolm Hulke. Director: Timothy Combe
The only serial to bear the words 'Doctor Who' as part of the official title, this programme also saw several other innovations introduced.

First and foremost was the technical process called colour separation overlay (CSO) whereby an image from one camera can be put on to the image seen by another camera and manipulated to create on-screen effects. The classic example of this is a person who appears to be floating several feet in the air. With 'Doctor Who and the Silurians' CSO is used for scenes requiring the Doctor to be in shot with a model dinosaur (as he and Liz Shaw explore the Silurians' caves), and where the Silurian monitor depicts the evolution of an ape into a man.

Like most of Malcolm Hulke's scripts, there are no true villains as such in this story. Indeed as the war between human and Silurian hots up, in the later episodes the Doctor is obliged to point out to his mammalian colleagues that the reptiles – viz. the Silurians – were the original owners of the Earth. This argument does not impress the Brigadier, however, who demonstrates his millions of years of evolution by blowing up the Silurian caves at the end of the serial.

The Ambassadors of Death (serial CCC) by David Whitaker with additional material by Malcolm Hulke. Director: Michael Ferguson

An unusual experiment was tried with this story. Instead of the title music and graphics following the usual thirty-second format, the opening sequence was faded out after the words *Doctor Who* had swirled in and swirled out again. The reprise from the previous episode was then run and at the cliffhanger moment the titles cut in again and the story title, writer and episode number were displayed.

Neither are the titles the only remarkable aspect of this seven-part story cataloguing the first arrival of benevolent alien ambassadors on Earth, whose powers are misdirected by hired mercenaries under the command of the insane General Carrington who fears the consequences should humans make contact with beings from space.

Not only were the space models once again excellent, having been built and shot by the Space Unit designers Ian Scoones and Peter Day, the story also benefited from the hauntingly beautiful location photography handled by seasoned BBC film cameraman A. A. Englander. Under the direction of Michael Ferguson and with an eerie musical soundtrack, provided by *Doctor Who's* resident composer/musician Dudley Simpson, the silhouetted movements of the space-suited amabassadors, with the sun behind them, achieve stunning visual impact.

Inferno (serial DDD) by Don Houghton. Directors: Douglas Camfield and Barry Letts

Nicholas Courtney (the Brigadier) confesses this to be his own personal favourite story in so far as he got to play two interpretations of his regular character. In the normal world he is the standard, up-front Brigadier acting as reluctant peacemaker between the Doctor and Professor Stahlman whose Project Inferno – to tap the gases and energies of the Earth's core – is UNIT's current security project. When the Doctor passes through a fold in the dimensions and arrives in a parallel world, he encounters the Brigade-Leader, a cold, ruthless, Mussolini-type figure immediately different from his other-worldly counterpart with an eyepatch and no moustache. Hampered by the autocratic Brigade-Leader and by the emergence of Primords (men transmogrified into monsters by the ooze brought up from the bowels of the Earth), the Doctor is unable to save this world from the holocaust unleashed by the 'success' of Project Inferno. His only hope is to get back and save the world he knows.

Two directors are credited on this serial. Producer Barry Letts took over halfway through when Douglas Camfield fell ill.

Terror of the Autons (serial EEE) by Robert Holmes. Director: Barry Letts

The arrival of a horse-box-shaped TARDIS at a fun fair, the theft of the one remaining Nestene energy unit from a museum, a macabre booby-trapped bomb and the sight of a corpse miniaturised to the size of a doll add up to a solemn realisation for the Doctor. His most deadly adversary – the Master – has returned to cause trouble on Earth.

Sure enough the bearded Master, who prefers others to do his dirty work, has allied with the Nestene Consciousness in a bid to open a channel for the second Nestene invasion of Earth. With a natural affinity for plastic, the Nestenes can turn almost anything into a deadly Auton killer: a plastic armchair, a bendy toy, a length of telephone cable, even the harmless plastic daffodils found in homes all over the land.

Although rightly regarded as a very good *Doctor Who* story, 'Terror of the Autons' was not without its problems. To begin with, stuntman Terry Walsh made one of the most spectacular falls ever seen in the series quite accidentally when he lost his balance and tumbled fifty yards down a quarry slope with the cameras still rolling. More serious were the complaints from parents at scenes showing policemen to be Autons, plastic armchairs to be capable of suffocation and toys to be deadly.

The Mind of Evil (serial FFF) by Don Houghton. Director: Tim Combe
At the time, and indeed for many years after, this was the most expensive *Doctor Who* story on record. The main source of expense was episode five's climax as UNIT troops storm Strangmoor Prison and do battle with the armed prisoners. To realise these scenes the BBC had to arrange filming in and around the grounds of Dover Castle and obtain the cooperation of a contingent of Marines who would, using ropes and grappling hooks, effect the scaling of the vertical walls. On screen it looked easy but the preparation was formidable.

Nor was this the only demanding section in Don Houghton's six-part script. Episode two required a whole scene to be spoken in Chinese (with subtitles), episode four had *Doctor Who*'s resident stunt team performing the hijack of a rocket transporter convoy and episode six's hardware requirements were a helicopter, a police van, an airfield and an operational ground-to-air missile.

Behind all this was the Master, planning to use a convict army, a stolen nerve-gas missile and an alien mind parasite to wreck a peace conference and plunge the world into nuclear war. Fortunately for the Doctor the mind of evil – the Keller Machine – proved to be a double-edged weapon.

The Claws of Axos (serial GGG) by Bob Baker and Dave Martin. Director: Michael Ferguson
Originally titled 'Vampire from Space', the plot of this story centres around an alien organism – Axos – which arrives on Earth intending to suck the planet dry of all its energy. This it would do by deceiving the human race into thinking Axos was benevolent and promising every continent a supply of Axonite, a biological compound supposedly capable of ending the world's food shortage. However, when activated, Axonite would become once more part of Axos, expanding and draining every source of energy to feed the creature's insatiable requirements.

Rather like 'The Web Planet' years earlier, this story demanded much that could not be supplied from stock – principally the interior of Axos, the living spaceship whose interior looked like the insides of a human heart.

Luckily the designers for this story had better facilities and technology at their disposal than their 1965 counterparts. The out-of-this-world look of Axos was achieved using a blend of CSO, expandable foam plastic, coloured lighting and latex rubber.

Colony in Space (serial HHH) by Malcolm Hulke. Director: Michael Briant

The first crack in the mould setting all Jon Pertwee's stories on Earth in the present day. On a mission for the Time Lords, the Doctor is despatched, in the TARDIS with Jo Grant, to a barren planet some five hundred years in the future. The planet has become barren thanks to radiation emitted by the Doomsday Weapon. The Master plans to gain control of this apocalyptic device despite the protection afforded it by the race who built the machine and then sank back into savagery as its baleful influence withered their minds too. The savages are not the Master's only problems. There are also a band of human colonists, the Doctor and Jo, plus the heavily armed IMC Miners who want the planet for its minerals.

Amongst the IMC equipment was a mining robot operated by John Scott Martin – an actor who has not lightly forgiven his appointed role in this story. To move the robot easily along rough terrain, large pneumatic tyres were fitted inside, giving the prop some weight. Consequently, when the robot encountered a steep slope for the first time the combination of gravity and mass gave it an unstoppable acceleration once the large wheels had begun rolling. As John Scott Martin drew his own legs up and prayed, the camera crew ran for their lives . . .

The Daemons (serial JJJ) by Guy Leopold (Barry Letts and Robert Sloman). Director: Christopher Barry

The beautiful English village of Aldbourne in Wiltshire was taken over by the BBC for the filming of this all-time *Doctor Who* classic as the Master strives to awaken and control the powers of an alien Daemon – a giant horned beast who has slept for centuries beneath a barrow termed the Devil's Hump by the inhabitants of nearby Devil's End.

Only the third five-part story in *Doctor Who*'s history, 'The Daemons' never suffered a dull moment. From the opening shot of a dark and stormy night, as rain lashes the pub sign of the Cloven Hoof (done with the assistance of the Fire Brigade), to the joyous maypole scenes at the end the story absolutely speeds along as the Doctor, Jo, Captain Yates and Sergeant Benton fight the Master, his satanist followers and the animated gargoyle Bok to prevent the final appearance of Azal.

So realistic was the destruction of Devil's End church at the end of the story, that one irate viewer was compelled to write in protesting at the BBC's callous attitude in blowing up an architectural masterpiece for the sake of drama. To the model builders of the visual effects department this letter was praise indeed.

The Day of the Daleks (serial KKK) by Louis Marks. Director: Paul Bernard

The much heralded return of the Daleks, after their five-year absence from the small screen kicked off with a very misleading set of trailers for the serial. Conscious, perhaps, that this was to be the second Dalek invasion of Earth, the BBC publicity machine swung into action and virtually refilmed the famous 1964 trailer sequence showing Daleks gliding about famous landmarks in London. London Bridge, the Tower of London, they were all there and sure enough the story reaped a big audience in consequence. Only one thing was wrong. The Daleks were never seen in London throughout the entire four episodes!

The bulk of the plot concerns a squad of guerilla resistance fighters from the twenty-second century who travel back in time to the present day. Their intention is to murder a diplomat they believe responsible for paving the Daleks' path to invading Earth again. As it transpires it is the guerillas themselves whose actions ultimately lead to the coming of the Daleks and only through some last-minute intervention is the Doctor able to break the time loop.

Penned by Louis Marks, this story originally had the title 'The Time Warriors' and was not intended to be a Dalek story. It was Terrance Dicks and producer Barry Letts who recommended that the Daleks be included within Marks's framework of the time paradox leading to a military dictatorship in the future.

The Curse of Peladon (serial MMM) by Brian Hayles. Director: Lennie Mayne

All those who ever met and spoke with Brian Hayles before his sad death in 1979 attested him to be one of that rare breed – the gentleman writer. Although better known for his film scripts, Hayles was always quietly amazed by the recognition he received for his *Doctor Who* story lines, particularly those which featured his creations, the Ice Warriors.

In this serial Hayles added a twist to their appearance by making them, for once, the goodies, who, although technically superior, find themselves under threat from the reactionary forces of a backward planet and political ramifications should they use their superiority to restore order to Peladon. Politics was very much the keynote in this period drama-cum-ghost story. King Peladon wishes his planet to enter the Galactic Federation. The Federation sends in an assessment committee in the form of Alpha Centauri (the hermaphrodite hexapod), Arcturus ('a box of tricks'), the Ice Warriors and a delegation from Earth – whom the Doctor and Jo replace accidentally. But the more conservative elements on Peladon fear cultural contamination from these aliens and, led by the High Priest, go about reactivating the curse of Aggedor to try to bring their monarch to his senses in time.

The Sea Devils (serial LLL) by Malcolm Hulke. Director: Michael Briant

Rightfully regarded as one of the definitive Pertwee serials, the story succeeds in part thanks to the eye-catching design of its title monsters. The Sea Devils, six of them in all, were sculpted and cast in latex rubber by designer John Friedlander who used the structure of a turtle's head as inspiration for his alien creations. Each Sea Devil head was worn as a hat by the actors playing them, therefore they were able to see out through a concealed mesh in the elongated necks.

And neither were the Sea Devils the only stars in this story. Cementing his immense popularity as the Master, Roger Delgado returned for his sixth tussle with the Doctor in possibly his most demanding story for the series. Most of the locations were set in and around the coastline of Portsmouth and the Isle of Wight with many scenes taking place in the sea itself. With a profound fear of water and as

a total non-swimmer Delgado nevertheless agreed to do all his own scenes in the sea and in doing so won himself the admiration and respect of his fellow cast and crew members.

The story, by Malcolm Hulke, sees the Master attempting to awaken a colony of aquatic Silurians with the aim of instigating a war between them and humankind. As always, the Doctor saved the day.

The Mutants (serial NNN) by Bob Baker and Dave Martin. Director: Christopher Barry

Armed with a tremendously inventive plot device 'The Mutants' opens with the Doctor and Jo being despatched by the Time Lords to Solos where colonial rule from Earth is about to end, handing power back to the Solonians. This event is rued by the acting Marshal who regards Solos as his own small empire and the Solonians as a species which must be wiped out after the recent spread of a disease which mutates the medieval humanoids into insect-like monsters. What no one realises, not even the Doctor at first, is that the mutations are part of the natural evolution process on Solos as the planet shifts from its 500-year-long summer into its 500-year-long autumn. As the environment changes, so too do the Solonians. Only in the last episode is this fully shown as warrior Ky sheds his insect chrysallis and becomes a glowing, superhuman being.

The musical mood effects for this story were composed and played by Tristram Cary whom director Christopher Barry had worked with on the very first Dalek serial. As in 'The Daleks', Cary veered away from using conventional instruments and composed his soundtrack using some of the early synthesisers just coming on to the market at this time.

The Time Monster (serial OOO) by Robert Sloman. Director: Paul Bernard

A gallery of famous names decorate the cast list for this six-parter, not least being that of Dave Prowse, now universally known as the body of Darth Vader from *Star Wars*. Still five years from that celebrated role, Prowse appears only in the first few minutes of episode six playing the Minotaur in this the Minoan explanation for the fate of Atlantis. Hammer Films star Ingrid Pitt plays the ruthless Queen Galleia whose ambitions ultimately doom her people, while the role of her handmaiden is taken by actress Susan Penhaligon, later of *Bouquet of Barbed Wire* fame.

'The Time Monster' has few equals, in *Doctor Who's* long history, as an action adventure story which really delves into the twin concepts of space and time. Using the TOMTIT machine the Master summons up armoured knights, Roundhead musketeers and even a V1 Flying Bomb to thwart the convoy bringing the TARDIS to Cambridge where the Doctor is attempting to stop him gaining control of the Crystal of Kronos.

Later, battling from within their two TARDISes, the Doctor and the Master discover that each TARDIS can be within the other, a mathematically impossible notion which nearly ends the Doctor's life when the Master brings the Time Monster, Kronos, aboard their twin vessels.

The Master (Roger Delgado), the Doctor's implacable enemy, with the Crystal of Kronos in 'The Time Monster' (1972)

The Three Doctors (serial RRR) by Bob Baker and Dave Martin with Terrance Dicks. Director: Lennie Mayne

What is there left to say about this anniversary-marking serial which has not been written, discussed or documented in umpteen fanzines, books, journals and newspapers so many times before?

With *Doctor Who* entering its tenth year on screen, the show's producers celebrated the event by bringing the past into the present with a plot vaguely reminiscent of *The Wizard of Oz*.

As the universe faces an energy drain into a black hole the desperately weakening Time Lords take a gamble and pitch the Doctor (William Hartnell), the Doctor (Patrick Troughton) and the Doctor (Jon Pertwee) against their powerful renegade, Omega.

Once a Time Lord himself, Omega has gone mad living alone in the universe of anti-matter and sees the Time Lords as the source of his misery. The Doctors manage to defeat him and the universe is saved. But of Omega, there is no sign . . .

As an anniversary serial, 'The Three Doctors' attains classic status if only for its hilarious scenes of acid dialogue and point scoring as Doctor argues with Doctor, proving the maxim about your worst enemy being yourself. The only sad moment in this story is the diminished role played by Hartnell whose illness at the time would only allow him to appear briefly as an adviser for several scenes.

Carnival of Monsters (serial PPP) by Robert Holmes. Director: Barry Letts

An unusual story in so far that it treads to perfection the borderline between drama and comedy. The plot is very strait-laced. An ambitious commissioner sees a means to depose the President of Inter-Minor by releasing dragonish carnivores from the zoo-in-miniature operated by visiting showman Vorg and his pretty assistant Shirna. The Doctor and Jo have arrived within the machine, unaware, at first, that they are carnival exhibits. Only when they ascend to the outside does the truth dawn, and by then Commissioner Kalik's plans are well advanced.

The comedy element is supplied through Robert Holmes's tremendously witty script and by the performances given by comedians Leslie Dwyer (*Hi-De-Hi*) and Tenniel Evens with whom Jon Pertwee had worked during his years in *The Navy Lark*.

An interesting addition to the cast was Ian Marter playing the role of the upper-crust First Officer Andrews, a year or so in advance of his regular part in *Doctor Who* as Harry Sullivan.

Repeated in 1981 as part of the *Five Faces of Doctor Who* package, this serial achieved an audience of over seven million people in an off-peak time slot on the minority channel opposite the main evening news broadcasts.

Frontier in Space (serial QQQ) by Malcolm Hulke. Director: Paul Bernard

With none of the fanfare surrounding the 1965 epic, *Doctor Who*'s production team managed, in 1973, to turn out a very good sequel to 'The Daleks' Master Plan'. The length was the same, so too were the principle 'baddies'. Only the title was altered and yet, amazingly, so many missed the tree for looking at the wood.

Centrepiece for the illusion was splitting the plot into two six-part stories. The first part, 'Frontier in Space', starts innocuously with the Doctor materialising the TARDIS into a cargo hold to avoid a mid-hyperspace collision. The freighter is later attacked by a raiding party of Ogrons, yet strangely only the Doctor and Jo see them as Ogrons. To the Earth crew the attackers are Draconians, representatives of the other great space empire in the galaxy. At present there is a wary peace between Earth and Draconia but now all this is threatened by accusations of raids and counter-raids.

Behind it all, needless to say, is the Master, but behind even him, as revealed in episode six, are the Daleks who plan to attack the galaxy with the biggest Dalek army every assembled. Thwarting the Master, the Doctor's next task is to follow the Daleks to their base and prevent the invasion.

The only serial of the Pertwee era to end on a cliffhanger this story was also the last to feature Roger Delgado as the Master. Shortly after its transmission the news came through of his sad death in a car crash in Turkey.

Planet of the Daleks (serial SSS) by Terry Nation. Directors: David Maloney and Paul Bernard

With 'The Three Doctors' having been recorded directly after 'Frontier in Space', for artists' contractual reasons, the complex links into this story were maintained by allowing Paul Bernard to record all the TARDIS scenes for 'Planet of the Daleks' on the set of 'Frontier in Space' – hence episode one is credited to two directors and the overlap is indistinguishable.

Chasing after the Daleks, the Doctor and Jo land on the jungle world of Spiridon. The Daleks have invaded this world to secure the secret of invisibility from the planet's inhabitants. With that the Dalek army will be able to strike freely at all targets in the galaxy. Luckily help is at hand for the two time travellers, in the form of a military task force from Skaro mounted by the old enemies of the Daleks, the Thals.

Despite dwindling numbers and the arrival of a Supreme Council Dalek on Spiridon, the Doctor, Jo and the Thals succeed in freezing the Dalek army and wrecking their base. But the Daleks are only delayed, not defeated.

The Green Death (serial TTT) by Robert Sloman. Director: Michael Briant

Nearly all *Doctor Who* stories have the germ of their ideas rooted in the writer's simple wish to entertain an audience. This story was an exception. Commissioned by producer Barry Letts, out of discussions with his script editor Terrance Dicks, part of its intention was to bring home to people the horrors of pollution and the damage to the environment uncontrolled exploitation of the land by big companies will cause.

The environmentalists, in this story, are represented by the alternative technologists of the Nut Hutch: prize-winning scientists led by young Professor Cliff Jones who have come to the Welsh valleys to research non pollutant sources of energy and food.

On the other side is Global Chemicals, a multi-national oil company

whose ruthless drive for efficiency and productivity leads to wholesale pollution of the surrounding area and the emergence of giant mutated maggots whose bite causes a long and agonising death.

Of course humankind's humanity is finally seen overcoming the heartless dictates of the machine, but not before *Doctor Who* has presented its viewers with one of the most thought-provoking and moving serials seen during the programme's long run.

The Time Warrior (serial UUU) by Robert Holmes. Director: Alan Bromly
Unaware that he would be creating one of the big five most popular monsters for *Doctor Who*, Robert Holmes was somewhat reluctant at the prospect of handling a historical story for the series, albeit with alien overtones. But, having been 'bodily dragged into the Middle Ages' – as Terrance Dicks recalls the incident – Holmes presented his story line to the script editor in a very novel form. It is customary, before an actual first draft script is commissioned, for the writer to submit a detailed plot synopsis to the producer and script editor for them to assess whether the ideas will work on television. In the case of 'The Time Warrior' Holmes elected not to write a straightforward episode-by-episode breakdown. Instead he penned the story's events in the form of a lengthy military communiqué from Sontaran Officer Hol Mes to his earthbound counterpart Terran Cedicks.

The style of the communiqué very much reflected the style of the finished serial, directed by former *Out of the Unknown* producer Alan Bromly. Linx, a Sontaran Warrior, crash-lands his scout craft in medieval England where he is forced to seek temporary shelter from a robber bandit named Irongron. Though fearsome fighters and plunderers, Irongron's men are sadly lacking in intelligence, a fact which makes for moments of great humour during the Doctor's adventure to prevent Irongron gaining twentieth-century weapons from the time-hopping alien.

Invasion of the Dinosaurs (serial WWW) by Malcolm Hulke. Director: Paddy Russell
The only *Doctor Who* story of the Jon Pertwee era never to be screened beyond the shores of Great Britain. By the mid-seventies over twenty-six countries worldwide were buying *Doctor Who*, many of them on a regular basis. This serial, however, could not be sold, due to a clerical error on the part of the BBC.

The story outlines the events following the return of the Doctor and Sarah Jane Smith to London after their medieval trip. The capital is deserted and only at the end of episode one is it revealed that the cause of the mass evacuation has been the sudden appearance of dinosaurs in the city streets. It is later revealed that the dinosaurs are merely part of a much greater plot by an idealist politician and a scientist to roll Earth's time back to the mythical Golden Age – before pollution ruined the planet.

Careful to preserve the secret of the dinosaurs' appearance at the end, episode one was titled just 'Invasion', not 'Invasion of the Dinosaurs'. Listed as such on BBC records, the first episode was accidentally destroyed when the directive was given to purge the prints and master negatives of the Patrick Troughton story 'The Invasion', the sales rights to which had already expired.

Death to the Daleks (serial XXX) by Terry Nation. Director: Michael Briant

After the harrowing events of Operation Golden Age, the Doctor decides Sarah needs a holiday and programmes the TARDIS to take them to the planet Florana. As always, they miss and arrive instead on the mist-covered world of Exxilon. The cause of their abrupt materialisation is the power emanating from a self-contained city built centuries ago by the Exxilons who then regressed into pagan worship of the edifice. One of the Seven Hundred Wonders of the Universe, the city almost has a claim to life and is as such a subject for investigation, firstly by the Doctor and then by a squad of Daleks who land on Exxilon to mine the only source of a mineral known to cure a space plague currently sweeping the galaxy.

Three actors are credited with playing the Daleks in this serial: Murphy Grumbar, Cy Town and John Scott Martin. At this time the BBC only had three working Dalek casings, as had been painfully obvious in 'The Day of the Daleks'. Seven 'dummy' Daleks were built for 'Planet of the Daleks' to swell the ranks of the all-conquering species but these were solid and did not have an operator. Thus in this story, where at least four are visible in the early stages, a great deal of care had to be exercised to cover up the fact that only three of the Daleks could move.

The Monster of Peladon (serial YYY) by Brian Hayles. Director: Lennie Mayne

Nothing succeeds like excess and for those who revelled in 'The Curse of Peladon' this serial was an absolute second helping. The writer, the director, the designer, even most of the main costumes were the same. Alan Bennion returned for his third appearance in the Ice Lord costume, this time restored again to the status of a villain.

The story line was surprisingly topical after the previous winter of discontent with Britain besieged by a miners' strike and a three-day week. The miners of Peladon down tools when they are apparently attacked by the vengeful spirit of Aggedor – their Holy Beast. The Doctor tries valiantly to act as mediator between them and the growing aristocracy to whom the miners represent the lowest of the low. Behind it all are, predictably, the Ice Warriors, who want Peladon's rich veins of the mineral trisilicate. Using their own weapon against them, the Doctor defeats the Warriors but not before a strong object lesson has been given to miners and aristocrats alike on the benefits of equality and fair shares for all. *Doctor Who* was once more back on a soapbox.

Planet of the Spiders (serial ZZZ) by Robert Sloman. Director: Barry Letts

As early as February 1974, Jon Pertwee declared an intention to leave *Doctor Who* after completing this his final season. 'Planet of the Spiders' was the story which wrapped matters up for the era of the third Doctor and, in true Pertwee style, it was done with much gusto and panache. Barry Letts temporarily vacated his producer's seat to direct a finale for the Doctor he had worked with for over five years. Both Letts and Pertwee shared a love of exotic gadgetry and they spent the greater part of this serial's budget on a glorious chase in episode two featuring a police panda car, 'Bessie', a hovercraft, an autogyro, a motor launch and Pertwee's own exotic car, the Whomobile. For most of these location-shot scenes, Jon Pertwee himself drove or piloted the multifarious crafts, perhaps mindful that this would be his last opportunity for some time to come.

The story line, too, bore hallmarks of Barry Letts, concerning itself with monsters of the mind which became corporeal as giant spiders, brought to Earth by the chanting of a group of Buddhist disciples. Many eastern philosophies were reflected in the Doctor's climactic confrontation with his fear – the Great Spider whose cave of crystals damaged his body to the point where regeneration was necessary for him to survive.

Robot (serial 4A) by Terrance Dicks. Director: Christopher Barry
The opening episode of this story gave many followers of the long-running series cause for alarm. Where Jon Pertwee had been a comedian playing the Doctor straight, former National Theatre actor Tom Baker seemed likely to reverse the trend and go all out for laughs. Somewhat erratic after his regeneration, the Doctor at one point emerges from the TARDIS dressed first as a viking warrior, then as a robed monarch, a Pierrot clown and finally as a curious mixture of tramp, Toulouse Lautrec and Harpo Marx.

The fears were groundless as later episodes were to prove. Still feeling some effects of the transformation, the Doctor is called on by the Brigadier to solve the riddle of stolen plans for a disintegrator gun. Further thefts occur – parts for the gun and then the top secret codes for firing the world's supply of nuclear missiles. In each case there are clues left behind which gradually point to the true culprit – a giant robot of enormous power whose original purpose is being subverted by a group of fanatical scientists. UNIT and the Doctor must strive to prevent world annihilation.

'Robot' pioneered another first for *Doctor Who*. Just as 'Spearhead from Space' had been shot entirely on film, so 'Robot' was recorded solely on tape – even the location scenes – thanks to a new form of lightweight video camera.

The Ark in Space (serial 4C) by Robert Holmes, based on an idea by John Lucarotti. Director: Rodney Bennett
Nearly eight years later, this story still holds the record for attracting the highest audience ever for a *Doctor Who* serial. Over 14 million tuned in to watch the Doctor's, Sarah's and Harry's desperate measures to protect the sleeping survivors of global holocaust on Earth from the devouring intentions of the parasite Wirrn. A gigantic cryogenic station has been built in space to house the chosen few until such time as the Earth is habitable again. But something has gone wrong and the sleepers have long overslept. Now the station has been invaded and infected by the grubs of a mother Wirrn and if the Doctor cannot drive them out into space again then the human race faces the prospect of being eaten 'like a

lot of jelly babies' . . .

Nobody who worked on this serial can understand quite why it was so popular. Even John Friedlander's insect-like Wirrn are not the most memorable of the Doctor's foes. Nevertheless it was a perfectly executed story with an atmosphere of mounting tension and suspense worthy of Alfred Hitchcock. The flavour of the next three years had been established with the arrival of new producer Philip Hinchcliffe.

The Sontaran Experiment (serial 4B) by Bob Baker and Dave Martin. Director: Rodney Bennett

Another oddity for *Doctor Who* – a story planned and recorded entirely on location, again using the portable system of video cameras. Shot immediately after 'Robot', despite its transmission order, it was Tom Baker's second opportunity to go on location for the series, this time out into the wilds of Dartmoor which doubled for post-holocaust London in the wake of the solar flares. Unfortunately for Tom Baker, three-quarters of the way through production he slipped on a rock, fell and broke a collar bone. The crew had to carry him almost a mile on a makeshift stretcher to the nearest road and, although the injury was not too serious, several scenes had to be replanned either so that the Doctor could stand immobile or his place could be taken, in long shot, by his stunt double, Terry Walsh.

Kevin Lindsay again played the Sontaran; this one, Major Styre, having come to Earth to subject a group of Earth colony astronauts to a series of nightmarish tortures to assess the human race's potential for withstanding a Sontaran assault. A new mask was designed for Kevin Lindsay by John Friedlander after the actor's complaint in 'The Time Warrior' of having difficulty in breathing.

Genesis of the Daleks (serial 4E) by Terry Nation. Director: David Maloney

It had to happen. After twelve years of warring sporadically against his most indestructible foes, the Doctor is brought to Skaro by the Time Lords at a point just before the genetically engineered evolution of the Daleks.

After a thousand years of war between the Kaleds and the Thals, both sides are near to exhaustion, staking all on their final secret weapons. In the case of the Thals, this takes the form of a superbomb. The Kaleds, spearheaded by their chief scientist Davros, have devised special travel machines for the creatures they will eventually mutate into, thanks to the effects of chemical and germ warfare. But Davros has accelerated the process and developed his own species of Kaleds he terms Daleks. Without conscience, pity or sound moral values the Daleks ultimately commit genocide on the Thals, dispense with the useless Kaleds and finally turn on their own creator.

Billed as a Dalek story the Daleks actually appear on screen for less than half an hour in this epic six-part serial. Spurred to write 'a morality play', much of Nation's script is a carefully balanced argument between two sides of moral reasoning which culminates in the Doctor's belief that, although the Daleks will cause untold misery for thousands of years, out of their evil will come something good.

The fourth Doctor, Tom Baker, confronts Davros (Michael Wisher), the creator of the Daleks, in 'Genesis of the Daleks' (1975)

Revenge of the Cybermen (serial 4D) by Gerry Davis. Director: Michael Briant

Recorded back-to-back with 'The Ark in Space', this story uses the same sets as its predecessor, although redressed with props and fittings to suggest the space station at an earlier point in its existence.

At this time space station Nerva is a navigating beacon recently striken by a terrible plague which has killed most of its crew. The Doctor recognises the plague from a previous encounter with its propagators. Later, beating off an attack by a Cybermat, the Doctor realises the Cybermen are at work – their intention this time being to destroy the nearby world of Voga: the Planet of Gold.

Gold is inimicable to the Cybermen's functioning and, after subduing resistance on the beacon, the Cybermen coerce the Doctor and two officers into transporting three deadly Cyberbombs deep into the heart of Voga, where they will later be detonated.

With the Vogan masks designed by John Friedlander and with the latest version of Cyberman (entrusted to the Alastair Bowtell Effects Company), the major battle between the two combatants was staged on location in the potholes of Wookey Hole. To this day, guides at the famous tourist attraction speak of the moment when a gleaming Cyberman lost his balance and tumbled headlong into a pool of muddy water.

Terror of the Zygons (serial 4F) by Robert Banks Stewart. Director: Douglas Camfield

Question: When is Scotland not Scotland at all? Answer: When it is Sussex doubling for Scotland to meet the budget needs of a *Doctor Who* story. By 1975, *Doctor Who*'s budget was far in excess of the legendary £2,000 per episode figure with which Verity Lambert had initiated. Even so, expensive trips to exotic locations were just as impractical with 'Terror of the Zygons' as they had been with 'The Highlanders' nine years earlier. Nevertheless, with convincing rolling hills, a convenient lake, over-dubbed bagpipe music and the BBC's stock Scottish actor Angus Lennie, the illusion of life on the Loch Ness shores was well maintained.

The story details the Doctor's return to present-day Earth and a struggle against the crew of a Zygon spaceship who have existed beneath the waters of Loch Ness for centuries. The Zygons control a gigantic armoured cyborg which, over the years, has gained an international reputation as the oft-seen, rarely photographed Loch Ness monster. The activities of the North Sea oil rigs have made the Zygons decidedly belligerent and, after a brush with UNIT, they decide to take their complaints, in the form of the Skarasen monster, to a government meeting by the banks of the Thames.

Originally recorded for inclusion in the twelfth season, this story was moved when Philip Hinchcliffe elected to change the dates of the seasons from a winter to an autumn start.

Planet of Evil (serial 4H) by Louis Marks. Director: David Maloney

Visual effects designer Dave Havard is justifiably proud of the exotic jungle set built at the BBC's Ealing film studios for this four-part deep-space horror story. Elaborately lit in rich purples, browns and reds this dense jungle, festooned with unearthly vines, shrubs and plants, was so convincing as to be greatly instrumental in *Doctor Who*'s ratings victory over the much more expensive *Space 1999* being screened opposite by ITV.

'Planet of Evil' is also one of *Doctor Who*'s more terrifying adventures, in some ways anticipating the film *Alien* in some of its content.

A supply of anti-matter crystals is brought aboard a space probe sent to rescue a geological party from Zeta Minor – the furthest planet in the known universe. But the forces present on Zeta Minor will not allow any anti-matter to leave the planet and as the probe tries to do just that the crew discovers, to their cost, that they have a monster on board which strikes silently and swiftly in the dark. Faced with an obstinate commander and a scientist afflicted by a terrible biological instability, the Doctor races against time to save the few remaining crew.

Pyramids of Mars (serial 4G) by Stephen Harris (Robert Holmes and Lewis Griefer). Director: Paddy Russell

Acclaimed as one of the all-time great *Doctor Who* serials, this story pulls few punches in picking all the best ingredients from all the Egyptian Mummy films ever made.

Possessed by the power of the dark god Sutekh, Professor Marcus Scarman is transported back to England to oversee the operation which

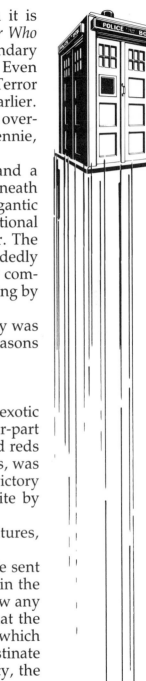

will free his master from a tomb in Egypt to which he was consigned by his brother Horus. The Doctor becomes aware of this when the TARDIS materialises inside the priory – Marcus Scarman's family residence. There in the courtyard servicor robots – looking uncannily like enbalmed mummies – are assembling a pyramid-shaped rocket to fire at Horus's pyramid on Mars: focal point of the power restraining Sutekh. Destroying the rocket would end the menace, is the Doctor's evaluation, but to do this he must enter Sutekh's tomb and confront the most powerful adversary he has ever faced.

Like all of the *Doctor Who* classics, 'Pyramids of Mars' succeeds because all the ingredients were blended to perfection. Highest of all the ingredients was the superb characterisation supplied by Gabriel Woolf as Sutekh. Although not required to move much, Woolf's sibilant voice conveys more harsh, sadistic menace than a whole army of Daleks and Cybermen combined.

The Android Invasion (serial 4J) by Terry Nation. Director: Barry Letts
For only the second time in his *Doctor Who* career, Terry Nation veered away from the Daleks to conceive a new race of galactic conquerors – the Kraals.

Seen as somewhat of an anomaly in a season otherwise so heavily steeped in nightmarish horror, 'The Android Invasion' is a somewhat gentle story of the Doctor's arrival in an apparently deserted rural English village. The few inhabitants he does discover, both in the village and the nearby space research centre, are strangely dispassionate and distant. Only later do he and Sarah uncover the truth. The village, in fact the whole surrounding countryside, is just an elaborate testing site for an invasion force of Kraal androids who will be used to infiltrate and disrupt the defences of Earth prior to a full attack by the Kraal space fleet. Mankind will be ex-ter-min-ated by a lethal virus carried by the androids.

Location filming for this story was done at the picturesque village of East Hagbourne, six miles from Evesham, the town which houses the BBC's big staff training centre. The centre itself is no stranger to *Doctor Who*, being used as a location for the stories 'The Invasion', 'Spearhead from Space', and 'Robot', to name but a few.

The Brain of Morbius (serial 4K) by Robin Bland (Terrance Dicks). Director: Christopher Barry
Script-writer Terrance Dicks is now greatly mellowed in attitude towards this story than he was back in 1975 when he felt the production team had made too many changes to his original teleplay. His original notion was to parody the Frankenstein story but twist it so that it was a monster that was trying to create a man rather than vice versa. When Mary Shelley's concept was re-applied, Dicks felt unhappy with the script and instructed a pen name be attached to it. Hence Robert Holmes's neat alias befitting Dicks's mood at the time.

The finished script is very much a revisit of *Frankenstein* with the deluded Doctor Mehendri Solon toiling fanatically within his lonely castle, aided only by his brutish manservant Condo. The body that will house the brain of the war criminal from Gallifrey is ready; all it needs now is a suitable head to crown the achievement. Enter the Doctor, seeking shelter from the rain, and the scene is set for a true homage to Universal Studios even down to the ultimate destruction of the monster at the hands of the torch-bearing local population – in this case the mystic circle of the Sisterhood of Karn.

With some ingenious sets from Barry Newbery and a fine performance by Philip Madoc as Solon, the only person disappointed at the end of the day was Terrance Dicks!

The Seeds of Doom (serial 4L) by Robert Banks Stewart. Director: Douglas Camfield

A remake of *The Thing from Another World* was not even a gleam in John Carpenter's eye when Douglas Camfield directed the first two episodes of this memorable six-parter.

Robert Banks Stewart had written his script concerning a mad botanist who brings to England a seed pod from space. Contact with the plumule causes instant infection, with the luckless human gradually transforming into a full manifestation of a Krynoid plant – a gigantic tentacled creature large enough to crush even a mansion. The Doctor and UNIT, in their last team-up together, fight to save humanity from the consequences of the fully matured Krynoid shedding thousands of seeds into the atmosphere which would doom all animal life on Earth. Luckily a squadron of RAF Phantoms is at hand to administer some timely defoliation.

The story was designed as a six-parter but on evaluation the content of the scripts was considered weighty enough only for four. Thus the first two episodes were rescripted to include a lengthy prologue showing the events surrounding the opening of the first pod in an Antarctic scientific research base. For the second time *Doctor Who*'s producer had cause to be grateful to Howard Hawkes's celebrated work in the fifties.

The Masque of Mandragora (serial 4M) by Louis Marks. Director: Rodney Bennett

'A nice thing about television, though it doesn't happen often, is the ability of an old series to perk up and surprise you. It's happening at this moment to *Doctor Who*. Do take a look at next week's episode for the Pre-Raphaelite costumes and settings, gorgeous in colour, that make the most diverting frame for the customary space opera nonsense. The latest chunk must have been bidding for some sort of record, ending in a triple cliffhanger no less.'

So wrote The *Daily Mail* after episode two's climax had seen the gallant Duke Giuliano preparing to do solo battle with the evil Count Federico's men, Sarah recaptured by the deadly Brotherhood of Demnos and the Doctor trapped in a temple by the powers of the Madragora Helix. For director Rodney Bennett, later to direct many of the BBC's prestige Shakespeare productions, that favourable and ratings-boosting review paid off a major gamble staked on this story. To recreate the period feel of Renaissance Italy, so vital to this story, the crew went further out on location than usual, to Wales – to the Italianate village of Portmeirion, created by architect Sir Clough Williams-Ellis and famous for its background in the ITV series *The Prisoner*. Even the costumes worn by the principle leads were more than usually sumptuous, having been flown in specially from Italy.

The Hand of Fear (serial 4N) by Bob Baker and Dave Martin. Director: Lennie Mayne

From the orange groves of Renaissance Italy to the steel gantries of Oldbury nuclear power station near Bristol and Sarah Jane's last appearance as a regular in *Doctor Who*. The scene is a quarry where recent blasting has unearthed a fossilised human hand. But the hand is alive and capable of possessing anyone who comes into contact with it. Sarah is the first victim, driven to taking the hand towards its chosen destination: the heart of a nuclear reactor which will provide the energy necessary to regenerate the form of Eldrad – a silicone-based alien life form who, aeons ago, caused the downfall of his/her race.

Two people played Eldrad in this story, Judith Paris and giant actor Stephen Thorne. The first Eldrad, the female, was supposedly based on Sarah's body print. The BBC costume department turned out a remarkable costume for Judith Paris – slim, plastic-encrusted suit that was so tight the actress had to be sewn into it and thereafter could not sit down. Her voice was modulated by a device called a Vocorder to give it a deeper, more masculine tone, thereby hinting that Eldrad was really a male before the final form was unveiled in part four. The male Eldrad costume was more economic than its counterpart due to the sheer time, effort and money that had gone into the first one.

The Deadly Assassin (serial 4P) by Robert Holmes. Director: David Maloney

Time Bandits costume designer James Acheson, and Joan Ellacott, were responsible for the Time Lord costumes featured in this story which have since been used in all subsequent Time Lord serials. This was the first to probe in depth the mysteries of the Time Lord civilisation and, because of the vast quanity of mythology injected into it by Robert Holmes, the serial has become something of a cult classic.

With episode three, most of which was shot on film, achieving the highest ratings ever for a *Doctor Who* episode, the serial concerns the circumstances of the Doctor's return to his home world of Gallifrey. He is framed for the assassination of the outgoing President and, in a desperate bid to clear his name, volunteers to merge his mind into the Amplified Panatropic Computations Network from which he will, if he survives, discover the true assassin.

The killer is revealed as the Time Lord Chancellor, Goth, but behind him is an even more sinister enemy – the Master. Not the handsome, commanding figure of old, but a decrepit half-cadaver hell-bent on destroying both the Doctor and the Time Lords.

A story with some unusually violent scenes, *The Deadly Assassin* was the subject of a major row between Mrs Mary Whitehouse and BBC head Sir Hugh Curran which culminated in the series being given some stricter guidelines on the use of gore, horror and violence.

The Face of Evil (serial 4Q) by Chris Boucher. Director: Pennant Roberts
Ever since Polly (Anneke Wills) donned her mini skirt for the first time in
the Hartnell era, *Doctor Who*'s girl companions had been tagged with the
label 'sex appeal to bring in the older viewers'. True or not, fathers
flocked back to the series in droves with the advent of Leela, played by
Louise Jameson. It was not hard to appreciate why. With a plunging
neckline, leather boots and an ample display of leg Leela was a hefty piece
of artillery in *Doctor Who*'s ratings arsenal.

Her début story was no mean contender either. Originally titled 'The
Day that God Went Mad' the story's focal point is a giant computer
housed within a long-crashed spaceship. A superbly built machine, the
computer – Xoanon – has evolved into a living, free-thinking life form
but, in doing so, has become unbalanced, enslaving the subconscious
thoughts of the Technicians and the Survey Team and setting them at war
against one another. Now, years later, both sides have sunk into
barbarism with the Tesh mortal enemies of the Sevateem tribe. Only
when he sees his own face carved on a mountainside does the Doctor
perceive how much he is responsible for all that has happened.

The Robots of Death (serial 4R) by Chris Boucher. Director: Michael
Briant
Ploughing across the landscape of a rocky, desert world, the giant shape
of a sandminer is harvesting minerals for its small contract-hired crew. In
running the huge landship, the nine-man team can rely on their
substantial complement of robot operators, ranging from the simple
D-Class (dum) single-function robots to the multi-capable SV7
(super-Voc) Coordinator. But, as the TARDIS arrives, the inexplicable
has happened – one of the crew has been murdered. At first accusations
run among the other team members – after all, his death represents one
less to receive the commission. Then the Doctor and Leela are suspected.
What none of them even dares to contemplate is the possibility that the
culprit could be a robot. In a robot-dependent culture such an occurrence
could spell the end for that civilisation.

Although no one knew it at the time, this story saw the last
appearance of the wooden walled control room aboard the TARDIS. It
had its début in 'The Masque of Mandragora' as a replacement for the
more familiar room seen since 1963. However, while it was felt to be very
atmospheric, the set suffered from being too static (i.e. too little going on
visually) and too reliant on wood which warped when the walls were put
into storage for a few months.

The Talons of Weng-Chiang (serial 4S) by Robert Holmes. Director:
David Maloney
This was David Maloney's last *Doctor Who* serial as director before the
impetus of producing *Blake's Seven* caught up with him. Certainly as an
'epitaph' this story has few peers. Once again with a keen eye for
locations and costumes, the *Doctor Who* team searched out superb period
backdrops at Wapping in the heart of London's dockland, and backstage
and in the flies of the Victorian Repertory Theatre at Northampton.
Prior to his appearance as Sherlock Holmes in a Sunday serial, Tom

Baker was delighted to find himself dressed in the manner of the Baker Street sleuth courtesy of John Bloomfield, previously known for his costume designs for *The Six Wives of Henry VIII*.

Set in Victorian London, the story sees the Doctor up against the sinister Magnus Greel – a war criminal from the fifty-first century whose home-made time machine has brought him here. But the experiment was only partially successful and now Greel is dying. Only by absorbing the life essences of young women, obtained for him by a loyal band of Chinese Tong members, can Greel (alias Weng-Chiang) hope to stay alive long enough to recover his time machine, innocuously in the possession of a prominent surgeon, Professor Charles Litefoot.

The Horror of Fang Rock (serial 4V) by Terrance Dicks. Director: Paddy Russell

Having dragged Robert Holmes bodily into the Middle Ages with *The Time Warrior*, Terrance Dicks received some of his own medicine in return as Holmes handed him one of his pet ideas – a *Doctor Who* story set in a lighthouse.

An alien spacecraft crashes into the sea close by the lonely off-shore lighthouse of Fang Rock. The vessel's pilot reaches the small outcrop and sets about a series of grisly experiments, killing off, one by one, the lighthouse keepers and a party of shipwrecked day-trippers. Also present on the rock are the Doctor and Leela, the former uncovering the alien culprit as a Rutan scout, one of the sworn enemies of the Sontarans. The Rutans plan to use Earth as a staging post for an attack on their opponents – an attack that will surely result in the Earth's destruction.

In the climax, the Doctor uses the modified light of the rotating beacon to destroy an approaching Rutan mother ship. So bright is the explosion that it alters the pigment of Leela's eyes from brown to blue. In reality this was done to satisfy Louise Jameson who had complained for some time of discomfort at having to wear the special brown contact lenses made for her when she accepted the role of Leela.

The Invisible Enemy (serial 4T) by Bob Baker and Dave Martin. Director: Derrick Goodwin

It is a rare exception when the major onus of a *Doctor Who* story is given over to special effects. This serial was one of those rare exceptions. Using Gerry Anderson's old studios at Bray, model builders Mat Irvine and Ian Scoones constructed a large space panorama, a shuttle craft and the elaborate moonscape of Titan base for some of the most complex miniature work seen in the series.

Set designer Barry Newbery needed to work very closely with the electronic effects operator whose work would play a key role in realising a journey the cloned Doctor and Leela make through a human body when they are reduced to microscopic size in racing against time to remove a deadly space virus from the Doctor's brain.

The most elaborate special effect though was unquestionably the prodigy of effects designer Tony Harding. With its own traction system, a series of servo-motors and an eight-channel radio control unit K9 blazed on to the screens in episode two and instantly became an overnight hit with the show's younger viewers. With the show's new producer Graham Williams unsure at first of K9's potential as a regular, two endings of 'The Invisibile Enemy' were recorded – one with K9 staying with Professor Marius, one with him going with the Doctor. And, as in the case of Jamie, it was the latter option which was taken up.

Image of the Fendahl (serial 4X) by Chris Boucher. Director: George Spenton-Foster·
'Like one who on a lonely road, doth walk in fear and dread / And having turned once, turns no more his head / Because he knows a frightful fiend doth close behind him tread.' Coleridge's celebrated poem formed the basis of Boucher's thinking when he wrote this four-part script to bring out all the fears that lurk at the heart of every nightmare. The opening scenes captured this to best effect as a lone hiker on a dark, empty road gradually becomes aware of something in the blackness stalking him. He tries to run but, as in true nightmare tradition, finds his legs paralysed and as a result is devoured by a gigantic slug.

And this was only a prelude to the main plot about a scientific team's attempts to investigate a mysterious ancient skull. Armed with a bit of foreknowledge the Doctor recognises the skull as that of the Fendahl, a creature which is death – and how do you kill death? He is unable to prevent the Fendahl manifesting itself in its full majestic glory through the body of a beautiful woman but, thanks to some tampering with a sonic time scanner, he is able to stop the creature absorbing all life on Earth.

The Sunmakers (serial 4W) by Robert Holmes. Director: Pennant Roberts
Millions of years into the future, the Doctor finds a very sophisticated colony existing on Pluto, warmed by the light of several artificial orbiting suns. Most of the people living on, or rather in, Pluto are human beings. But the rulers are the executives of the Sun Company, an alien-controlled business operation that is expanding through the galaxy and subjugating other races by misuse of commercial power. The workers are not free. The curiously intricate and devious methods of tax payments to the Company ensure that they are permanently enslaved. They never see the light of day; their dreary existences are spent in the windowless network that forms the working and living quarters. But there are rebels who, in spite of the constant electronic surveillance, have managed to escape to little-penetrated levels of the complex.

It is not improbable that Robert Holmes's inventive mind and flair for dry wit devised this story as a consequence of receiving a particularly bad assessment from the Inland Revenue. Beneath the obligatory sci-fi overtones, 'The Sunmakers' is a thinly disguised acid parody on the British tax system with all its idiosyncrasies and complexities. The guards are the Inner Retinue, the corridors are coded with such numbers as P45 and even the Tax Gatherer himself wears a costume reminiscent of a giant humbug. The storyline may have confused the young but to any who have ever filled out the dreaded yearly tax return this serial gave positive proof that the pen is mightier than the sword.

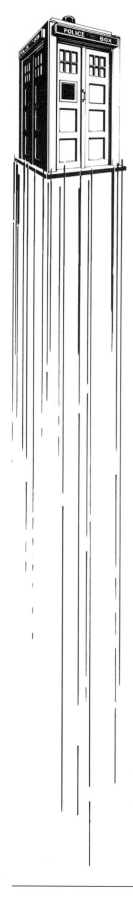

Underworld (serial 4Y) by Bob Baker and Dave Martin. Director: Norman Stewart

An ingenious premise forms the background to 'Underworld'. Just as an oyster forms a pearl around a piece of grit, so, Baker and Martin propounded, cosmic debris could form around a spaceship until its original outlines are submerged beneath mounting layers of dust and rock that will ultimately fuse into the shape of a planet.

The Doctor, Leela and K9 encounter a group of astronauts who are searching for the lost gene bank of their race. It disappeared a hundred thousand years ago aboard another space vessel – the P-7E. With some help from the time travellers, the astronauts locate the P-7E but find it at the heart of a recently formed planet on which are living the descendents of the ship. The race has now subdivided into three castes – the Trogs, the Guards and the Seers, all of whom serve the ship's computer, the Oracle; worshipping it as an idol now that its original purpose has been forgotten.

That this story is not so well remembered is perhaps attributable to the bold experiment conducted with it. The greater majority of the cave scenes were done using CSO but while it certainly succeeded as a cost-cutting measure, the lack of depth of field reduced the serial's realism.

The Invasion of Time (serial 4Z) by David Agnew (Graham Williams and Anthony Read). Director: General Blake

This was the sequel to 'The Deadly Assassin' with a vastly increased sense of scale for the Time Lords' home planet accomplished by filming most of the Gallifrey scenes on location. Settings as diverse as Hammersmith Swimming Baths and a disused hospital near Redhill, Surrey, were commandeered to give this show its larger-than-life proportions.

The first four episodes baffle the audience into believing the Doctor has gone mad. He returns abruptly to Gallifrey, claiming the title of President rightfully his after the demise of Chancellor Goth in the previous tale. Armed with his powers as President, he appears to turn traitor by allowing an attack force of Vardan invaders to take control of the planet. Only is it gradually made apparent that the Doctor is collaborating with these invaders to gain their confidence. Once he has that, he is able to despatch them. Even then the threat is not ended. A new attack begins, but this time from a far more sinister adversary. The Sontarans have come to Gallifrey to plunder the secret of mastering time.

Much of the last two episodes is taken up with an extensive chase through the TARDIS but it was this chase which led to much criticism of this serial due to its showing the TARDIS interior to be made up of Victorian brickwork and latticed lift shafts.

The Ribos Operation (serial 5A) by Robert Holmes. Director: George Spenton-Foster

The highly skilled ladies of the BBC's make-up department have had their fair share of unusual assignments over the years with *Doctor Who*, but probably few were as eyebrow-raising as the day Tom Baker walked into the studio for the final sessions on 'The Ribos Operation' sporting a dog-bitten, hugely swollen lip. So while the script editor adjusted the script for the following story to reflect an explanation, the make-up supervisor for this story undertook the careful job of covering up the bite mark for this one to maintain essential continuity.

And continuity was to be the theme of this landmarking season, the first to feature an on-going theme throughout all six stories. The White Guardian of Light and Time summons the Doctor and instructs him to hunt down and assemble the six segments to the all-powerful Key to Time. With this the Guardian can prevent chaos overtaking the universe and thus foil his counterpart – the Black Guardian. Armed with a tracer device and a new assistant – Romanavoratrelunder (Romana for short) – he locates the first segment on the medieval planet of Ribos, disguised as a nugget of a rare and valuable mineral called Jethrik. Before he does so, though, he has to outwit the exiled prince of a warlike race and a pair of scheming con-men who intend to 'sell' Ribos to the Prince.

The Pirate Planet (serial 5B) by Douglas Adams. Director: Pennant Roberts
The huge tide of income from *The Hitch-Hiker's Guide to the Galaxy* was but a trickle into Douglas Adam's account when he was offered the opportunity to pen a script for *Doctor Who* on the strength of his highly popular radio series.

The Pirate Planet displays much of Adam's flair for inventive and often oblique writing. Aiming for the planet Calufrax, site of the Second Segment, the Doctor is puzzled when the TARDIS lands instead on Zanak, a prosperous planet ruled over by the mysterious figure, the Captain. He is appalled to discover the secret of Zanak's prosperity is its plundering of other worlds. For Zanak is hollow and through a series of gigantic transmat engines has materialised around Calufrax, crushing it into a condensed ball of matter and sucking from it all its life and wealth. When he learns the next target is Earth, the Doctor, K9 Mark II and his Time Lady companion must do battle against the half-human/half-machine Captain, the reclusive ex-monarch of Zanak, Queen Xanxia, and a lethal death robot innocuously designed in the shape of a parrot. An even bigger problem looms thereafter when the travellers learn that the whole planet Calufrax is indeed the Second Segment of the Key to Time.

The Stones of Blood (serial 5C) by David Fisher. Director: Darrol Blake
When this story topped their annual season poll, the Doctor Who Appreciation Society presented its writer, David Fisher, with a beautiful award fashioned into the shape of the serial's main baddie, the Cailleach, by sculptress Susan Moore. It was fitting that this story should have received such an award as, apart from being a fine combination of black magic story and science fiction adventure, it was also *Doctor Who*'s one hundreth story, an event occurring within its fifteenth year on screen.

The Third Segment is revealed as a pendant worn by one Vivien Fay who, as the Cailleach, holds sway over a circle of modern Druids. The strength of her position is maintained by a ring of animated standing stones which demand constant intakes of warm blood. Vivien Fay's own

apparently magical powers are derived from harnessing the energies of a stranded space cruiser hovering above the stone circle but invisible due to its being in a different spatial dimension. Only when he is able to bridge the hyperspace gap is the Doctor able to uncover Vivien Fay's true identity as an escaped alien criminal, Cessair of Diplos.

A memorable anniversary story, though a scene was cut showing Romana presenting the Doctor with a birthday cake in episode one.

The Androids of Tara (serial 5D) by David Fisher. Director: Michael Hayes

Anyone familiar with Stewart Granger's double performance as the commoner and king-apparent in *The Prisoner of Zenda* would have no trouble in recognising the source used for this only partially serious *Doctor Who* adventure. Only the location was changed with Leeds Castle, embellished with a glass painting, doubling for the Ruritanian fortress.

Finding the Fourth Segment – disguised as part of a statue – presents no problems for Romana. Getting away with it though is quite another matter when she encounters the mighty-nosed Count Grendel. For Romana is the exact double of the Princess Strella, the promised future wife of the Taran Monarch-to-be Prince Reynart. With both Strella, Romana and, later, Reynart as his prisoners, Grendel hopes to be crowned king in place of the rightful heir. His plans are foiled though when the Doctor is able to repair and re-activate an android double of the Prince and sends him to the coronation, thus gaining time for Reynart's aides to seek out the true monarch.

As a final confrontation with Grendel looms, it takes all of the Doctor's ingenuity and a great deal of remarkable swordsmanship to determine who's who with the double-dealer's doubles.

The Power of Kroll (serial 5E) by Robert Holmes. Director: Norman Stewart

Stepping up from all fours, K9's voice, alias John Leeson, got to play a more organic role in this story as the technician Dugeen, one of several engineers present on the third moon of Delta Magna operating a pilot plant to collect methane from the swamp surroundings.

The refinery's presence is resented by the swamp people who have been given this moon as a kind of reservation. They see the coming of the Earthmen as an intrusion and their leader, Ranquin, is far from dismayed when the vibrations from the plant's machinery awaken the wrath of their dormant god Kroll.

Kroll is a savage monster squid nearly two miles across and hundreds of feet high. Worse, it harbours within it an ancient relic which is the Fifth Segment of the Key to Time. It is this which has caused Kroll's giant dimensions and, as the creature envelops the refinery in the last episode, it is the Doctor who must grapple with the beast and effect the trans-mutation of the relic into the segment before Kroll crushes the entire platform.

With much of 'The Power of Kroll' taking place on location in Iken Marshes, K9 was confined to the TARDIS for this adventure.

The Armageddon Factor (serial 5F) by Bob Baker and Dave Martin. Director: Michael Hayes

Five down, one to go and, as the Doctor materialises the TARDIS midway between the two warring planets of Zeos and Atrios, he fears that the Black Guardian, who has so far not shown his hand, may rise to oppose them now that the quest is nearing its conclusion.

Sure enough the Doctor does find his stiffest opposition so far in the form of the Shadow, a wraith-like creature serving the Black Guardian whose evil designs have caused the devastating war of attrition between the two worlds. At first both the Doctor and the Shadow are uncertain as to the guise of the Sixth Segment but, as events progress, the terrible truth dawns. The Segment is the living person of the gentle Princess Astra and therefore she must die if the Key is to be complete. It is an agonising decision for the Doctor to make but one made easier when the Guardian who appears before him at the end turns out to be the Guardian of Chaos. Dispersing the Key once more, Princess Astra is restored to life, but the Doctor knows in return he will be the target of vengeance by one of the most powerful beings in existence.

It was only during recording that Mary Tamm – Romana – made clear her intention to leave after the story to begin a family. Unable to insert a departure scene in time producer Graham Williams decided to maintain a form of link by having Romana, next season, regenerate into the form of Princess Astra, alias Lalla Ward.

Destiny of the Daleks (serial 5J) by Terry Nation. Director: Ken Grieve

The BBC's Press Office swung into action with a vengeance promoting this serial as the return of the Daleks after an absence of more than four years. Picture articles of the Movellans, with rising star Suzanne Danielle very much to the fore, appeared in all of the tabloid newspapers, while on the day of the first episode the *Daily Mail* presented an interview with the one person who could equally claim to be the creator of the Daleks, BBC designer Ray Cusick.

A well-kept secret in the show was the return of the fictional Dalek creator, Davros, played this time by actor David Gooderson due to the unavailability of Michael Wisher. Only viewers in Wales knew he would make a sudden reappearance in episode two when that region's *Radio Times* unintentionally 'blew the gaffe'.

The first two episodes chronicle the arrival of the Doctor and Romana II on a radioactive wasteland planet they later discover to be Skaro. The Daleks are there too, burrowing into the ruins of the old Kaled city with the aim of unearthing their only partially dead creator. The Daleks, being creatures of pure logic, have been unable to overcome an impasse in their war with the equally logical Movellans. They hope Davros will aid them in overcoming this. But when the Movellans, in turn, 'recruit' the Doctor, a frightening game of real-life chess ensues.

The City of Death (serial 5H) by David Agnew (Douglas Adams and Graham Williams). Director: Michael Hayes

The show stopper of the season, 'City of Death' had everything: an all-star cast including Julian Glover, Catherine Schell, John Cleese and

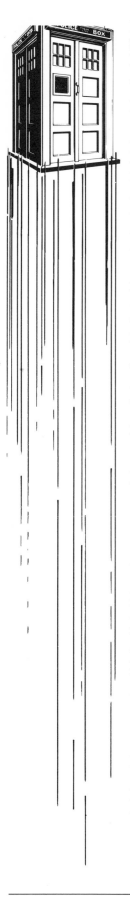

Eleanor Bron, some of the best model effects work ever, supervised by Ian Scoones, and an ingenious script which, while exceptionally rich in humour, never quite went over the top. And, the biggest selling point of all, it was the first *Doctor Who* serial to take the cast and crew overseas to a foreign location, in this case Paris 1979, described in a wine analogy by the Doctor as something of a 'table vintage year'.

The story begins with the destruction of the Jagaroth spaceship on Earth millions of years ago in pre-history. The explosion fragments its pilot, Scaroth, into identical splinters of himself, scattered across many time zones in the future. Each splinter is in contact with the others and together they are trying to galvanise the human race into constructing a time machine that will enable the furthermost splinter, in the guise of Count Scarlioni, to return to the past and stop the ship's initial destruction.

But the only way Scarlioni can afford the technology to build his time machines is by pulling off the greatest art fraud of all time. He intends to steal the *Mona Lisa* from the Louvre and then sell it and several copies, all commissioned from Da Vinci by another Scaroth splinter, for untold millions of pounds.

The Creature from the Pit (serial 5G) by David Fisher. Director: Christopher Barry
The problem confronting the designers of this show was its monster, about five tons in weight, which was basically a shapeless translucent blob capable of extruding limbs at will like a giant amoeba.

Faced with this headache and a strictly limited budget, the only practical solution was to build the creature, named Erato in Fisher's script, as a giant inflatable plastic bag with various appendages protruding from it.

To everyone's amazement the show was generally well received by the public, a feat due in part to the superb jungle set, again built at the film studios in Ealing.

A rare occurrence in *Doctor Who*, the main baddie was a woman. A matriarch of the planet Chloris, the key to Lady Adrasta's power lay in her total monopoly on the world's metal. Chloris, although overabundant in planet life, is almost devoid of ore minerals, hence when alien ambassador Erato arrives offering metal in return for vegetation Adrasta is greatly displeased and promptly has the creature imprisoned in a pit. When the Doctor lands on Chloris he finds Erato has been transmitting a distress signal to his people for some time, with the result that a neutron star has now been set on a collision course with the planet's sun . . .

Nightmare of Eden (serial 5K) by Bob Baker. Directors: Alan Bromly and Graham Williams
An unusual story line for *Doctor Who*, 'Nightmare of Eden' deals heavily with the misuses and consequences of the drug trafficking racket. Viewers, including children, were even shown the effects of a drug trip from the euphoric 'highs' to the violently unstable conditions of withdrawal although, as always with *Doctor Who*, it was handled with a careful eye on the show's younger audience.

The TARDIS lands aboard a luxury space liner recently in hyperspace collision with another vessel. The crash has left the two ships merged together and the instabilities of the interface points have led to creatures called Mandrels being able to escape from a machine called a Continuous Event Transmuter.

The Doctor's investigations convince him that someone aboard the two ships is involved in trafficking Vraxoin – the most dangerously addictive drug in the galaxy. Later, framed as the smuggler himself, the Doctor has to find the true culprit before the Eden law enforcer can catch him.

Bob Baker's highly inventive script had the Mandrels themselves as the source of the drug. Whenever one is killed, it rapidly decomposes to leave a fine white powder – Vraxoin. Sadly a lengthy visual effects scene showing this decomposition had to be edited to a few seconds to avoid the episode over-running.

The Horns of Nimon (serial 5L) by Anthony Read. Director: Kenny McBain

Christmas time is traditionally the time for panto entertainment and, as the festive month of December 1979 entered the Yuletide week, so *Doctor Who* unfurled its homage to generations of Widow Twankeys and Abanazers.

Part of the fun of pantomime is spotting the legion of in-jokes and certainly with *The Horns of Nimon* there was no shortage of these. In penning his script, Anthony Read dipped back into Greek legend for his characters and situations, just as he had authorised Bob Baker and Dave Martin to do with 'Underworld' a few seasons earlier (P-7E equals Persephone, get it?). In this instance budding aviator Daedalus becomes Soldeed, a role sent up in gloriously eye-rolling fashion by actor Graham Crowden. The principle-boy hero is Seth – losing two syllables from the source name Theseus – the young prince of Anethe (Athens), who, spurred on by his people, is travelling to Skonnos (Knossos) as part of the tribute to the Nimon (Minotaur) with the ambition of slaying the beast.

The Nimon Monster has promised the Skonnons a return to their former glory as a military empire if they, in turn, will provide him with a quantity of the energy-giving mineral hymetusite. What not even the awe-struck Soldeed realises is that the Nimon plans to use the hymetusite energy to energise a hyperspatial bridge that will allow the rest of his race access to Skonnos. If that happens the planet, and many others, will be plundered by this race of life-sucking parasites.

Shada (serial 5M) by Douglas Adams. Director: Pennant Roberts

Who, what or where is Shada? This was to have been the mystery surrounding this planned final story of the seventeenth season. Conceived as a six-part story by Douglas Adams, its style and presentation was along the lines of the very successful 'City of Death' serial with large emphasis being placed on the location backgrounds. In this case the location was Emmanuel College, Cambridge, the name being altered to St Cedds for purposes of the plot. For writer Douglas Adams, *Shada* was almost a homecoming as he himself had studied at Cambridge before

taking up the more rewarding pursuit of hitch-hiking.

In the plot Adams virtually puts himself into the story with his character of Chris Parsons, a post-graduate student who finds himself in possession of an ancient book accidentally given to him by his tutor Professor Chronotis. The book is printed on a parchment unknown on Earth, an observation later confirmed when it is revealed the book is in fact *The Ancient Law of Gallifrey*, a tome written at the time of Rassilon and stolen by a Time Lord criminal named Salyavin. Chronotis himself is a retired Time Lord living incognito on Earth. Very worried on discovering he has mislaid the book, Chronotis summons aid from the Doctor and Romana. The book contains information on such matters as Shada and now Chronotis feels it might be better if the book was returned to the Time Lords.

But no sooner has Chronotis sent the Doctor on his way to find the book, than he has another visitor – Skagra.

Skagra is a megalomaniac scientist who has developed the power to steal minds. An alien, Skagra intends to go one step further and place an imprint of his mind inside every sentient being in the universe, thereby controlling them absolutely. To do this, however, he requires the knowledge possessed by Salyavin and to find Salyavin he must first find Shada.

And so the scene is set for a desperate confrontation between Skagra, armed with a flying globe that steals minds and his monsterish servants the Krargs and the Doctor. Shada, it transpires, is the prison world maintained, but denied, by the Time Lord High Council. Salyavin was imprisoned there centuries ago and soon the chase is on to reach this small rock world. But even then a surprise awaits the victor. For Chronotis is much more than he seems . . .

The technical expertise applied to this story is as high as anything previously seen in *Doctor Who*, with special effects being particularly to the fore. Episode two, for example, was to have featured a lengthy sequence, all done on film, with the Doctor racing through the streets of Cambridge on a bicycle (what else?) pursued by the flying sphere. Other sequences required the Doctor to make a hazardous crossing between two TARDISes (Chronotis's study is his own TARDIS disguised inside as well as out) while still in the time vortex. Finally, on Shada, there is an extended battle of wills between the Doctor and Skagra using other prisoners there as combatants. Among these prisoners are many familiar faces to *Doctor Who* viewers, including a Dalek, a Zygon and a Cyberman.

Being a six-part story, shooting 'Shada' required a few days' filming on location and then three blocks of taping sessions in the BBC Television Centre studios (a block being two or three days of recording). The filming was all completed satisfactorily as was one of the three recording blocks. However, on the week the second one was due to commence, a lengthy and costly strike of studio staff began at the BBC, bringing all programme production to a halt. As ever when this occurs, a big backlog of shows soon accumulated such that, when production was eventually resumed, priorities had to be established as to which shows needed to be done and which could be safely scrapped.

Sadly, 'Shada' was among those rostered for scrapping, although all its filmed and recorded material was preserved in the event of the producer being able to reschedule the show for another season. Incoming producer John Nathan-Turner tried hard to get 'Shada' completed as a special one-off show but failed. Later on, cast changes precluded the programme ever standing a chance of completion.

Thanks to the efforts of the BBC's internal film library though, what does remain of 'Shada' is kept for posterity and will possibly be featured in future documentaries about the series.

The Leisure Hive (serial 5N) by David Fisher. Director: Lovett Bickford
In a review for the Wider Television Access Group's magazine *Primetime*, a writer very astutely labels *Doctor Who*'s plots as comprised of 'intricate layering'. Few instances more ably demonstrate this key ingredient than 'The Leisure Hive'. Here the shape of its teleplay derives equally from the writer, the director, the producer and the musicians.

David Fisher's original script – was a vaguely tongue-in-cheek spoof of the Mafia protection racket system and as such appears in the W. H. Allen novelisation, penned by Fisher himself. However, new producer John Nathan-Turner, who had devised the original scenario, and director Lovett Bickford saw the show in a completely different light, switching the style of its presentation radically towards a more lyrical and glossy appearance.

The plot remained essentially the same. The Argolins, a people made barren by the effects of a nuclear war, have built the Leisure Hive as a means to teach others how to exist in harmony. But the stability of the hive is threatened, firstly by an over-ambitious junior Argolin named Pangol and principally by an alien business cartel whose way of operating verges on the criminal. Where this story scores its greatest impact is with the stylish use of camerawork coupled with an all-pervading musical soundtrack, supplied by Peter Howell of the BBC's Radiophonic Workshop.

Meglos (serial 5Q) by John Flanagan and Andrew McCulloch. Director: Terence Dudley
A frequent problem with using CSO for backgrounds, so 'Underworld's' production crew would attest, lies in its inability to present depth of field and freedom of movement to the camera. These problems proved in this story to be curable, with the experimental use of a process called Scene-Sync.

Using a system of computer-linked cameras moving in perfect synchronisation, both model and live action sets could be perfectly integrated, thereby enabling figures on the latter to move freely about the former.

In the case of 'Meglos' Scene-Synch was used for the exterior scenes set on the planet Zolpha-Thura – a desert wasteland concealing the underground laboratory of the last Zolpha-Thuran, Meglos. At the touch of a switch Meglos's laboratory can rise from the dunes to tower above the Gaztak pirates and their kidnapped human.

By putting his conciousness into the body of the human, Meglos can imitate the Doctor's face and form and so gain entry to the city of the

Tigellans unopposed. The Tigellans are panicked by the apparent failure of their city's power source – the Dodecahedron. In truth the multi-faceted artifact is a vastly complex device which, when used properly, can generate enough power to destroy a planet – and Meglos plans to do just that, beginning with Tigella.

Full Circle (serial 5R) by Andrew Smith. Director: Peter Grimwade
The beginning of a trilogy of stories for the Doctor as the TARDIS tumbles helplessly through a Charged Vacuum Emboitement to emerge into the universe of E-Space – a radically smaller spatial zone recognisable by the greenish tint to the sky. Unaware of this at first, the Doctor, Romana and K9 arrive on a world they believe to be Gallifrey, only to find out that it is really the lush, verdant world of Alzarius.

At the time of their arrival the dreaded period of Mistfall has just begun – a climatic condition causing dense fogs and a savage species of marsh creatures to appear. The inhabitants of a crashed Starliner fear the coming of Mistfall for reasons they are not quite sure of. Delving into the problem, the Doctor is amazed to find that the linking factor between the Starliner personnel and the marshmen is a lot closer than any of them could imagine.

The writer for this story, Andrew Smith, was still in his teens when he had his freelance script for 'The Planet That Slept' (the working title for 'Full Circle') accepted by John Nathan-Turner. Interviewed quite early on in his reign as producer, Nathan-Turner stated his aim to introduce more young talent into the series and, as well as Andrew Smith, 'Full Circle' also saw the début of teenage actor Matthew Waterhouse as the junior companion Adric.

State of Decay (serial 5P) by Terrance Dicks. Director: Peter Moffatt
Still trapped in E-Space, the Doctor and Romana are searching fruitlessly for an exit when K9's sensory equipment registers a nearby planet capable of supporting life. Sure enough the planet does indeed prove to be inhabited – by a community of peasants whose ceaseless toil serves the needs of their rulers, the three aristocrats who live in the Tower. With a metallic spire pointing heavenwards the Tower resembles a huge missile. The Doctor is the only one not to show surprise when he learns that the Tower is indeed a long-stranded space vessel, brought to this desolate world by the power of an unseen giant. Finding the ship's fuel tanks the Doctor and Romana are horrified to discover inside vast quantities of human blood. For the three original crew members are still alive and preserved in the bodies of vampires – serving their dark lord until the time of his arising.

Even as far back as his *Doctor Who* script-editing days, Terrance Dicks had wanted to write a vampire story for the programme and, with 'State of Decay', he finally achieved his goal. It was a hard-won battle though. Originally Dicks had penned episode one of a script for the 1977/78 season and was greatly dismayed when it got cancelled by the upper echelons of the BBC who feared its production might pre-empt their major adaption of *Dracula* that autumn.

Warriors' Gate (serial 5S) by Steve Gallagher. Director: Paul Joyce
Like a good wine, 'Warriors' Gate' has improved in palatability since its
first confused screening in January 1981. Then everyone understood that
it was the wind-up to the E-Space trilogy and that it was the story which
said farewell to Romana and K9 Mark II. What very few comprehended
were all the bits in the middle that ostensibly made no sense whatsoever.
It took until spring 1982 and publication of the W. H. Allen novelisation
for the truth to be explained fully: that here indeed was one of the
cleverest stories ever to go out under the *Doctor Who* banner.

Attempting to escape E-Space, the TARDIS arrives at the midway
point between positive and negative space – the Zero Point. It gets stuck
there as does a privateer spaceship owned by a band of slavers under the
command of Captain Rorvik.

In the case of the TARDIS it arrives there as a result of a hijack by a
lion-like alien called a Tharil. The Tharils are time sensitives and can ride
the time winds and jump the time lines at will. To them the past, the
present and the future are all one and hence all ordained. With some
guidance from the Tharil Biroc and from the Gundan robots who all but
murdered the Tharil race, the Doctor is allowed a privileged insight into
the history and future of a race who were one-time rulers over a vast and
ruthlessly controlled empire.

The Keeper of Traken (serial 5T) by Johnny Byrne. Director: John Black
The beginning of another trilogy – this time aimed towards reintroducing
one of *Doctor Who*'s most colourful enemies – the Master.

With a very strong sense of continuity (a hallmark of Nathan-Turner's
era) the Master is brought back at first in the decrepit form last seen in
'The Deadly Assassin'. Armed with two TARDISes, he has disguised one
of them as a statue set in the royal garden of the Traken counsellors'
palace.

The Master, as the statue Melkur, knows the demise of the current
Keeper of Traken grows near. When the Keeper dies his great powers are
handed over to his successor and it is these powers the Melkur Master
seeks. To achieve this he sets about the systematic corruption of the
Traken rulers – using bribery, threats and even the possessive love of a
woman counsellor as weapons in his insidious campaign.

The Doctor foils him, but only just. Escaping retribution in his second
TARDIS, the Master pauses *en route* to commandeer a new body in the
form of Counsellor Tremas. The Master's new body is a frightening
combination of Tremas and the old Master.

Logopolis (serial 5V) by Christopher H. Bidmead. Director: Peter
Grimwade
Few people could initially accept the announcement of Tom Baker's
retirement from the role of the Doctor when it was announced on the nine
o'clock news one wet October evening. For so long had he played the part
– nearly seven years – that it was thought his stamp on the series was
indelible.

But time flies, even for the Doctor, and it was in sombre mood that
many viewers tuned into the first episode of 'Logopolis' some months

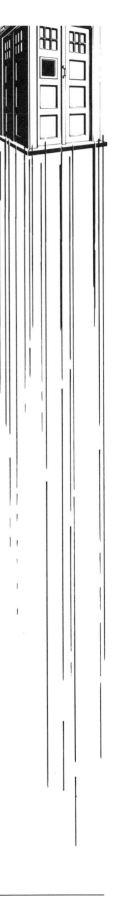

later. Perhaps conscious of this, director Peter Grimwade gave 'Logopolis' an almost funereal atmosphere, right from the opening moments, as a policeman is dragged to his doom inside the Master's TARDIS, to the close of episode four with the crushed, battered body of Tom Baker giving way to the youthful frame of Peter Davison.

When not writing or script-editing for *Doctor Who*, Christopher H. Bidmead's other literary endeavours are towards those scientific and technical journals which deal in the main with computers. Logopolis, the planet, was a giant computer – a city of chanting wizards whose every city, pathway, alcove and passage formed a network of registers and addresses for the single function of calculating the equations to maintain the structure of the universe. When the Master sought control over the universe by subverting the operation of Logopolis, he unwittingly unleashed devastation on a galactic scale.

Castrovalva (serial 5Z) by Christopher H. Bidmead. Director: Fiona Cumming
The longest-ever inter-season gap separated the end of 'Logopolis' and the beginning of this serial, although, thanks to the efforts of producer John Nathan-Turner, the wait was made more bearable by the BBC's screening of *The Five Faces of Doctor Who* in the autumn. This five-week season comprised at least one story from each Doctor's era, culminating with a re-run of 'Logopolis' to set the scene for Peter Davison's début in 'Castrovalva'.

However, if audiences thought they would be getting the new Doctor straight away they were wrong. Not only did the new Doctor remain in an unstable frame of mind for one episode, as in 'Robot', or even for two episodes, as in 'Spearhead from Space', he remained erratic and unpredictable throughout all four twenty-five minute segments, finally pinning on his stick of celery and adopting his infectious grin only in the last minute. Right up to then the Doctor's personality had wavered between total irrationality and the mannerisms of his former incarnations, including a stunning impersonation of Patrick Troughton in the opening episode.

The story title, 'Castrovalva', hails from a print of the same name by the artist M. C. Escher. Adopting this and several of Escher's other prints as inspiration Bidmead's teleplay has the recovering Doctor trapped, by the Master, in a city where space literally folds back in on itself. Unless he can locate the key to a way out he will remain trapped there for eternity.

Four to Doomsday (serial 5W) by Terence Dudley. Director: John Black
Although preceded by 'Castrovalva', 'Four to Doomsday' was the first Peter Davison serial to be recorded, as the length of his hair gives hint. 'Castrovalva' was recorded fourth in order of making to allow Davison time to settle into his character, thereby knowing how he wanted to end up before he worried about the mechanics of getting there.

'Four to Doomsday' is therefore a more straightforward plot with an emphasis on action and fast pace.

The TARDIS deposits the four travellers aboard a giant Urbankan spaceship set on a course for Earth. The Urbankan ruler, Monarch, intends to pillage Earth of its mineral resources, especially silicon, so that he may further develop his already quite considerable technology. The Doctor and his friends get a first-hand demonstration of the Urbankans' abilities when they find that all the non-reptile people aboard the ship, far from being human as was first supposed, are actually very sophisticated androids. In the final battle the Doctor uses this knowledge to lock many of the lesser androids into permanent displays of ritual dancing (termed 'recreationals') while he and Adric confront Monarch with his own deadly poison.

With a heavy emphasis on dance, this story is virtually unique in listing a choreographer – Sue Lefton – among the credits.

Kinda (serial 5Y) by Christopher Bailey. Director: Peter Grimwade
Like some of the best works of Tolkien, *Doctor Who*'s story lines can often be seen on two levels. On the one hand, there is the undemanding level of pure entertainment. On the other, is the more elusive pursuit of indentifying ideas and influences the writer has used in the development of his screenplay. 'Kinda' highlights this multi-level of appreciation with its often puzzling but ultimately enthralling screenplay. In an early scene, for example, Tegan has fallen into a trancelike state due to the mesmeric influences of the wind-chimes. With her mind freed from her body, she journeys into a black void where she encounters two people playing draughts by the side of an abstract piece of sculpture. While these two obstinate know-all figures appear to have no relevance to the plot, their presence is intended to reflect Tegan's subconcious opinion of her two companions, Adric and Nyssa (seen playing draughts earlier in the episode), and her confusion at the impossible dimensions of the TARDIS.

Allegories such as this abound in 'Kinda' as it traces the threat posed to the gentle people of Deva Loka by the coming of an Earth expeditionary force. The predictions of a Wise Woman, forseeing the Kinda's destruction, look to come true as the evil, serpentine presence of a Mara passes into the real world through the mind of Tegan and possesses one of the Kinda malefolk.

The Visitation (serial 5X) by Eric Saward. Director: Peter Moffat
When an escape pod carrying four Terileptil criminals beaches close by an Elizabethan manor house in the year 1666, a series of events is precipitated which leads, perhaps inevitably, to the start of one of the most famous fires in history. One of the Terileptils is killed shortly after the landing. Another stays in occupation of the manor to develop a deadly bacillus capable of eradicating the humans who killed its companion. But the other two go in search of a hiding place in the capital city of London. And only in the closing seconds of the story is it shown that their bakery hideout is in the narrow, winding streets of Pudding Lane . . .

The most location-bound story of the season, 'The Visitation' made use of one of the most popular spots in British cinema for its forest exteriors. Black Park near Iver, Berkshire, background to many a Hammer Film, doubled for the seventeenth-century landscape while nearby Tithe Barn in Hurley became Squire John's residence.

Pioneering another first for *Doctor Who* visual effects designer Peter Wragg used a system of radio-controlled servos to effect facial movement and expression on the mask of the Terileptil leader.

Black Orchid (serial 6A) by Terence Dudley. Director: Ron Jones
The only science fiction element present in this story is the TARDIS. In all other respects 'Black Orchid' is a return to the pure historical stories last seen with 'The Highlanders' in 1966.

The attention to period detail in manufacturing an Agatha Christie 1920s background is immaculate even down to the very careful editing in of stock steam locomotive footage for an early scene on a now disused railway station.

True to the spirit of Agatha Christie, 'Black Orchid' is a whodunit with a series of grisly murders pointing very markedly at the Doctor who must then prove emphatically who-hadn't-done-it. Identifying the true culprit is not easy, as the one witnessed murder takes place during a fancy-dress ball held after the annual cricket match at Dalton Hall. The murderer was dressed in the costume originally presented to the Doctor who, in turn, was at the match solely due to a case of mistaken identity to begin with.

Only later on is the true culprit revealed as the hideously mutilated other son of Lady Cranleigh. Once a noted botanist, a skirmish with some unfriendly Amazon Indians has left him ill in both mind and body, obsessed with the girl Ann Talbot, whom he was due to marry, who is identical facially to the Doctor's companion Nyssa.

Earthshock (serial 6B) by Eric Saward. Director: Peter Grimwade
A truly remarkable story, 'Earthshock' is one of the rare instances where the Doctor is seen to lose more than he gains. True he is able to save a vital conference from the apocalyptic effect of an anti-matter nuclear explosion, but in doing so he witnesses the event which kills off the dinosaurs millions of years earlier. Worse, the progenitors of the explosion, the Cybermen, are left dispersed but not defeated and in the cause of the struggle one of the Doctor's companions – Adric – is lost, fighting till the end to prevent the collision between Earth and the explosive contents of a space freighter.

Easily the showpiece of the season, 'Earthshock' is relentless in not letting up the suspense until the final roll of the credits in episode four – done without the customary theme music to enhance the effect of Adric's death.

The eight costumes built for this latest generation of Cybermen by the Imagineering Effects Company – whose work is also to be seen in the new Gerry Anderson puppet series *Terrahawks* – are shot to their best advantage by director Peter Grimwade whose main problem on this show was recording almost double the number of scenes per episode to achieve its lightning pace.

Time-Flight (serial 6C) by Peter Grimwade. Director: Ron Jones
Switching hats rapidly from director to writer Peter Grimwade had conceived his Concorde story some years earlier during Tom Baker's tenure as the Doctor. Location footage shot in and around Concorde and

the Heathrow Airport terminals feature predominantly in the first and last episodes. As the serial opens, the Doctor finally gets Tegan to her destination at Heathrow just as one of the Concordes has gone missing – vanishing abruptly from the radar screens as it approached the runways. Using his UNIT credentials, the Doctor and company are passengers on another Concorde which is sent out to fly the same route. Sure enough it too vanishes, reappearing 140 million years back in time on a remote heath, empty save for the imposing sight of a distant citadel. The two aircraft have disappeared as a result of an elaborate conjuring trick and as the Doctor maintains, 'behind every illusion is a conjuror'. However, even he is unprepared when the conjuror – a wizard named Kalid – turns out to be his arch-enemy, the Master . . .

Arc of Infinity (serial 6E) by Johnny Byrne. Director: Ron Jones

Twenty continuous years in the life of a series is something of an event in television circles, so to mark the event producer John Nathan-Turner planned this season to include something from the Doctor's past in each of the stories.

The reference point in this show was Omega – the one-time Solar Engineer last seen in the bench-marking serial of the tenth season, 'The Three Doctors'. Starting with the premise of 'How do you kill someone who isn't?' Omega was shown to have survived the super nova of 'The Three Doctors', and was once again seeking a doorway back to physical existence in the normal universe. To this end he had conspired with a member of the High Council, the Time Lord Hedin, to bond his anti-matter body with that of the Doctor, creating a stable material body for himself.

After an initial failure to merge with him, the Time Lords summoned the Doctor back to Gallifrey to take steps to avert a second attempt. Now holding the rank of Lord President, the Doctor's one-time teacher Borusa decreed the only sure way to prevent the bonding would be the summary execution of the Doctor. However, even Borusa was unaware of the 'mole' in their midst. Thanks to Hedin's actions, the attempted destruction of the Doctor merely resulted in the time traveller being placed further in the power of Omega . . .

Snakedance (serial 6D) by Christopher Bailey. Director: Fiona Cumming

Reunited with the Doctor after the affair of Omega, Tegan's second voyage in the TARDIS began with a journey to the planet Manussa; an occurrence baffling to the Doctor in so far as Tegan herself had mysteriously mapped the coordinates for the flight. Very quickly it became apparent why. Far from being free from her possession on the Kinda world, the Mara force within her mind had remained and was now once more asserting itself.

Becoming separated from her companions on Manussa, Tegan's will eventually capitulated, turning her into a vanguard for the evil intelligence's bid to reform a body for the Mara on its own home planet.

To this end the Mara was almost successful. Subverting the mind of a bored, young nobleman – Lon – the Mara conspired to acquire the Great Crystal from its Guardian – Ambril – and have it used at the Janissary ceremony commemorating the banishing of the Mara from Manussa. Only the Doctor understood that the use of this Crystal in the ceremony would open a path for the Mara to regain physical existence.

In this story even the serpent visual effects – which had dogged 'Kinda' – were not forgotten, with real snakes being used for the all-important explication scene between the Doctor and the sage Dojjen.

Mawdryn Undead (serial 6F) by Peter Grimwade. Director: Peter Moffatt. There is not just one element from the Doctor's past in this story, but two. After a gap of several years, John Nathan-Turner was lucky enough to re-cast satanic-voiced Valentine Dyall in his role as the Black Guardian for the long-awaited dual between the two adversaries. In this adventure, though, the cosmic manipulations of the Guardian were invisible to the Doctor, who could only remark on the uncanny number of coincidences which seemed to be happening.

Becoming enmeshed in the problem of a group of scientists who had sought to become Time Lords, the Doctor was forced to help their leader, Mawdryn, to achieve their goal of immortality. Previous failures to attain this had left Mawdryn and his associates trapped in a cycle of perpetual mutation from which there was no respite. Ultimately, though, the Doctor was able to grant the mutants a gift more precious to them than immortality – death – thanks to the misguided intervention of his old friend, the Brigadier.

The inclusion of Nicholas Courtney, as Lethbridge-Stewart, in this *Doctor Who* story proved to be as popular a move, with long-term viewers, as the inclusion of a past Doctor in a serial. Having now played opposite Messrs Hartnell, Troughton, Pertwee, Baker and Davison, Courtney holds the unique record of being the only actor to have managed this feat. And, despite a gap of over seven years since his last appearance, Courtney found his characterisation of the deadpan Brigadier was still as popular as ever with the fans.

Terminus (serial 6G) by Steve Gallagher. Director: Mary Ridge
Accepted aboard the TARDIS as a companion, the Black Guardian's agent Turlough tried once more to destroy the Doctor, this time by tampering with the TARDIS; a dangerous pursuit – and disaster was only averted by a melding of the ship with another drifting space vessel. Eventually all four travellers were cut off from their craft, leaving them stranded on an apparently deserted ship. Turlough's further efforts to destroy the Doctor were thwarted when he and Tegan became trapped in the vessel's under-floor ducting system. Far more serious were the problems faced by Nyssa and the Doctor. Far from being abandoned, the spaceship proved to be a transport ship for sufferers of Lazar's Disease – a leprosy-like condition supposedly curable on the Terminus Station. It took the Doctor to find out that victims of the infection were far from cured on this base, but by that time his own companion, Nyssa, had joined the pitiful ranks of the Lazars.

Directing this serial was almost a case of *déjà vu* for Mary Ridge, whose best-known work had been for the series *Blake's Seven*. There she once directed an episode titled 'Terminal'.

New fashions for the Doctor's two lovely companions, Tegan (Janet Fielding) and Nyssa (Sarah Sutton) in 'Terminus' (1983)

Enlightenment (serial 6H) by Barbara Clegg. Director: Fionna Cumming That this story finally reached transmission intact and on time was something of a miracle. Due originally to be recorded after 'Terminus' production came to a grinding halt when an industrial dispute lasting nearly two months shut down studios at the BBC's Television Centre. Consequences of this strike were the curtailing of the planned seventh story of the season and for a time it looked as though 'Enlightenment' might follow along the same path.

Fortunately the strike ended in mid-December 1982 but even then it was not plain sailing for the ships of 'Enlightenment'. With a heavy backlog of programmes to be cleared, the show did not go into the studio until mid-January. That meant, once shooting had finished, there was just five weeks to do all the editing, dubbing, syphering (addition of music and effects) before the first episode went out on 1 March 1983. The production team made it, but only just . . .

The importance of getting this story out on air was its climax to the struggle between the Doctor and the Black Guardian. The setting for this was a race between a number of sailing ships. What made it strange was that these ships were flying in space using planets and moons as marker buoys. The answer lay in their captains, all of whom were Eternals – powerful immortals in human guise. Whoever won the race received the gift of Enlightenment. Opposed both by Turlough and another Black Guardian agent, Wrack, the Doctor was able to draw on some support from the other Guardian – the White Guardian, again played with finesse by Cyril Luckham.

The King's Demons (serial 6J) by Terence Dudley. Director: Tony Virgo
As with 'Enlightenment' this two-part, predominantly historical serial only got done by the skin of its teeth. The crippling industrial dispute at the BBC ended just in time for this serial to fulfil its scheduled recording dates.

The theme for this story owed something to 'The Time Meddler' in that it dealt with a plot, by the Master, to change history by preventing King John from signing the Magna Carta. With help from an android called Kamelion, taken from the planet Xeriphas, the Master intended to halt the signing by having Kamelion impersonate King John. The first hint the Doctor got that something was amiss was when he met a traveller from London who was perplexed as to how the King could be in London and yet there in the countryside at the same time.

The involvement of the Master was not made known until the end of episode one – the secret being kept in the *Radio Times* by an even more cunning anagram of the Master's identity than usual.

The sequence from 'Shada', featuring Tom Baker as the Doctor, which was utilised in 'The Five Doctors', November 1983

THE DOCTOR WHO LIBRARY

TARGET NOVELISATIONS

by Terrance Dicks
1 **Abominable Snowmen**

2 **Android Invasion**

3 **Androids of Tara**

by Ian Marter
4 **Ark in Space**

by Terrance Dicks
5 **Armageddon Factor**

6 **Auton Invasion**

7 **Brain of Morbius**

8 **Carnival of Monsters**

by Malcolm Hulke
9 **Cave Monsters**

by Terrance Dicks
10 **Claws of Axos**

by David Fisher
11 **Creature from the Pit**

by David Whitaker
12 **Crusaders**

by Brian Hayles
13 **Curse of Peladon**

by Gerry Davis
14 **Cybermen**

by Barry Letts
15 **Daemons**

by David Whitaker
16 **Daleks**

by Terrance Dicks
17 **Dalek Invasion of Earth**

by Terrance Dicks
18 **Day of the Daleks**

19 **Death to the Daleks**

20 **Deadly Assassin**

21 **Destiny of the Daleks**

by Malcolm Hulke
22 **Dinosaur Invasion**

23 **Doomsday Weapon**

by Ian Marter
24 **Enemy of the World**

by Terrance Dicks
25 **Face of Evil**

by Andrew Smith
26 **Full Circle**

by Terrance Dicks
27 **Genesis of the Daleks**

28 **Giant Robot**

by Malcolm Hulke
29 **Green Death**

by Terrance Dicks
30 **Hand of Fear**

31 **Horns of Nimon**

32 **Horror of Fang Rock**

by Brian Hayles
33 **Ice Warriors**

by Terrance Dicks
34 **Image of the Fendahl**

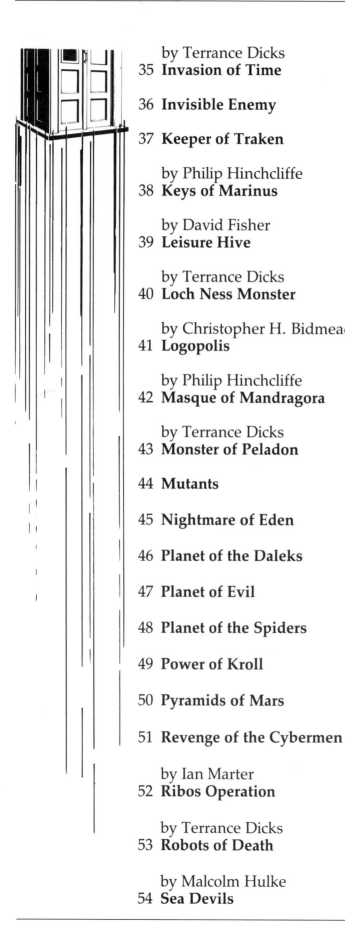

by Peter Grimwade
74 **Time-Flight**

by John Lydecker
79 **Terminus**

by Terrance Dicks
75 **Meglos**

by Terrance Dicks
80 **Arc of Infinity**

by Christopher H. Bidmead
76 **Castrovalva**

81 **Five Doctors**

by Terrance Dicks
77 **Four to Doomsday**

by Peter Grimwade
82 **Mawdryn Undead**

by Ian Marter
78 **Earthshock**

TARGET NON-FICTION DOCTOR WHO
by Terrance Dicks
The Adventures of K9 and Other Mechanical Creatures

by Nigel Robinson
The Doctor Who Crossword Book

by Terrance Dicks
Doctor Who Dinosaur Book

by Terrance Dicks and Malcolm Hulke
The Making of Doctor Who

by Terrance Dicks
The Second Doctor Who Monster Book

by Jean-Marc Lofficier
The Doctor Who Programme Guide Volume 1

The Doctor Who Programme Guide Volume 2

by Nigel Robinson
The Doctor Who Quiz Book

The Second Doctor Who Quiz Book

by Terrance Dicks
Terry Nation's Dalek Special

W. H. ALLEN DOCTOR WHO BOOKS NOT AVAILABLE IN TARGET
by Terrance Dicks
Doctor Who – Dalek Omnibus

by Peter Haining
Doctor Who – A Celebration: Two Decades through Time and Space

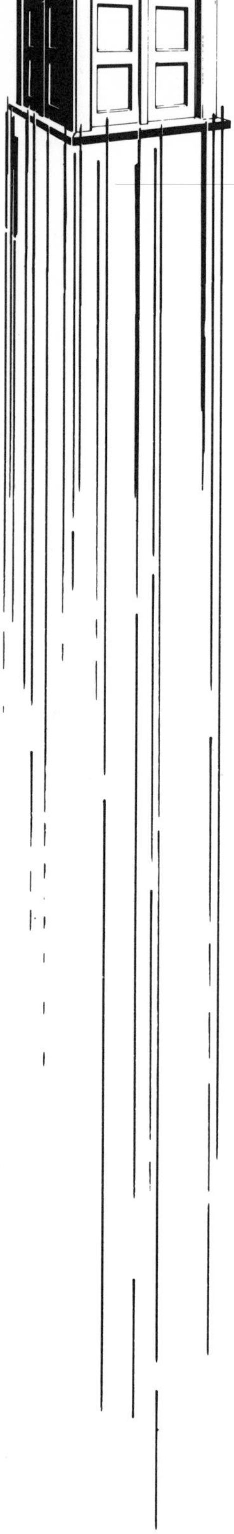

THE PEOPLE WHO

CODE	SERIAL TITLE	WRITERS

The Doctor played by William Hartnell
Produced by Verity Lambert and Mervyn Pinfield
Script editor: David Whitaker

CODE	SERIAL TITLE	WRITERS
A	An Unearthly Child (The Tribe of Gum)	Anthony Coburn (C. E. Webber)
B	The Daleks	Terry Nation
C	Beyond the Sun (The Edge of Destruction)	David Whitaker
D	Marco Polo	John Lucarotti
E	The Keys of Marinus	Terry Nation
F	The Aztecs	John Lucarotti
G	The Sensorites	Peter R. Newman
H	The Reign of Terror	Dennis Spooner
J	Planet of Giants	Louis Marks
K	The Dalek Invasion of Earth	Terry Nation

Script editor: Dennis Spooner

L	The Rescue	David Whitaker
M	The Romans	Dennis Spooner

Produced by Verity Lambert

N	The Web Planet	Bill Strutton
P	The Crusade	David Whitaker
Q	The Space Museum	Glyn Jones
R	The Chase	Terry Nation

Script editor: Donald Tosh

S	The Time Meddler	Dennis Spooner
T	Galaxy Four	William Emms
T/A	Mission to the Unknown	Terry Nation

MADE DOCTOR WHO

DIRECTORS	DESIGNERS
Waris Hussein	Peter Brachacki Barry Newbery
Christopher Barry Richard Martin	Raymond Cusick Jeremy Davies
Richard Martin Frank Cox	Raymond Cusick
Waris Hussein John Crocket	Barry Newbery
John Gorrie	Raymond Cusick
John Crocket	Barry Newbery
Mervyn Pinfield Frank Cox	Raymond Cusick
Henric Hirsch	Roderick Laing
Mervyn Pinfield Douglas Camfield	Raymond Cusick
Richard Martin	Spencer Chapman
Christopher Barry	Raymond Cusick
Christopher Barry	Raymond Cusick
Richard Martin	John Wood
Douglas Camfield	Barry Newbery
Mervyn Pinfield	Spencer Chapman
Richard Martin	Raymond Cusick John Wood
Douglas Camfield	Barry Newbery
Derek Martinus	Richard Hunt
Derek Martinus	Richard Hunt Raymond Cusick

CODE	SERIAL TITLE	WRITERS
Produced by John Wiles		
U	The Myth Makers	Donald Cotton
V	The Daleks' Master Plan	Terry Nation Dennis Spooner
W	The Massacre	John Lucarotti Donald Tosh
Script editor: Gerry Davis		
X	The Ark	Paul Erickson Lesley Scott
Produced by Innes Lloyd		
Y	The Celestial Toymaker	Brian Hayles
Z	The Gunfighters	Donald Cotton
AA	The Savages	Ian Stuart Black
BB	The War Machines	Ian Stuart Black (Kit Pedler)
CC	The Smugglers	Brian Hayles
DD	The Tenth Planet	Kit Pedler Gerry Davis
The Doctor played by Patrick Troughton		
EE	The Power of the Daleks	Terry Nation (Dennis Spooner)
FF	The Highlanders	Elwyn Jones Gerry Davis
GG	The Underwater Menace	Geoffrey Orme
HH	The Moonbase	Kit Pedler
JJ	The Macra Terror	Ian Stuart Black
KK	The Faceless Ones	David Ellis Malcolm Hulke
Script editors: Gerry Davis and Peter Bryant		
LL	The Evil of the Daleks	David Whitaker
Produced by Peter Bryant Script editor: Victor Pemberton		
MM	The Tomb of the Cybermen	Kit Pedler Gerry Davis
Produced by Innes Lloyd Script editor: Peter Bryant		
NN	The Abominable Snowmen	Mervyn Haisman Henry Lincoln

DIRECTORS	DESIGNERS
Michael Leeston-Smith	John Wood
Douglas Camfield	Raymond Cusick Barry Newbery
Paddy Russell	Michael Young
Michael Imison	Barry Newbery
Bill Sellars	John Wood
Rex Tucker	Barry Newbery
Christopher Barry	Stuart Walker
Michael Ferguson	Raymond London
Julia Smith	Richard Hunt
Derek Martinus	Peter Kindred
Christopher Barry	Derek Dodd
Hugh David	Geoffrey Kirkland
Julia Smith	Jack Robinson
Morris Barry	Colin Shaw
John Davis	Kenneth Sharp
Gerry Mill	Geoffrey Kirkland
Derek Martinus	Chris Thompson
Morris Barry	Martin Johnson
Gerald Blake	Malcolm Middleton

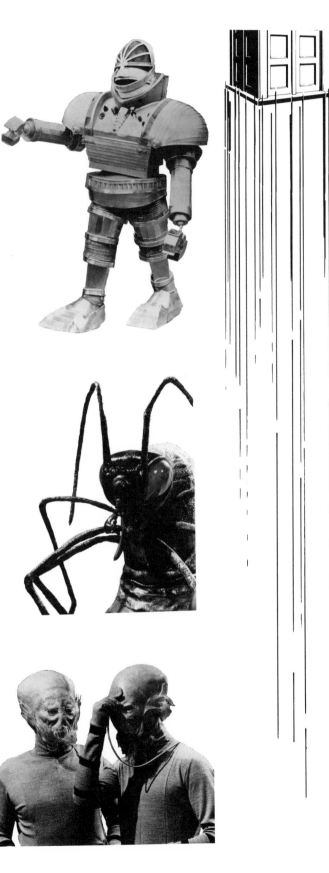

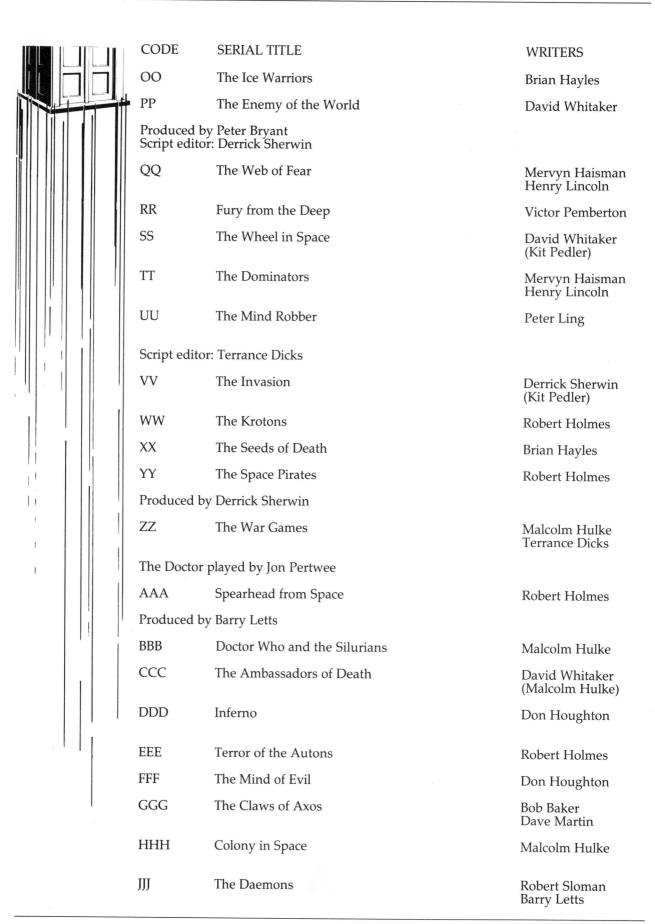

CODE	SERIAL TITLE	WRITERS
OO	The Ice Warriors	Brian Hayles
PP	The Enemy of the World	David Whitaker

Produced by Peter Bryant
Script editor: Derrick Sherwin

CODE	SERIAL TITLE	WRITERS
QQ	The Web of Fear	Mervyn Haisman Henry Lincoln
RR	Fury from the Deep	Victor Pemberton
SS	The Wheel in Space	David Whitaker (Kit Pedler)
TT	The Dominators	Mervyn Haisman Henry Lincoln
UU	The Mind Robber	Peter Ling

Script editor: Terrance Dicks

CODE	SERIAL TITLE	WRITERS
VV	The Invasion	Derrick Sherwin (Kit Pedler)
WW	The Krotons	Robert Holmes
XX	The Seeds of Death	Brian Hayles
YY	The Space Pirates	Robert Holmes

Produced by Derrick Sherwin

CODE	SERIAL TITLE	WRITERS
ZZ	The War Games	Malcolm Hulke Terrance Dicks

The Doctor played by Jon Pertwee

CODE	SERIAL TITLE	WRITERS
AAA	Spearhead from Space	Robert Holmes

Produced by Barry Letts

CODE	SERIAL TITLE	WRITERS
BBB	Doctor Who and the Silurians	Malcolm Hulke
CCC	The Ambassadors of Death	David Whitaker (Malcolm Hulke)
DDD	Inferno	Don Houghton
EEE	Terror of the Autons	Robert Holmes
FFF	The Mind of Evil	Don Houghton
GGG	The Claws of Axos	Bob Baker Dave Martin
HHH	Colony in Space	Malcolm Hulke
JJJ	The Daemons	Robert Sloman Barry Letts

DIRECTORS	DESIGNERS
Derek Martinus	Jeremy Davies
Barry Letts	Christopher Pemsel
Douglas Camfield	David Myerscough-Jones
Hugh David	Peter Kindred
Tristan de Vere Cole	Derek Dodd
Morris Barry	Barry Newbery
David Maloney	Evan Hercules

Douglas Camfield	Richard Hunt
David Maloney	Raymond London
Michael Ferguson	Paul Allen
Michael Hart	Ian Watson
David Maloney	Roger Cheveley

Derek Martinus	Paul Allen
Timothy Combe	Barry Newbery
Michael Ferguson	David Myerscough-Jones
Douglas Camfield Barry Letts	Jeremy Davies
Barry Letts	Ian Watson
Timothy Combe	Raymond London
Michael Ferguson	Kenneth Sharp
Michael Briant	Tim Gleeson
Christopher Barry	Roger Ford

CODE	SERIAL TITLE	WRITERS
KKK	The Day of the Daleks	Louis Marks
MMM	The Curse of Peladon	Brian Hayles
LLL	The Sea Devils	Malcolm Hulke
NNN	The Mutants	Bob Baker Dave Martin
OOO	The Time Monster	Robert Sloman
RRR	The Three Doctors	Bob Baker Dave Martin
PPP	Carnival of Monsters	Robert Holmes
QQQ	Frontier in Space	Malcolm Hulke
SSS	Planet of the Daleks	Terry Nation
TTT	The Green Death	Robert Sloman
UUU	The Time Warrior	Robert Holmes
WWW	Invasion of the Dinosaurs	Malcolm Hulke
XXX	Death to the Daleks	Terry Nation
YYY	The Monster of Peladon	Brian Hayles
ZZZ	Planet of the Spiders	Robert Sloman

The Doctor played by Tom Baker
Script editor: Robert Holmes

4A	Robot	Terrance Dicks

Produced by Philip Hinchcliffe

4C	The Ark in Space	Robert Holmes
4B	The Sontaran Experiment	Bob Baker Dave Martin
4E	Genesis of the Daleks	Terry Nation
4D	Revenge of the Cybermen	Gerry Davis
4F	Terror of the Zygons	Robert Banks Stewart
4H	Planet of Evil	Louis Marks
4G	Pyramids of Mars	Robert Holmes Lewis Greifer
4J	The Android Invasion	Terry Nation
4K	The Brain of Morbius	Terrance Dicks
4L	The Seeds of Doom	Robert Banks Stewart

DIRECTORS	DESIGNERS
Paul Bernard	David Myerscough-Jones
Lennie Mayne	Gloria Clayton
Michael Briant	Tony Snoaden
Christopher Barry	Jeremy Bear
Paul Bernard	Tim Gleeson
Lennie Mayne	Roger Liminton
Barry Letts	Roger Liminton
Paul Bernard	Cynthia Kljuco
David Maloney Paul Bernard	John Hurst
Michael Briant	John Burrowes
Alan Bromly	Keith Cheetham
Paddy Russell	Richard Morris
Michael Briant	Colin Green
Lennie Mayne	Gloria Clayton
Barry Letts	Rochelle Selwyn
Christopher Barry	Ian Rawnsley
Rodney Bennett	Roger Murray-Leach
Rodney Bennett	Roger Murray-Leach
David Maloney	David Spode
Michael Briant	Roger Murray-Leach
Douglas Camfield	Nigel Curzon
David Maloney	Roger Murray-Leach
Paddy Russell	Christine Ruscoe
Barry Letts	Philip Lindley
Christopher Barry	Barry Newbery
Douglas Camfield	Roger Murray-Leach Jeremy Bear

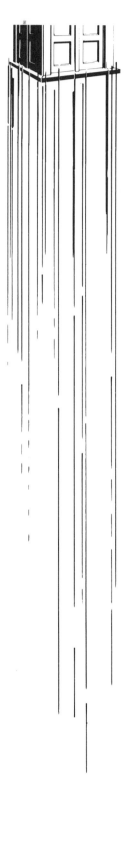

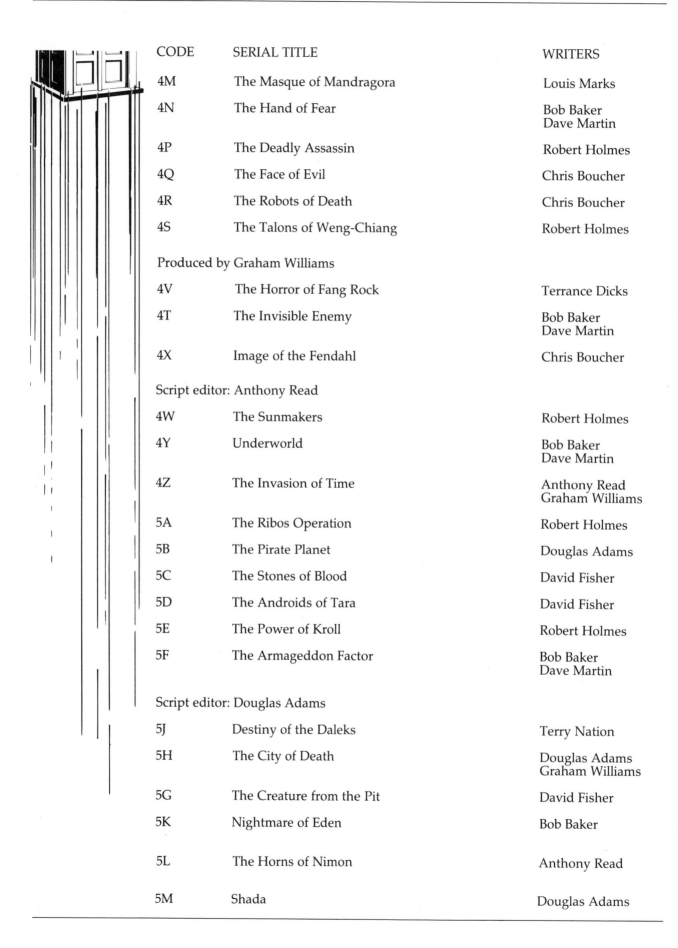

CODE	SERIAL TITLE	WRITERS
4M	The Masque of Mandragora	Louis Marks
4N	The Hand of Fear	Bob Baker Dave Martin
4P	The Deadly Assassin	Robert Holmes
4Q	The Face of Evil	Chris Boucher
4R	The Robots of Death	Chris Boucher
4S	The Talons of Weng-Chiang	Robert Holmes

Produced by Graham Williams

4V	The Horror of Fang Rock	Terrance Dicks
4T	The Invisible Enemy	Bob Baker Dave Martin
4X	Image of the Fendahl	Chris Boucher

Script editor: Anthony Read

4W	The Sunmakers	Robert Holmes
4Y	Underworld	Bob Baker Dave Martin
4Z	The Invasion of Time	Anthony Read Graham Williams
5A	The Ribos Operation	Robert Holmes
5B	The Pirate Planet	Douglas Adams
5C	The Stones of Blood	David Fisher
5D	The Androids of Tara	David Fisher
5E	The Power of Kroll	Robert Holmes
5F	The Armageddon Factor	Bob Baker Dave Martin

Script editor: Douglas Adams

5J	Destiny of the Daleks	Terry Nation
5H	The City of Death	Douglas Adams Graham Williams
5G	The Creature from the Pit	David Fisher
5K	Nightmare of Eden	Bob Baker
5L	The Horns of Nimon	Anthony Read
5M	Shada	Douglas Adams

DIRECTORS	DESIGNERS
Rodney Bennett	Barry Newbery
Lennie Mayne	Christine Ruscoe
David Maloney	Roger Murray-Leach
Pennant Roberts	Austin Ruddy
Michael Briant	Kenneth Sharp
David Maloney	Roger Murray-Leach
Paddy Russell	Paul Allen
Derrick Goodwin	Barry Newbery
George Spenton-Foster	Anna Ridley

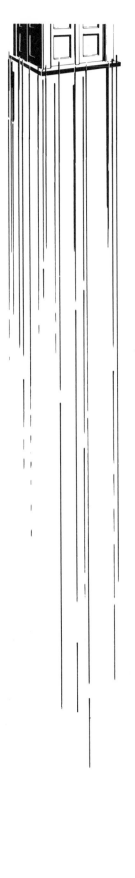

Pennant Roberts	Tony Snoaden
Norman Stewart	Dick Coles
Gerald Blake	Barbara Gosnold
George Spenton-Foster	Ken Ledsham
Pennant Roberts	Jon Pusey
Darrol Blake	John Stout
Michael Hayes	Valerie Warrender
Norman Stewart	Don Giles
Michael Hayes	Richard McManan-Smith

Ken Grieve	Ken Ledsham
Michael Hayes	Richard McManan-Smith
Christopher Barry	Valerie Warrender
Alan Bromly Graham Williams	Roger Cann
Kenny McBain	Graeme Story
Pennant Roberts	Victor Meredith

CODE	SERIAL TITLE	WRITERS

Produced by John Nathan-Turner
Executive producer: Barry Letts
Script editor: Christopher H. Bidmead

CODE	SERIAL TITLE	WRITERS
5N	The Leisure Hive	David Fisher
5Q	Meglos	John Flanagan Andrew McCulloch
5R	Full Circle	Andrew Smith
5P	State of Decay	Terrance Dicks
5S	Warriors' Gate	Steve Gallagher
5T	The Keeper of Traken	Johnny Byrne
5V	Logopolis	Christopher H. Bidmead

The Doctor played by Peter Davison
Produced by John Nathan-Turner
Script editor: Eric Saward

5Z	Castrovalva	Christopher H. Bidmead

Script editor: Antony Root

5W	Four to Doomsday	Terence Dudley

Script editor: Eric Saward

5Y	Kinda	Christopher Bailey

Script editor: Antony Root

5X	The Visitation	Eric Saward

Script editor: Eric Saward

6A	Black Orchid	Terence Dudley

Script editor: Antony Root

6B	Earthshock	Eric Saward

Script editor: Eric Saward

6C	Time-Flight	Peter Grimwade
6E	Arc of Infinity	Johnny Byrne
6D	Snakedance	Christopher Bailey
6F	Mawdryn Undead	Peter Grimwade
6G	Terminus	Steve Gallagher
6H	Enlightenment	Barbara Clegg
6J	The King's Demons	Terence Dudley

DIRECTORS	DESIGNERS

Lovett Bickford	Tom Yardley-Jones
Terence Dudley	Philip Lindley
Peter Grimwade	Janet Budden
Peter Moffatt	Christine Ruscoe
Paul Joyce	Graeme Story
John Black	Tony Burrough
Peter Grimwade	Malcolm Thornton
Fiona Cumming	Janet Budden
John Black	Tony Burrough
Peter Grimwade	Malcolm Thornton
Peter Moffatt	Ken Starkey
Ron Jones	Tony Burrough
Peter Grimwade	Bernard Lloyd-Jones
Ron Jones	Richard McManan-Smith
Ron Jones	Marjorie Pratt
Fiona Cumming	Jan Spoczynski
Peter Moffatt	Stephen Scott
Mary Ridge	Dick Coles
Fiona Cumming	Colin Green
Tony Virgo	Ken Ledsham

The *Doctor Who* Celebration at Longleat, Easter 1983

THE DOCTOR WHO EXHIBITIONS

According to all the actors who have played the Doctor, the single most fervent wish of the majority of fans they have met over the past twenty years has been to accompany the Time Lord in the TARDIS on one of his journeys of adventure! Of such wishes are dreams made, of course – but it *is* possible to experience a little of what life for the Doctor is like at the two now long-running exhibitions in England: at the seaside resort of Blackpool and deep in the Wiltshire countryside at Longleat House. For in both are a variety of items previously used on the programme which help conjure up some of its excitement and magic.

This year, the exhibitions at Blackpool and Longleat are celebrating an anniversary just like the series itself. For when they opened their doors at Easter for the daily run which took them through to the end of October, both were enjoying their tenth successive seasons. It is also ten years since the very first *Doctor Who* exhibition was staged – a comparatively modest affair which was part of the BBC Special Effects Exhibition at the Science Museum in Kensington, London. Visitors then were just given a glimpse of the interior of the TARDIS and several of the Doctor's adversaries, including, naturally, a Dalek.

But things have come a long way since that humble beginning, and the exhibitions are now extensive in size, wide-ranging in scope and do full justice to the imaginative skills that go into producing the programme.

The Blackpool exhibition, at 111 Central Promenade on the busy Golden Mile right in the shadow of the famous Tower, is both the biggest and most impressive of the shows. Entry through a TARDIS-shaped gateway takes visitors down stairs into a labyrinth of subterranean corridors, past various displays and into the Doctor's world. On display are props, costumes, special effects and an array of monsters and aliens, all of which are constantly being updated as the series progresses and characters change. Mementoes of the past are, however, retained and such favourites as the Daleks, Davros and K9 are ever-present, their impact highlighted by special sound and lighting effects.

A feature of the Blackpool exhibition are the small-scale models of landscapes, spaceships and space-flight equipment, built with such precise attention to detail it is no wonder they look so realistic – or so large – on television. At the heart of things is the main TARDIS control room which last year (1982) was being menaced by four Cybermen grouped around their Cyberscope. The features of Peter Davison naturally dominate the displays of photographs and a loop video shows the regeneration of the Doctor from his Tom Baker persona into that of Peter.

The setting for the second major *Doctor Who* exhibition could not be more different. Longleat House, the stately home of the Marquess of Bath, nestles in rolling hills near Warminster in Wiltshire. The house itself is an Elizabethan mansion containing a wealth of art treasures, rich furnishings and valuable paintings and books, while the gardens which surround it were laid out by the famous eighteenth-century landscape designer, 'Capability' Brown, and contain the first safari park to have been created in Britain. But for fans of *Doctor Who*, far richer treasures and excitements lie in the exhibition which was set up in 1973.

Once again the exhibition is entered by way of a TARDIS gateway and, though the show is smaller than that at Blackpool, it does contain an equally full coverage of the Doctor's activities and adversaries – with faithfuls like the Daleks, Cybermen and K9 prominently featured. These displays are also updated year by year with fresh items from the studios. The use of darkened sets, swirling electronic sounds and multi-coloured flashing lights makes a visit quite unforgettable.

Longleat, like Blackpool, is open from 1 April to 30 October and both contain wide-ranging selections of the latest examples of *Doctor Who* merchandise for sale. (This April, Longleat played host to two days of special festivities to mark the twentieth anniversary.)

To be celebrated in two permanent exhibitions is a rare, even unique, honour for a television character and certainly unparalleled in the twenty years in which *Doctor Who* has been shown. And who – if you will excuse the pun – is to deny that still more exhibitions might not open at other venues in the future?

THE DOCTOR WHO FAN CLUBS
The Doctor Who Appreciation Society
by David Saunders

The Doctor Who Appreciation Society is a non-profit-making organisation, which is run on an amateur basis. It is dedicated to the assimilation, preservation and distribution to its members of all matters pertaining to the concept of 'Doctor Who' for the information and entertainment of its members.

In 1975 a fanzine appeared in the world of comics fandom called *TARDIS*. It had been produced by a comics and *Doctor Who* fan named Andrew Johnson, who almost immediately passed on the magazine's editorship to another *Who* enthusiast called Gordon Blows. Gordon threw himself into publishing the magazine as often as was possible and was contacted by one of its readers with a view to contributing regularly to the publication, Jan Vincent-Rudzki. Gordon and Jan got together with a fellow student of Jan's, Stephen Payne, and together they decided to form a society of which *TARDIS* would become the magazine and membership was opened to the public at large in May 1976 with an initial group, spread throughout the country, numbering seventy.

In forming the DWAS, as it became known, Gordon, Jan and Steve quickly realised that to have a society along the lines they wanted would involve more than just the three of them in the organising and soon three other volunteers joined them as the main body of the society, Jeremy Bentham, Keith Barnfather and Stuart Glazebrook.

These six continued for just over four years in running the society. Others who also served in some capacity over the years include Chris Dunk, John Peel, Gary Russell, David Shackley, Mark Sinclair and Chris Slatter. One of the strengths of the society has been the willingness of others to lighten the workload of the nuclear group and thus, when time had taken its toll of the founders, a new group succeeded them towards the end of 1980.

Over the years, as more enthusiasts learned of its existence, the membership of the society has grown from that initial seventy to over 1,200 and with the international success of the programme it has not been confined to British shores; one of the members of the organising body is responsible for looking after the needs of those interested in the show in Europe, Africa and Australasia. A North American branch of the society, with almost as many on the books as its British parent, covers Canada and the USA. There are also strong links with the Australasian Doctor Who Fan Club through its president, Anthony Howe.

The society's organisation is divided into various departments, each run by a member of the society executive; these number nine and comprise Ian McLachlan, Gordon Roxburgh and Richard Walter, three gentlemen of Scottish extraction who edit one of the three regular magazines apiece, Tony Clark (art), Deanne Holding, the first and only lady to serve on the body (photographic), David J. Howe (reference), John McElroy (overseas) and Paul Zeus (convention). The society administration and the executive body are linked by the society coordinator, David Saunders, whose responsibilities range from liaising with the BBC and other outside bodies to acting as treasurer.

Membership of the society is on a yearly basis and currently the subscription rate is £5. This enables, once administration expenses for membership cards, information sheets, etc., have been met, the production of a monthly newsletter, *The Celestial Toyroom*, which is designed to keep all members up to date with society and *Doctor Who* news.

A sample of the numerous *Doctor Who* fanzines

TARDIS now appears quarterly and is the prime publication of the society. It features articles by members, photographs, a lively letters column, artwork, quizzes and interviews with cast and production staff, both present and past. The fan-fiction aspect is met by a twice-yearly-magazine called *Cosmic Masque*, which features stories about the Doctors and their companions in imaginative settings. As well as these, there is the society *Yearbook*, which reviews the year both on screen and off and documents the society's calendar of events.

The events are organised by the convention department, for which past episodes are hired for re-screening, guests from the programme's past and present are invited and at the annual two-day convention, known as PanoptiCon, awards are presented to the writer and director of that year's winning story, as polled by the members. Other one-day events also take place during the year, known as the Inter-Face (dedicated to the era of one particular Doctor, in turn) Series and also the Dwasocial Series, where, as the name suggests, the emphasis is on the socialising aspect.

The first convention of the society was a modest one-day affair, held in a church hall in Battersea, London, with attendances by Jon Pertwee, Tom Baker and Louise Jameson (Leela) during August 1977. Now the PanoptiCon begins very late on a Friday evening and lasts until around 7 p.m. on the following Sunday and takes place at a large provincial hotel. During 1983, the twentieth anniversary year, there was a stand at the BBC Longleat Event to publicise the society and special publications were brought out by the reference department organiser and the *TARDIS* editor. The occasion is also being marked by a celebration, again at a provincial hotel, where the emphasis will be on the fan aspect of the background to the programme, as near to 23 November as possible.

The address of the Doctor Who Appreciation Society is 38 Hazeldean Road, Harlesden, London NW10 8QU.

The Australasian Doctor Who Fan Club by Antony Howe

The Australasian Doctor Who Fan Club was formed in Sydney in August 1976 to save the *Doctor Who* series from being cancelled by the Australian Broadcasting Commission (ABC) due to 'poor ratings'. To this end our first activity was a public demonstration with placards and a Dalek at the ABC head office, followed by a letter-writing campaign. Late in 1977 the ABC policy was changed, and from 1978 *Doctor Who* has been regularly screened.

To publicise the series and our campaign to save it the club began to publish a magazine called *Zerinza* (allegedly a Dalek word meaning 'Good Success' which we needed to save *Doctor Who*). Publishing the magazine quickly became the main activity of the club as it enabled all members to receive news, articles, etc., concerning *Doctor Who*.

As most members are widely scattered across Australia, social activities can never be a major part of club activities. However, recently some fans have formed local groups, holding regular meetings and social outings in their towns or suburbs. To help these fans in isolated areas, a club member runs a mail order service for imported merchandise (mainly books).

In 1980 to improve services to members a newsletter was formed to keep them up to date with the latest news and gossip from anywhere about *Doctor Who*. This left *Zerinza* to concentrate on articles, story summaries and interviews and other non-news material. The newsletter is *not* available to overseas fans, except those in New Zealand.

Fans in some of our major cities have over the years organised *Doctor Who* parties and in 1980 Sydney fans were very lucky to have Jon Pertwee and, in 1981 Katy Manning as guests (both were visiting – the club cannot afford to fly guests in from overseas). Membership passed six hundred in 1982.

Letters should be addressed to: Club Secretary, 11 Lincoln Street, Stanmore, NSW 2048, Australia, and if a reply is needed must enclose an Australian stamp or three International Reply Coupons.

The Doctor Who Fan Club of America by Ron Katz

The Doctor Who Fan Club of America all came about because a friend of mine named Chad Roark, and I, wanted some *Doctor Who* T-shirts! Quite by chance we had seen the *Doctor Who* programme while on a sports car rally in the Rocky Mountains in May 1981. It had made us instant fans of Tom Baker – and very intrigued by the concept of the show.

Well, once we were hooked, we heard that there were *Doctor Who* T-shirts available and tried to get hold of some. After five months we finally succeeded – but were very disappointed. You see, we both know something about this area of merchandising. My background is in men's clothing sales, manufacture, merchandising and design. Chad's is in graphic design. So we decided to develop our own *Doctor Who* T-shirt and button (badge). Although neither of us had ever been a member of a fan club before, let alone run one, we still managed to recruit 39 members.

And that's how the Doctor Who Fan Club of America was born.

At the beginning of 1982, I was approached by an official of the local television station running the *Doctor Who* programme, KRMA TV, and asked if I and the other members would like to appear on television to raise money for the station. Of course, I accepted and on 21 March 1982 our entire fan club (all thirty-nine of us) were on television asking the viewing audience to donate money.

You have to understand that everyone we knew, our families, our friends, the people of KRMA TV, all thought we were crazy. After all, *Doctor Who* was supposed to be a children's show and we were all in our twenties and thirties! Chad and I thought, however, that the audience would be much more sophisticated than everyone had figured. We were right. We raised over $60,000 for the station, more than any other programme had ever raised for KRMA TV! They were absolutely flabbergasted (so were we, really!). What was even better, for us, was that in the next week, over eight hundred people wrote us letters, wanting to join DWFCA! We were on our way!

By June 1982 we had 1,200 members in Colorado. We needed money to expand but, of course, most people still thought we were crazy. I quit my job and so did Chad. We knew *Doctor Who* had something big in store for us and we were going to 'go for it'. We decided to have a *Doctor Who* party. In America, conventions are usually called 'cons'. I hate that word and all it stands for. Chad felt the same way. We decided on the word 'festival': it seemed to fit the *Doctor Who* feeling. We already called ourselves 'Whovians', so 'Whovian Festival' it was. We held it in the mountains, watched *Doctor Who* movies all day, and it was great fun. Children and old folk alike attended. No one knew anyone else. The only common bond was you know Who!

That festival gave us the money to broaden the scope of our club, and we started to promote *Doctor Who* and the DWFCA in other markets . . . successfully, I might add. By September 1982 the club had 3,000 members and (we were later told) we had become the largest *Doctor Who* organisation in the world *and* the largest 'pirateers' of *Doctor Who* merchandise. (In our defence I have to say that we had been trying to get permission without any luck.) Then, in the middle of that month at a convention in Denver, we had a meeting with John Nathan-Turner. He liked what we were doing. So did the Head of BBC Merchandising, Roy Williams, and Assistant Sales Director John Harrison. In fact, they were all very impressed with our merchandise and, of course, our numbers.

Following this, Chad and I made our biggest decision to date. We decided to invest all of our money into one festival. We invited Anthony Ainley and Sarah Sutton to be our guests at the Colorado Whovian Festival II on 21 November. We rented an arena, Mammoth Gardens, and knew we would either have a smash hit on our hands or the bubble would burst and we would fall flat on our 'Whovian' faces.

We opened the doors at 8 a.m. Soon family people were pouring in – unlike the sci-fi type of crowds our average age is thirty-one years old. By 9.30 a.m. there were 2,500 people at the Gardens and the festival was in full force. We ran *Doctor Who* stories no one had seen before, a local group did a specially written play and everyone, including Anthony Ainley and Sarah Sutton, had a great time. We raised another $1,200 for the local television station and, between the merchandise and gate receipts, it added up to a $25,000 day!

The Colorado Whovian Festival taught us a lot. We know now that festivals will be a big part of our organisation. We know how to make them even better. People love them; they love to be a part of them. Chad and I have devoted our lives (at least for right now) to *Doctor Who* and DWFCA. Our whole reason, we believe, for success is that we're having fun, really, lots of fun. We turn people on with our club and our festivals because we're turned on to it.

We work an average of eight hours a day on the club, its merchandise and its future. We are also devoted to the promotion of *Doctor Who* in the USA. When we first started out there were about fifty television stations in the country that aired the programme; there are currently over a hundred. We work closely with Lionheart Television International (the licensed distributors of the series). If they want to get into a new market with the programme, we assist them. If the television station is a commercial one, we become the first advertiser; if it's a Public Broadcast Station, we promote the show and help them raise money. This year we shall be travelling all over the country to raise money, and our goal for 1983 is $1,000,000 for PBS. We'll do it, too!

At this time (February 1983) there are 7,500 members of the DWFCA. If I told you our goals for membership this year, you would surely think we were crazy! We have plans to bring several of the Doctors to the USA and conduct Whovian Festivals in at least thirty American cities this year. By the end of 1984 *Doctor Who* will be on the lips of the 200,000,000 plus Americans in this country. We're going to work hard, meet a lot of people, make a lot of money and have a lot of fun.

That sounds like a great way to spend the next decade or so, doesn't it?

Membership of the Doctor Who Fan Club of America costs $5 and the address is PO Box 6024, Cherry Creek Station, Denver, Colorado 80206, USA.

The Doctor Who Information Network (Canada)

The Doctor Who Information Network has been in existence for several years under coordinator Dean Shewring of Peterborough, Ontario. The group has been particularly active in lobbying Canadian TV stations to run *Doctor Who* programmes and members have also proved themselves determined campaigners when any station has indicated that it might drop the show from their schedules.

DWIN runs two magazines, *Contact* and *Mark II*, which help in such campaigns, as well as carrying all the latest information concerning *Doctor Who* both in Canada and abroad. They also carry interviews with people concerned with the show, discussions on the stories and news of the activities of members. DWIN also has local 'chapters' in different areas of Canada where fans can meet from time to time.

The group also holds an annual 'Who Party' in Ontario in November, at which videos of *Doctor Who* programmes are shown and members discuss various aspects of the series.

The address of the Doctor Who Information Network is PO Box 1764, Peterborough, Ontario, Canada K9J 7X6.

The Italian Doctor Who Fan Club

W. H. Allen was delighted to be made an Honorary Member of the Italian Doctor Who Fan Club who can be contacted at the following address:
Via Bologna 33/23, Genova 16127, Italy.

THE DOCTOR WHO FILM ARCHIVES

A Complete Guide to the BBC Archives
of *Doctor Who* Films

By March 1983, a total of 601 episodes of *Doctor Who* had been televised, but, due to a variety of reasons (in the main the destruction or loss of film), 134 of these episodes are missing from the BBC archives. It is believed that copies of some of these may still exist in the hands of private collectors and, in order to complete the filmed history of the Doctor's adventures, Sue Malden, the archive selector of the BBC film library, would welcome any information that might enable her to trace and copy the missing episodes.

WILLIAM HARTNELL

Story title	Black and white	Colour	Story title	Black and white	Colour
Pilot Episode	all		The Space Museum	all	
An Unearthly Child	all		The Chase	all	
The Daleks	all		The Time Meddler	2	
Beyond the Sun	all		Galaxy Four	none	
Marco Polo	none		Mission to the Unknown	none	
The Keys of Marinus	all		The Myth Makers	none	
The Aztecs	all		The Daleks' Master Plan	none	
The Sensorites	all		The Massacre	none	
The Reign of Terror	6		The Ark	all	
Planet of the Giants	all		The Celestial Toymaker	none	
The Dalek Invasion of Earth	all		The Gunfighters	all	
The Rescue	all		The Savages	none	
The Romans	all		The War Machines	2	
The Web Planet	all		The Smugglers	none	
The Crusade	3		The Tenth Planet	1,2,3	

PATRICK TROUGHTON

Story title	Black and white	Story title	Black and white
The Power of the Daleks	none	The Web of Fear	1
The Highlanders	none	Fury from the Deep	none
The Underwater Menace	3	The Wheel in Space	6
The Moonbase	2,4	The Dominators	all
The Macra Terror	none	The Mind Robber	all
The Faceless Ones	1	The Invasion	2,3,5,6,7,8
The Evil of the Daleks	none	The Krotons	all
The Tomb of the Cybermen	none	The Seeds of Death	all
The Abominable Snowmen	2	The Space Pirates	2
The Ice Warriors	none	The War Games	all
The Enemy of the World	3		

JON PERTWEE

Story title	Black and white	Colour	Story title	Black and white	Colour
Spearhead from Space	none	all	The Mutants	none	all
The Silurians	all	none	The Time Monster	none	all
The Ambassadors of Death	all	1	The Three Doctors	none	all
Inferno	all	none	Carnival of Monsters	none	all
Terror of the Autons	all	none	Frontier in Space	all	4,5
The Mind of Evil	all	none	Planet of the Daleks	all	all bar 3
The Claws of Axos	none	all	The Green Death	none	all
Colony in Space	all	all	The Time Warrior	none	all
The Daemons	all	4	Invasion of the Dinosaurs	none	all bar 1
The Day of the Daleks	none	all	Death to the Daleks	none	all
The Curse of Peladon	none	all	The Monster of Peladon	none	all
The Sea Devils	all	all	Planet of the Spiders	none	all

TOM BAKER

Story title	Black and white	Colour	Story title	Black and white	Colour
Robot	—	all	Underworld	—	all
The Ark in Space	—	all	The Invasion of Time	—	all
Sontaran Experiment	—	all	The Ribos Operation	—	all
Genesis of the Daleks	—	all	The Pirate Planet	—	all
Revenge of the Cybermen	—	all	The Stones of Blood	—	all
Terror of the Zygons	—	all	The Androids of Tara	—	all
Planet of Evil	—	all	The Power of Kroll	—	all
Pyramids of Mars	—	all	The Armageddon Factor	—	all
The Android Invasion	—	all	Destiny of the Daleks	—	all
The Brain of Morbius	—	all	The City of Death	—	all
The Seeds of Doom	—	all	The Creature from the Pit	—	all
The Masque of Mandragora	—	all	Nightmare of Eden	—	all
The Hand of Fear	—	all	The Horns of Nimon	—	all
The Deadly Assassin	—	all	Shada (all studio and location work preserved)		
The Face of Evil	—	all	The Leisure Hive	—	all
The Robots of Death	—	all	Meglos	—	all
The Talons of Weng-Chiang	—	all	Full Circle	—	all
The Horror of Fang Rock	—	all	State of Decay	—	all
The Invisible Enemy	—	all	Warriors' Gate	—	all
Image of the Fendahl	—	all	The Keeper of Traken	—	all
The Sunmakers	—	all	Logopolis	—	all

PETER DAVISON

Story title	Black and white	Colour	Story title	Black and white	Colour
Castrovalva	—	all	Arc of Infinity	—	all
Four to Doomsday	—	all	Snakedance	—	all
Kinda	—	all	Mawdryn Undead	—	all
The Visitation	—	all	Terminus	—	all
Black Orchid	—	all	Enlightenment	—	all
Earthshock	—	all	The King's Demons	—	all
Time-Flight	—	all			

NOTES:
1) Before *Spearhead from Space* no episodes were recorded in colour.
2) After *Planet of the Spiders* no episodes were transcribed on to black and white film.

3) Some clips from lost episodes still exist, for example, the Hartnell/Troughton regeneration in *The Tenth Planet*.

A *Doctor Who* camera crew on location filming 'Tomb of the Cybermen' in June 1967